LONDON
DRY
DOLIN
VERMOUTH
DE
CHAMBÉRY

ELLA QUITTNER

OBSESSED with THE BEST

100+ *Methodically* PERFECTED RECIPES

Based on 20+ HEAD-TO-HEAD TESTS

WILLIAM MORROW
An Imprint of HarperCollins*Publishers*

For Nate and Mouse, my two most spirited kitchen companions.

For my mother and father, who introduced me to the pleasures of cooking, and the pleasures of writing.

For my fellow obsessives: anyone who was told they asked "too many questions" in grade school; anyone who is currently midway through an internet deep dive of a person your friend went on a date with one time four months ago; anyone who has a stack of 11 unfinished novels on their bedside table, who interrupts their own interrogations with side interrogations, who has been deemed "weird" or "intense," who has been told they talk too much and too fast, who can remember what their mom wore on their first day of school, down to the button. I hope you'll bring that energy to my dinner table one day.

CONTENTS

WHERE TO BEGIN?

FROM THE GROUND OR NEARBY

ATTENTION-SEEKERS

DESSERTS TO EAT IN BED

or Standing Over the Sink or Seated Like a Lady

YOU GOT TO THE END!!!

LIST OF RECIPES

Mother Recipes for each section are indicated by italics.

1.1 Whole peeled canned Tomatoes
5.1 Roasted
2.4 10
Roma Tom. Blanch
2.2 1 large red onion
4.3 Instant Pot
1.4 Roma Tom Frozen
1.6 Cherry Tom Food Mill
2.3 4 shallots
Tomato Master Sauce
3.2 whole onion
5.2 Roasted, 425F 30min
3.3 onion diced + sauteed
4.2
3.5 onion, seared
5.3 Anchovy
Tom Sauce Master
Tom Food Mill
2.1 1 large
3.4 onion diced raw

INTRODUCTION TO THE BOOK,
and What You'll Need

There is no such thing as "the best." I spent more than a year traveling around America and beyond to try to understand the urge so many of us have to rank and to qualify, to compete, to win. To consume as many meatballs as we can while doubled over a plastic folding table on the steps of a historic church as an emcee who calls himself "Lil Mo Mozzarella" screams "nobody moves, nobody gets hurt" into a megaphone over and over and the rapid artillery fire of a tee shirt gun punctuates the crowd's cheers.

I was, by the way, not immune. Who among us could scroll past a headline promising "the best" way to do anything? Who could walk past a billboard without glancing up when it blared a guarantee that the person pictured was "the best" in any class; who wouldn't want to know what that was like? Who could ignore advice about "the best" place to visit, "the best" deal for wagyu at Costco, "the best" way to look 10 or 15 percent hotter without trying, "the best" business plan to get rich from the couch? Who could commit to one of the two dueling ramen fests unspooling concurrently in different parts of Tokyo during the same week without first pressing local experts to learn which one was "better"? Who could look away from Lil Mo's gang of motley meatballers before a victor was crowned and the prize money of $111 changed hands?

It's human to want to get the most, at least the way that I was raised. (One of my grandfather's catchphrases was "free is free," and he was known to retrieve used golf balls from the course adjacent to his yard, scrub them with a toothbrush, and resell them in packs of three labeled "vintage.") And that can be true whether it applies literally to squeezing value from cost (the revenue from my grandpa's sales paid for his greens fees), or to courting the richest possible human experience. Like when "the best" is the least, as in the most exclusive. Or when it offers the mirage of value, delivering instead choice. It can be a community organizing principle or an algorithmic output.

I could drone on about late-stage capitalism and Hobbesian motivations for human behavior, but we'd both be bored. Instead, I want to tell you about the past year. My year of bests. Before I do that, though, here's something I can't stop thinking about: A friend recently asked me how home cooks knew which recipes to use before the internet existed and search engines emerged. I explained the way things used to work, as best I knew: People used to make the recipes that were available to them—the ones that their families passed down from older generations, or if their forebears couldn't cook, the ones they clipped from magazines or that they'd heard about from their one friend whose dinner parties always went the latest, who had to arrange special horse-drawn-carriage drivers to carry home the guests. They couldn't order dehydrated cheese powder from Nuts.com; instead, culinary patterns arose from local abundance and trade routes. When the chef Scott Peacock teamed up with the chef Edna Lewis to compile an anthology of Southern recipes, they reflected on how, even in the cuisine of one subregion of one country, so many of Peacock's childhood recipes revolved around peanut oil (he was raised in southern Alabama) and so many of Lewis's revolved around lard (she was raised near livestock).[1] Then came the internet, which despite what cultural critics who are better equipped than I to say might have you believe, was a good thing, at least the way I look at it: It made all sorts of information newly accessible to people. (Yes, it spawned QAnon, and yes, it may have flattened culture, but it also taught my grandpa who Malala was and made it so when people were dying of Covid alone in quarantined hospital units, they could press a button to see the faces they loved most.)

With search engines came search engine optimization, and with SEO came the end of a certain kind of storytelling. Maybe that's too macabre. That certain kind of storytelling was already dying, I guess. The advertising models were all broken. SEO only helped to kill it faster, because thoughtful stories didn't necessarily go viral the way that stories of putting tens of thousands of dollars in a shoebox and handing it to a stranger went viral. Which is not to say that the modern internet hasn't spawned some of the best stories out there, ones about food included. (And it's given rise to a whole host of new storytellers, whom we call "influencers," which has ushered in a new and yet familiar tradition of oral storytelling with its own thousands of subcultures.)

I tell you all of this not because I want to complain about what we've lost, or because I have the answer to where any of it is going, but because I want to explain how I got here. To the point of writing a book that is basically clickbait incarnate—though I really did find several excellent ways to roast chicken, and I stand by them—while it simultaneously inspects and criticizes my own drive to produce exactly that.

This whole project started with bacon and insecurity. I had left a Wall Street job for a nebulous career in "food media," which at the time mostly meant *Bon Appétit* staffers posting photographs of cappuccinos with the caption "copped," and which also portended lots of layoffs. Part of me was amused by the way that stylists in the test kitchen where I worked executed their chore load with the focus of emergency room surgeons, the way they delivered bad news in exactly the same style ("I'm so sorry but, your apple cake—it, it didn't make the inversion"). And the other part was terrified that whatever I had stumbled into (cupcakes in the middle of the day, an impromptu assignment to interview Magnus Nilsson, health insurance) was going to end very soon. So I set out to make myself indispensable. I went into the back end of the website I worked for and sorted all stories ever written in descending order of most comments. A top result was something about how to cook bacon, and the commenters were incensed and vocal about their own strategies. And so my former column, "Absolute Best Tests," was born.

This book couldn't be further from that column, technically speaking. That column crawled out of my sense of urgency and anxiety, and I wrote it with little reporting. But it taught me how to use my tendency toward obsession in a way that was, at least a bit, productive. My natural desire to spiral actually worked for me instead of against me when it came time to go down the internet wormhole of all of the different ways to boil eggs. It wasn't novel; publications like America's Test Kitchen and Serious Eats had pioneered a sort of science-inflected, iterative way to develop recipes long ago, and with far more scientific expertise. It was just my spin.

So is this book. I'm not charting new territory; I'm compiling my research. About how there are so, so many ways to do any task in the kitchen, about what happens when I pluck the pieces I like best from each method and weave them together. And about the people, places, and things obsessed with excellence. I went to the State Fair of Texas to learn about how deep-fried butter came to win an award. I visited Des Moines for the Blue Ribbon Bacon Festival—then trailed its architect around the world to Japan, for more bacon. I drove into the black belt of Alabama to become a "biscuiteer," under the watchful eye of Scott Peacock. I pored over cookbooks and history books and stories about culture. I spent days gorging at the last remaining all-you-can-eat buffets on the Las Vegas strip. I traveled through Italy to learn techniques for making fresh pasta chewy, and got my rental car locked in a private parking garage indefinitely in the process. I interviewed three generations of one family who run a tiny senbei shop in Kichijoji and attended dueling ramen festivals in Tokyo. I trawled all over the structures of "the best" that had been built before me, before I began to build a few myself. By which I mean I tried to catch one of Lil Mo's tee shirts as it shot through the air. It slipped through my fingertips.

SO, WHAT IS THIS BOOK? HOW SHOULD YOU USE IT?

This whole project was nebulous and sweeping, and at times it became personal. Instead of ending up with some tightly packaged answer about why certain people (me, and maybe you) are intrinsically obsessed with a vague idea of "the best," in the end, I arrived mostly at more questions.

I wanted to know about the finest ways to cook things, and I wanted to inspect the cultural forces that had led me to that inclination—that had driven so many of you to tussle in the comments sections and my inbox, telling me I had missed something, or telling me you had located an obscure technique, or encouraging me to keep going.

Just as there is no such thing as "the best," broadly, there is no "best" way to do any one thing in the kitchen. I set out to identify culinary methods that produce maximal flavor with minimal technique. So at the top of each section where I detail my findings, you'll see I've included a bit about my "mission." From there, I guide you through the findings of what I call "head-to-head trials," basically pitting many cooking methods or ingredients or tools against one another to analyze the varying results. Each section of head-to-head findings leads into at least one Mother Recipe, combining the elements of my trials I liked most for the desired result, plus several additional recipes that either iterate on the Mother or make use of other methods that didn't make sense in the Mother.

Use the book however suits you: If you prefer to cook or bake without a recipe, the head-to-head findings will still offer insight and save you a good bit of home testing. If you prefer not to get into the weeds and just want the best method, as I saw it, flip right to the Mother Recipe; check out the headnote and difficulty level. If I'm recommending a recipe that seems like a project, trust me, it's worth it. And if you love the Mother Recipe but want to dive even deeper, try the next few recipes. Each one is designed for flexibility, meaning there's room to play with seasonings, toppings, platings, and pairings throughout, because that's how I like to cook and bake.

And then, there are reported essays. At first, I wanted to understand if those cultural forces I mentioned were predominantly American. That was a question that came up a lot as I reported this book, from kind strangers on elevators and organizers of festivals to which I had flown: Are Americans *really* more obsessed with the best than any other culture?

Absolutely not. No culture is a monolith, but even if one were, America is no more obsessed with excellence than any other place; it's just obsessed in a unique way. But there are people everywhere who are obsessed with the best: Sometimes that means knowing about it, sometimes that means being it, sometimes that means avoiding it or scowling at the fixation with it. In every country, in every subculture—in every family, even—there are singular views of superiority and excellence, informed by identity and experience and history. (By the way, I'll admit here that I, too, am completely obsessed with the best. I danced around that admission for most of the past year, while I reported this book. When I sold the book proposal, the publishing announcement said I would be exploring Americans' obsession with the best—as though I wasn't one of them. The truth is, I am so competitive that I recently had to self-eliminate from a friend's birthday scavenger hunt, because I came to in the chalk aisle of a CVS as I was saying to my husband that he was "lagging on purpose, forcing us to throw this thing." I have always known this about myself, and yet I resisted the connection between my own disposition and the central question of this project, because I could not stomach the idea of personally declaring "the best" any one way of doing anything in the kitchen. Because it's not—context is integral to everything, and especially to the way we cook and eat.)

But what began as an attempt to unravel certain mysteries of culinary excellence evolved into a broader exploration of the human experience. We eat so we can survive, but we also eat to connect with our heritage, to feel things, to express our creativity, to forge bonds. In the end, this book is not just about "the best" recipes, it's about celebrating the diversity of culinary traditions and the universal human quest for meaning.

WHAT YOU'LL NEED

You won't need much to execute most of the recipes in this book. Although I included tools like a sous vide and an air fryer where it made sense in my trials, I would only ever recommend special equipment to you in a recipe if it was really, really worth it. I'm a flavor maximalist and a technique minimalist. I want to save you money for ingredients and, when you're too tired to cook, for fancy cured meat to drape throughout layers of your chip towers! (See page 353.)

I do occasionally call for the food processor when I think it's really worth lugging out, as in my Triple-Secret Meatballs on page 175 or the Dark Chocolate Pretzel Buttercream on page 324. And many of my baking recipes call for a stand mixer, or else a hand mixer. I also recommend you use an inexpensive kitchen scale (I love Escali!) and sometimes an instant-read thermometer. Both are great additions to the obsessive's kitchen.

A NOTE ON INGREDIENTS

There are a few special pantry items I think you should stock up on right now, which my mother recently said were "all finely milled specialty powders, like cocaine." They are:

DIAMOND CRYSTAL KOSHER SALT: My salt of choice! If you like to use Morton's kosher salt instead, start with about two-thirds as much as I call for, and scale up to taste.

DUTCH-PROCESS COCOA POWDER: It tastes like the outside of Oreos! The nuts and bolts: This is cocoa that has been alkalinized, which means it's less bitter than natural cocoa. I call for it anytime I ask you to use cocoa powder. My favorite brands are Droste and Gerbs.

"00" FLOUR: I call for "00" flour in the Egg Pasta Dough on page 228. The name refers to the fine grind of the wheat, which makes for super-tender but stretchy, glutinous noodles. It absorbs water more readily than a coarser flour. As Scott Peacock taught me, you can also use "00" for excellent biscuits.

MALTED MILK POWDER: Malted milk powder is basically whole milk powder with super-nutty, savory notes from ground-up malted barley. I call for it as a way to make my Gooey Malted Cookie Dough Chocolate Chunk Bars on page 294 taste like the dough has been hydrating for days, and to add complexity and chew to the Chewy Malted Chocolate Shortbread on page 343. You could also make an incredible whipped cream by adding a few spoonsful as you reach the soft peak stage, while the mixer runs. Or, add it to the panna cotta on page 282 and top with crushed malted milk balls. I buy enormous tubs of Carnation malted milk powder, and I'm constantly shocked by how quickly I go through them.

TOASTED MUSHROOM POWDER: You will not regret familiarizing yourself with toasted mushroom powder, which gives so much layered depth to roasts, chicken skin, broths, my Triple-Secret Meatballs on page 175, and more. You can buy a concentrated, finely ground mushroom powder online—I like shiitake powder. But I prefer to make my own by blending dried mushrooms into fine dust in a powerful blender, then toasting that dust over dry heat in a skillet for 5 to 10 minutes while I stir, until it's gone from pale beige to dark taupe and is super fragrant. For more on mushroom powder, see page 162.

WHOLE MILK POWDER: This is essentially just evaporated milk. It can make baked goods more tender, or a milkshake incredibly creamy, but in this book I use it mostly to boost flavor. You'll find it in my Overachiever Extra-Browned Butter Bakery-Worthy CCCs on page 290, in the first variation for my Shortbread Mother Recipe on page 340, and in my Milk and Honey Whipped Cream on page 270. It's the most delicious way to stabilize whipped cream, and incredibly savory and rich in a buttercream frosting. You can also play around with it once you've secured a bag. Try it in my Under-Pressure Flaky Biscuits on page 17 or add it to the Fluffy No-Special-Equipment Pancakes on page 48. I like Judee's Brand Whole Milk Powder, which is what the recipes were tested with, though King Arthur also makes a version that gets rave reviews.

WHERE
TO
BEGIN?

1

Tender Layered

BISCUITS

MISSION

A formula for buttery biscuits that emerge from the oven layered like a Victorian lady's fan, and which can be executed without special machinery. Even if the biscuit-maker is weirdly nervous and clammy.

WHAT I TESTED

Fat integration • Other additions
Baking temp • Cut method
Chilling and/or freezing dough

GRATED BUTTER
CUBED BUTTER
GRATED + CUBED BUTTER
LARD
EGG YOLK
VODKA
MILK
BUTTERMILK
WHITE WINE
CHEESE
FOOD PROCESSOR
STAND MIXER
350°F
375°F
400°F
BISCUIT CUTTER
SHARP KNIFE
BENCH SCRAPER
DROP BISCUITS
PRE-FREEZE
PRE-FREEZE + FREEZE DOUGH
JUST FREEZE DOUGH
JUST CHILL DOUGH
MAKE BY HAND

I BECAME A "BISCUITEER" ON A SUNNY MORNING IN APRIL.

It was the first day of an eight-day holiday about avoiding risen bread. I set out for a long drive to see Scott Peacock—the Southern chef so prolific he was once flown out to make biscuits and fried chicken for the birthday party of a celebrity who lives in a seaside town in California that rhymes with "mosquito" and who has many favorite things. (Always abide the NDA.) I had my first biscuit of the day in Birmingham at 7:15 a.m. for $1 at Salem's Diner, where my server, Joyce, called me "baby." I gushed about its tender belly to Wayne, who owns the diner. He told me it came frozen. (Joyce had recommended I order the bacon, egg, and cheese breakfast wrap and I hadn't listened; when one went by to another table, Joyce pointed and said, "Now look, baby, *that* is the *wrap*.")

I arrived several hours later seventy-three miles away in Marion, Alabama, the historic town in Alabama's black belt where Coretta Scott King was married, and where Peacock now teaches what he calls "biscuiting" to hopeful "biscuiteers," in the kitchen of a Greek Revival mansion that looks like the one in *Hush . . . Hush, Sweet Charlotte.* "We need biscuit more than it needs us," Peacock told me. "And there is nothing that expresses the touch of the baker more than the biscuit; the biscuit will express the baker whether you want it to or not."

Peacock's burnished biscuits and leavings (the scraps he adds to the sheet pan with the stamped-out rounds) express that he is a semi-reformed perfectionist, with a deep respect for tradition. In fact, Peacock nearly turned his focus to European cooking as a young man until a conversation with Edna Lewis set him straight; to this day he docks his biscuits with a fork like she did when they lived and cooked together, though he says, "We never discussed why she did it." As soon as a batch of biscuits enters Peacock's 500°F range, he abandons all small talk as he narrates the successive "blooms" in the oven like a preacher giving a sermon, the aroma stretching and tumbling through the kitchen, his voice reaching a crescendo right before he "rescues them from their agony" moments before they would burn. They come out of the oven looking prehistoric, arid and mottled with craggy seams from where Peacock's homemade single-acting baking powder labored mightily.

Peacock's biscuits are made with a level of drama and respect I came to recognize from the time I spent observing people obsessed with the best: They call for two different heritage-grain flours, extra-thick and extra-salty buttermilk, and the homemade baking powder he has long evangelized. Perhaps he respects biscuits so well because he grew up obsessed with them, first the kind from the Pillsbury can, which he tried and failed to replicate as a boy in Hartford, Alabama. Or perhaps it's because in the oral histories he's collected, the topic of biscuit as fantastical treat has surfaced again and again; he recalls a ninety-one-year-old subject explaining that cornbread was ubiquitous to a Southern child, but a biscuit meant a special occasion, and it had to be shared with siblings. Corn could be farmed all around, but flour cost money.

The stovetop cathead biscuits my mom remembers from her grandmother and aunts expressed something, too: a stubbornness worn by the Wolverton women, who chose to live in a tiny Appalachian town in Kentucky that flooded so badly each year that they had to move away for several weeks and rebuild their lives when it drained. No one liked to cook, but they all liked fresh biscuits with their coffee. So my mother's aunt, Butch—a woman so predisposed to caretaking that she kept a pen of stray dogs in case she had time to find one a home—dutifully ran the two-minute process to make a batch of dough several times a day, like someone might refill a Brita, with bacon grease from an old can on the countertop, all-purpose flour, and a little bit of milk. The ones my mom made us growing up, drop biscuits riddled with sharp cheddar, expressed that she had learned to put on airs in the North.

Zeb Stevenson's biscuits down in Atlanta expressed an innovation born of necessity. Stevenson, who became the chef at renowned Atlanta restaurant Watershed after Peacock, eventually spent years at the helm of his own spot. On certain days of the week, he began to sell towering, square-cut biscuits to lines of clamoring fans. They weren't angel biscuits (another classic Southern style that uses yeast as well as baking powder and soda), and they weren't quite the yeast-raised ones you'd find in an old cookbook. Stevenson closed down the restaurant late each night, so he needed a dough that he could prepare the night before and cold ferment in the refrigerator while he got a few hours of sleep; his overnight formula emerged.

The frozen biscuits I loved at Salem's Diner expressed Wayne's devotion. He had scoured the market for premade biscuits he could trust to bake dependably, so he was free to focus on what was more important to the regulars who had started to feel like family (extra-crispy hash browns, handmade sausage flecked with pepper, that *wrap*).

And mine express that I am a little frivolous, taken with the zeitgeist: biscuits that tower and teeter like Slinkies about to tip down a staircase, catnip for the internet generation. They express that despite everything I've learned as a biscuiteer, I still think maybe I can have it all, sweet and savory at once, a biscuit with more functions than most pairs of shoes. They say that I'm full of hubris, that my hands are often clammy, and that despite both of those damning qualities, this biscuit recipe is worth passing along.

About a week after I met Peacock, he came to New York City and invited me over for tea. I brought my frivolous biscuits, warm in a small box held together by a fuchsia ribbon, nervous to hear what he would make of the lamination. The room filled with his pals: Ruth Reichl; an advertising executive who had invented a slogan you've heard; a poet who described the tea beautifully ("it looks like it's holding candlelight") and who asked me to tell her about one of the essays in this book, then said she had read a similar essay elsewhere. I glanced sideways at my box of biscuits. Scott caught me looking. "Don't worry," he said. "There's no such thing as the one true biscuit."

We never cracked the box; his guests trickled out one by one and I spent the next couple of days glancing at my phone for some conclusion, maybe an indictment, but by the time Monday came, and still nothing, I knew I had already gotten what I needed.

It wasn't until I had baked maybe forty batches of biscuits that I had a revelation: Biscuits are just pie dough with a better personality. Maybe that's an oversimplification—there are, after all, so many ways to make a biscuit. There are the fluffy-but-flat single-layer Southern-style biscuits, angel biscuits, cathead biscuits. There are the hulking, tender yeast-raised biscuits that Stevenson spent years perfecting. There are biscuits made with lard, ones seared in hot bacon fat, ones made completely on the stovetop. There are biscuits made with shortening, like the ones Toni Tipton-Martin recorded in *Jubilee*.[1] The biscuits made with heritage wheat by Peacock in Alabama. Drop biscuits, biscuits with cheese in the dough, biscuits from a can.

But I wanted to develop a version of an accordion-flaky buttermilk biscuit with the kind of layers that would allow me to peel one apart, to watch steam from its belly billow up and away. Like the ones at Tandem Bakery in Portland, Maine, or Bird Dog Café, a few blocks from my apartment. And I wanted them to be foolproof for a home cook of any skill level. Key to this biscuit is its crusty top and tender interior. I learned pretty early on into my trials that making a tall biscuit with distinct folds really comes down to two things: (1) integrating the fat in such a way that enough pieces of it remain in solid shreds so that, like with a rough puff pastry, they melt and emit steam that causes layers to rise in the oven, and (2) folding the dough together so that it forms distinct layers rather than one fused lump with butter bits here and there. Grating the butter before you mix it with the dry ingredients—a trick that had been floating around restaurant kitchens and the internet for ages, and which was further popularized by Briana Holt's biscuits at Tandem Bakery after my friend Eric Kim adapted the recipe[2] in 2023—worked far better than any other method of fat integration, because it produced consistent, cheerful wood-chip shreds of butter. The only issue was that the delicate grated butter could melt when handled with hot hands, but a few jaunts into the freezer, plus freezing-cold liquid, easily solved that. Freezing the biscuits before baking them also ensured the butter bits were solid.

I learned through trial and error that folding the dough over itself too many times can actually create too much cohesiveness, especially for a hot-handed baker like myself. I landed on a mixture of folds until most of the dry flour dust had been incorporated, then a few slice-and-stacks, to make sure the edges are clean and distinct and don't keep the biscuits from rising tall.

It took Zeb and Scott demonstrating their thoughtful versions for me to really think about the nuts and bolts of a biscuit. And how those nuts and bolts are the same ones you'd use to make piecrust. The proportions are a little different from those in pie dough, which contains less moisture than your average buttermilk biscuit, but the main players are there: butter or lard, all-purpose flour, salt, sugar, moisture. And the core tenet for flaky layers—keeping bits of butter intact, in just the right way—applies to both.

Which led me to another realization: For decades, home cooks in the know have been adding vodka to their pie dough for a more tender crust. (I tried to trace this back; the earliest tip I found was in a 2007 *Cook's Illustrated* article.) More than a dozen years ago, a Redditor named "hailtheface" offered a plausible explanation for how vodka helps piecrust[3]: Essentially, the formation of gluten causes shrinking and tightening during the bake; vodka inhibits gluten formation, keeping the crust tender and delicate.

Vodka-as-secret-ingredient knows no bounds: Chefs also add it to no-churn ice cream to keep it from turning icy (vodka has a lower freezing point than water), and to the batter for fried foods for extra crackle. I landed on replacing about ¼ cup of the buttermilk in my recipe with vodka, and the results are the most tender biscuit I've had the pleasure of peeling apart.

I used a similar sugar ratio to the Tandem biscuits, based on a recipe adaptation in *The New York Times,* but added brown sugar for a faint molasses-evoking sweetness that pairs perfectly with butter. For the rest of the liquid, I used buttermilk for its tenderizing acid and savory undertone. (My trial with wine produced wine-flavored biscuits that were actually surprisingly flaky, perhaps due to their alcohol content, and my trials with milk made for much denser biscuits.) Fat-wise, I settled on butter, but lard—per Lewis's recipe[4]—worked beautifully, too. Do swap it in if you've got some readily accessible. Ultimately, to combat wonky home ovens, I suggest heating to 400°F, then baking at 375°F to give your baking powder an early kick in the butt.

THE BEST METHOD

Use frozen grated butter, add vodka (!!!) to your buttermilk, and take advantage of the fold-and-stack, as on page 17.

MOTHER RECIPE

UNDER-PRESSURE FLAKY BISCUITS

LEVEL

Anyone can execute

TIME

1 hour

MAKES

6 big biscuits or 12 smaller ones

I wanted to develop a super-flaky, sweet, layered biscuit that would release steam from its belly when peeled in two, and I wanted them to be easy to perfect. The biggest antagonist to this style of biscuit is pressure. Timing pressure, attention from a crowd, or a lack of counter space. All of which create hot hands! Which reduces your ability to keep a good portion of the butter in solid form. The solution is not special equipment; anyone should be able to make a great biscuit with just forks, a knife, and either a pastry cutter or two spatulas. The solution is attention to temperature, and ingredient composition. These ended up close to the Tandem Bakery biscuits recipe with a few tweaks. My big three findings—which I discuss in detail on page 15—are that frozen grated butter is a sensation for a reason, too much folding can lead to overly sticky dough (and thus midway through I ask you to switch to a slice-and-stack), and vodka (!!!) contributes an extra measure of tender crumb. Since I know you (my mother) will ask: Yes, you could do all these steps in the food processor. Just be sure to scrape in any bits of butter that don't make it through the grating disc, and lower your expectations about 10 percent; the biscuits will still be delicious, but you'll end up with a dough that rises a little less. Either way, when pressing out the dough, press gently, and from the center; as Scott Peacock told me in Alabama, biscuit dough is but "a sponge full of water." When it comes time to cut, use the sharpest tool available and slice in a straight-down slice. Moving a blade back and forth to try to saw biscuits apart will make their layers stick (and ruin the rise).

1 cup (2 sticks/225 g) salted butter, frozen

3 cups (426 g) all-purpose flour

¼ cup (50 g) granulated sugar

¼ cup (49 g) light brown sugar

4 teaspoons baking powder

2 teaspoons Diamond Crystal kosher salt

¼ cup (49 g) vodka, chilled in the freezer

1 cup plus 1 tablespoon (250 g) cold buttermilk, shaken to combine

1. Grate the frozen butter on the medium side of a box shredder. Add to a large bowl, along with the flour, granulated sugar, brown sugar, baking powder, and salt. Freeze the bowl for 15 minutes, or up to 24 hours, covered.

2. Toss the mixture with two forks, not your hands (to keep it cold). You can stop when the ingredients are well-integrated, meaning the butter shreds are still intact, but they're coated in flour and sugar and evenly spaced throughout the bowl. Pour the vodka and buttermilk over the top (not all in one place) and stir to combine—just until you have big rocky clumps of dough and some floury bits on the rim and bottom. (Don't overmix.)

3. Dump the mixture onto a clean cutting board or countertop. (Bonus points if you have a cold surface, like a marble pasta board, but no worries if not.) Press it gently into a large (roughly 10 × 10-inch) square, pressing the floury dust into the top and sides as you go. You'll end up with a shaggy, not quite cohesive square a little more than 1 inch tall.

continued

4. Take a pastry cutter or your two widest spatulas and slide them under the neatest (most stuck together) side of the messy square, and as best you can, fold that side over the other, like you're closing a book. (It's fine if things are still messy and crumbly.) For those keeping track, you'll now have a crumbly 10 × 5-inch rectangle a little more than 2 inches tall. Gently repeat, folding one short side over the top, so you end up with a shaggy 5 × 5-inch square. With just barely damp (from the sink) hands, press in any remaining floury matter into the top and press out your 5 × 5 square back into a 10 × 10 square, like a more cohesive version of what you began with.

5. Repeat step 4 just until you have a 5 × 5-inch square. THIS TIME, press it out with your hands from its top and center (not sides) just until it's a little flatter, about 7 × 7 inches. Take a pastry cutter or sharp knife and cut straight down the center, and stack one half on top of the other. Press it down from the top and center (not sides) just until it's roughly cohesive and repeat: Slice it down the center and stack. Then, press it gently from the top back into a 7 × 7-inch square. Using a sharp knife or pastry cutter, divide the square into 6 tall biscuits (each will be about 3.5 × 2 inches wide and about 2 inches tall). (For more and smaller biscuits, just cut each of these in two.)

6. Freeze the biscuits for at least 20 minutes, uncovered, or tightly wrapped for up to 3 weeks.

7. When you're ready to bake, heat the oven to 400°F. Place the frozen biscuits on a metal sheet pan or in a cast-iron skillet; give them at least 1 inch of space to rise properly. Place in the oven and lower the heat to 375°F. Bake for 24 to 28 minutes, until browned in places across the top, fluffy, and set on the sides.

A BERRY COBBLER

LEVEL

Anyone can execute

TIME

1 hour

MAKES

Cobbler for 6 to 8

I originally called this recipe "A Better Berry Cobbler." I meant "better to me," because this one gets a roof of flaky-tender buttermilk biscuits rather than the denser drop biscuits of my youth. (It turns the cobbler into more of an upside-down berry shortcake instead of the more commonly seen flat cake-topped one. For tips on maximizing biscuit rise, see page 14.) But the more I dug into the classic cobbler, the more I wanted to crabwalk away from that title. The dish came about in the British colonies as a sort of corollary to suet pudding. Today, variations have a host of names, like the "slump" or the "grunt." Even within the American South, there are a number of cobblers. As Scott Peacock wrote in The Gift of Southern Cooking*, to Edna Lewis, "'cobbler' meant a kind of deep-dish pie with fruit baked between a bottom and top layer of pastry."[5] For Peacock, the "cobbler" was a dish of fruit that had cream biscuits baked into its top like dumplings, but also occasionally meant canned peaches covered with a box of Duncan Hines Yellow Cake Mix with melted butter poured on top of it, then baked. So in lieu of starting something I can't finish (I love to nap), I'm going to just call this recipe A Berry Cobbler and leave it at that.*

1 recipe Under-Pressure Flaky Biscuits, prepared through recipe step 4 on page 17 (don't bake them!)

Roughly 8 cups mixed berries, frozen (fresh is fine but frozen will get jammier)

⅓ cup (64 grams) light or dark brown sugar, plus 3 tablespoons for topping the biscuits

2 tablespoons cornstarch

3 tablespoons freshly squeezed lemon juice

1 tablespoon vanilla bean paste or pure vanilla extract

½ teaspoon Diamond Crystal kosher salt

1 large egg

Vanilla bean ice cream, for serving

1. Prepare the Under-Pressure Flaky Biscuits recipe through step 4.

2. Repeat the folding motion: Take a pastry cutter or your two widest spatulas and slide them under the neater (more stuck together) side of the square, and fold that side over the other, like you're closing a book. Do it again, folding the short side over the short side so you end up with another 5 × 5-inch square. THIS TIME, press it out from its top and center (not sides) with your hands just until it's a little flatter, about 7 × 7 inches, and then take your pastry cutter or a sharp knife and cut straight down the center, and stack one half on top of another. Press it down from the top and center (not sides) just until it's roughly cohesive, and repeat: Slice it down the center and stack. Press it gently from the top back into an 8 × 8-inch square, then take a sharp knife or pastry cutter and divide the block into 8 square biscuits (each will be about 2 inches × 2 inches wide, and a little under 2 inches tall).

3. Freeze the biscuits, uncovered, for at least 20 minutes, or tightly wrapped, for up to 3 weeks.

4. When you are ready to bake, make the fruit layer. Heat the oven to 400°F.

5. Butter a 9 × 13-inch baking dish (Pyrex is fine, so is metal). Add the fruit, ⅓ cup of the brown sugar, the cornstarch, lemon juice, vanilla, and salt. Toss with a fork to combine and coat the fruit evenly; lightly mash to release some

continued

juices. Let sit for at least 15 minutes to macerate, aka release more juice. (If you're using fresh fruit, let it sit closer to 45 minutes and wait to preheat the oven.)

6. Bake for about 15 minutes, to give the fruit a head start. Meanwhile, whisk the egg in a small bowl to use in a few minutes as an egg wash.

7. After 15 minutes, carefully remove the dish from the oven and top with the frozen biscuits. Distribute them evenly across the surface so that when they rise and spread and topple sideways, they'll fan out and cover most of the top. Use a pastry brush or the back of a spoon to paint the tops of the biscuits with egg wash. Sprinkle the tops with the remaining 3 tablespoons brown sugar.

8. Return the dish to the oven and reduce the heat to 375°F. Bake for 20 to 26 minutes (timing will vary based on your berry type), until the berry mixture is thickened and bubbling around the edges and the biscuits are beginning to brown on top. If they show a hint of burning, you can lower the temperature and bake for longer or tent with foil.

9. Serve warm, scooped from the baking dish, topped with ice cream.

2

Crispy-Chewy BACON

MISSION

Bacon with clearly perceptible stretches of chew and crispy edges.

WHAT I TESTED

Bacon thickness
Cooking methods
Coatings

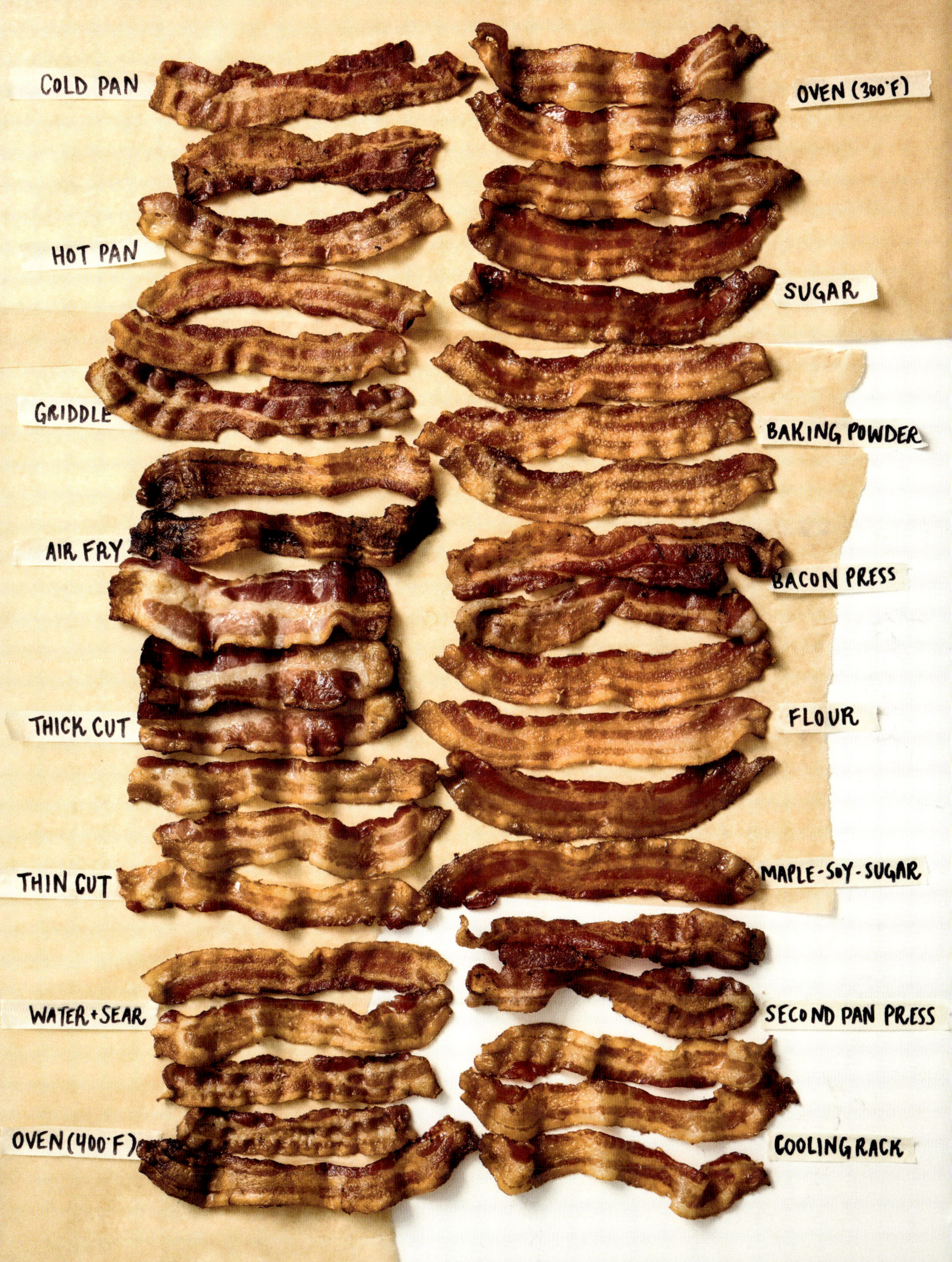
COLD PAN
OVEN (300°F)
HOT PAN
SUGAR
GRIDDLE
BAKING POWDER
AIR FRY
BACON PRESS
THICK CUT
FLOUR
THIN CUT
MAPLE-SOY-SUGAR
WATER+SEAR
SECOND PAN PRESS
OVEN (400°F)
COOLING RACK

BACON IS AN INGREDIENT THAT NEEDS VIRTUALLY NO NUDGING TO BECOME THE MOST DELICIOUS VERSION OF ITSELF.

I heard that message clearly when I flew to Des Moines, Iowa, for the Blue Ribbon Bacon Festival: The best way to cook bacon, I was told, is any way that is at your immediate disposal. I learned that lesson again at the Porktoberfest in Kofu, Japan, where bacon four times as thick as I'd ever seen it was threaded onto skewers and turned over an open fire until its edges prickled with char and its belly wept with rendered fat.

Bacon is, in a sense, self-saucing—the fat is going to melt into the rest of the meat as you cook it, so you need not prepare a pan with cooking fat. Almost any type of skillet or griddle or pan will get the job done; differences in vessel merely encourage various degrees of crispiness depending on contact and air circulation.

Against the advice of everyone I interviewed about bacon—flagging this for therapy—I still wanted to add something to the conversation. I hoped to find a way to cook bacon that maximized the qualities I loved, even if they were mostly naturally occurring. So I committed to finding a method that produces chewy swaths and crispy bits within the same bacon strips.

I tested a range of techniques, which all worked well; my favorite used a cast-iron pan, for its even temperature and seasoned surface. I experimented with coating bacon in flour, sugar, a glaze, and baking powder. Sugar and flour took a good thing and made it a little too sodden. I was delighted by the effectiveness of the baking powder in producing crisp; if you like your bacon like a pretzel stick, do try it. The soy-sugar glaze swept me off my feet. It enhanced without overwhelming, and when applied later on, didn't cause the bacon to burn.

I ultimately settled on a technique without special equipment. As with most bad behavior, this method works best with thick-cut bacon. (Thin tended to stick together when overlapped.) For thin-cut bacon, I preferred the oven method, straight on the sheet pan at 400°F.

THE BEST METHOD

Start thick cut bacon in a cold cast iron pan or griddle, overlapping the strips with intention for spots of chew.

8

MOTHER RECIPE

"B.E.C." BACON
(aka Chewy-Crispy Bacon)

LEVEL

Anyone can execute

TIME

15 minutes

MAKES

Bacon for 4 to 6

All bacon is good bacon. Bodega B.E.C. bacon, with its chewy sections and moments of crisp, is perfect bacon. To achieve this Platonic ideal at home: (1) use thick-cut bacon, (2) start with a cold pan, (3) cook in a cast-iron skillet or on a griddle, and (4) for the chewiest bits, layer the bacon strips with a couple crosswise strips. For more crisp, I recommend using a second pot or pan like a giant bacon press to finish your strips. To take this to the next level, I add a glaze toward the end, but you can skip that bit if you want pure pork.

2 tablespoons soy sauce

2 tablespoons pure maple syrup

1 tablespoon packed dark or light brown sugar

One 12- to 16-ounce package thick-cut bacon (roughly 8 to 12 strips)

1. In a small bowl, whisk the soy sauce, maple syrup, and brown sugar. Set aside.

2. Place your largest cast-iron skillet or griddle over a burner, but don't turn on the heat. Lay the bacon slices out like a pound symbol: half of the strips side by side with only about ½ inch of space between them, and the other half of the strips perpendicular on top of the first half. (Depending on your pan size, you can cook your bacon in batches, rather than trying to cram a whole package in at once if it doesn't reasonably fit.) Turn on the heat to medium. Burner strength varies, so you'll want to watch the bacon throughout and adjust heat as needed to avoid burning.

3. Cook for 6 to 8 minutes, until the bottoms of the bacon strips have begun to render fat and have developed some browning. Use tongs or forks to flip the strips, and if using a pound symbol formation, keep it intact as you flip (or reform it should the pieces get jumbled). Lower the heat to medium-low and cook for about 5 minutes, until the bottom side has rendered and begun to brown. Place a second pan or Dutch oven—the heavier the better (I use a 5-quart Dutch oven)—over the bacon, like an extra-large bacon press. Cook for about 1 minute. Lift and check for crispness; the bacon should be mostly browned with undercooked parts where overlapping. Remove the second pan. Move any overlapping strips to be parallel with the others, to give the undercooked parts another minute or two of heat so they're chewy but not raw. (If any stick, flip again and cook over medium-low heat until they split easily.)

4. About 1 minute before you're ready to pull the bacon from the skillet, use a pastry brush or the back of a spoon to glaze the strips, then flip. Glaze the other side. Cook each side for 30 seconds, cutting the heat before the bacon begins to burn.

5. Drain on a wire rack, not on paper towels (the bacon will stick to paper towels).

B.L.T. with P.

LEVEL

Anyone can execute

TIME

20 minutes

MAKES

4 sandwiches

As its name suggests, the "B.E.C." Bacon on page 26 is at home on a breakfast sandwich—but it's even better on a B.L.T., where texture is so important given the few ingredients. Here I add a loud fourth to the mix, with wrinkly pepperoncini. If they don't ring a bell, you will definitely recognize the flavor from Mississippi roast, antipasto plates, and top-notch turkey subs. Save the leftover brine for a fluorescent, ascerbic martini.

1 large ripe tomato, heirloom or whatever you like

Diamond Crystal kosher salt

½ head iceberg lettuce

8 pepperoncini in brine, drained

One 12- to 16-ounce package thick-cut bacon (roughly 8 to 12 strips)

8 slices milk bread, white bread, or whatever you like

½ cup Hellmann's mayonnaise (or more if desired)

1. Slice the tomato into 8 slices and sprinkle both sides with salt. Slice 4 roughly ½-inch-thick discs from the lettuce. Slice the pepperoncini into roughly ⅛-inch-thick rings; no need to be too precise.

2. Prepare the bacon as on page 26.

3. Transfer the bacon to a plate and adjust the heat down to low. If there's more than about ¼ inch of grease in the pan, carefully pour it into a bowl and set aside. To the rest of the grease, add as many pieces of the bread as you can fit and griddle for a few minutes on each side, until golden brown. Repeat in batches, adding reserved grease as needed. Sprinkle each slice of bread with salt.

4. Assemble the sandwiches: Apply thick swipes of mayonnaise onto every slice of griddled bread. On half, add two slices of tomato. Add 2 to 3 strips of bacon and a disc of lettuce. Sprinkle the sliced pepperoncini onto the remaining four slices of mayonnaise-swiped bread and stack the slices on top of the lettuce. Cut each sandwich down the center.

3

Foolproof Poached

EGGS

MISSION

Straightforward poached eggs with molten yolks and cohesive, evenly cooked whites.

WHAT I TESTED

Cooking methods • Additions to water
Technique variations • Temperatures

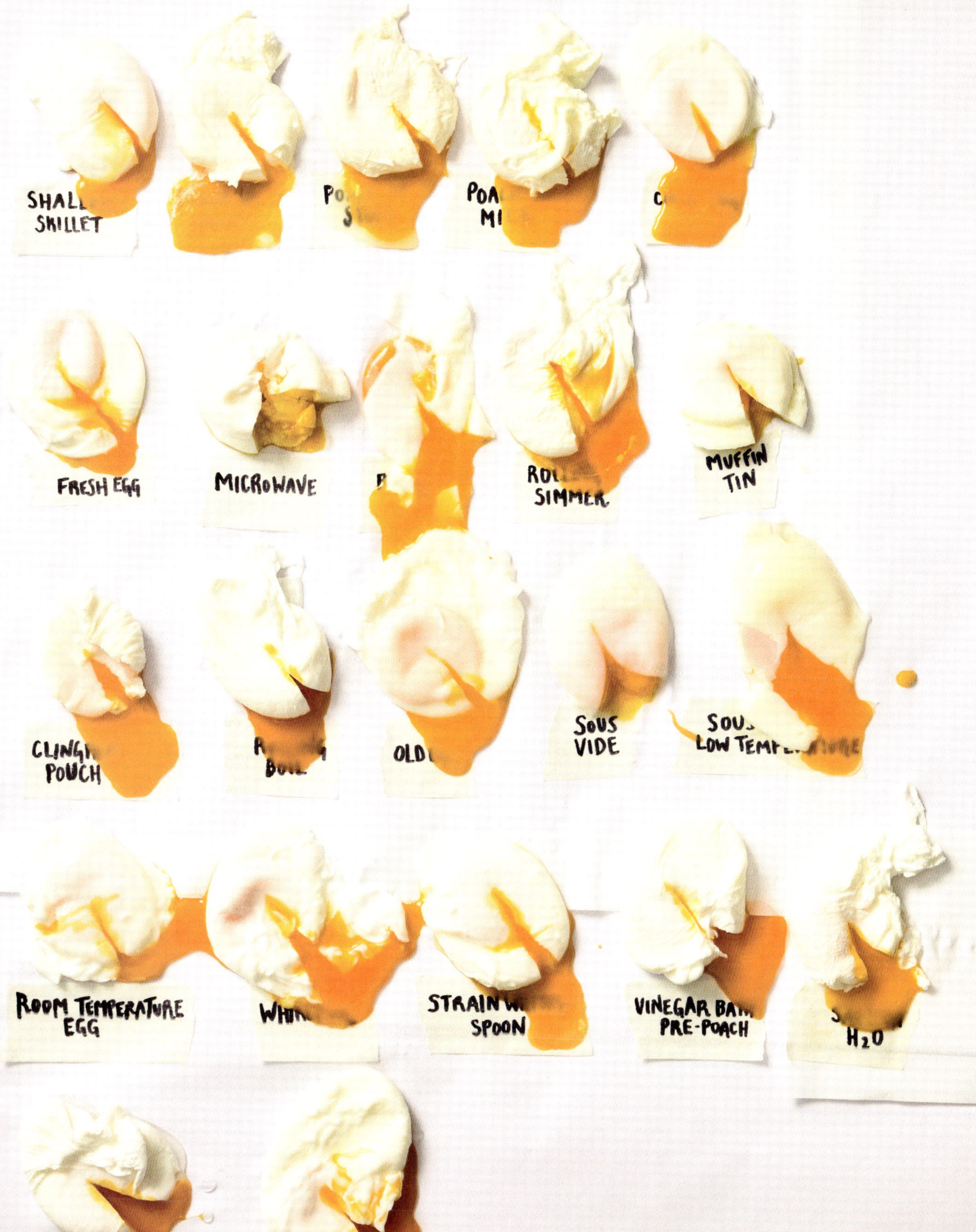

SKILLET
FRESH EGG
MICROWAVE
SIMMER
MUFFIN TIN
POUCH
SOUS VIDE
SOUS
ROOM TEMPERATURE EGG
STRAIN
SPOON
PRE-POACH
H_2O
IN H_2O
STRAIN
SIEVE

THE FOLLOWING SENTENCE WILL TELL YOU EVERYTHING YOU NEED TO KNOW ABOUT HOW MANY FRIENDS I HAD AS A CHILD.

When I was in elementary school, I spent two years fixated on poaching eggs in complete silence by using an As-Seen-On-TV device that some family member had purchased and immediately abandoned. It was a pot with a removable inset layer that consisted of four separate, insulated compartments into which the user could crack eggs. The top layer could then be nestled into boiling water, for four puck-shaped "poached" eggs. A quick perusal reveals that Williams Sonoma still sells a fancy version of this contraption, though I've moved past it for a few reasons. One is conceptual: It does not truly poach; the egg never directly touches hot water, which is the point of the cooking technique and is key to achieving delicate, tender whites. The second is that I am patently against equipment that has a single use, unless that single use occurs all the time, as with a rice cooker or martini shaker.

I have abandoned that instrument of As-Seen-On-TV sorcery in favor of the real, mercurial thing. A true poached egg is, by definition, somewhat fussy. Its name accurately implies the helicopter-cheffing required to maintain a simmer, rather than the hands-off approach of letting it (a pot of water) rip (I'm desperate to seem cool), at a full boil over high heat.[1] A true poached egg is an exercise in freeform sculpture. Whereas a soft-boiled egg cooks in its own shell for shape insurance, a poached egg cannonballs unsheathed into a pot of hot water and firms up before one's eyes, sometimes into a taut teardrop with a perfectly centered core of yolk, but more often assuming the form of a lopsided Frisbee wearing a Victorian nightgown.

It's no wonder that the average poached egg fan is, apparently, an optimist. Some 1,500 years after the first poached egg entered the communal record in Marcus Gavius Apicius's cookbook *De Re Coquinaria*, the British Egg Industry Council commissioned[2] a report on a topic that has never once crossed my mind organically: gauging personalities by egg predilection. The BEIC had hired a consumer research firm to poll 1,010 adults on both their traits and their preferences in egg preparations. Then-chairman Andrew Jorêt was quoted in a publication called *Farmers Weekly*, calling the findings "the 'eggs factor.'"

Some of their data is utterly irrelevant to an egg enthusiast who has little knowledge of the UK's geographical sprawl. ("Scrambled egg-eaters are most likely to live south of Birmingham.") But others are revealing: "The average poached egg-eater is likely to have two children and no more than one older brother or sister. . . . A taste for poached eggs increases as one gets older. . . . They may have a tendency to wear decorative clothing and prefer upbeat and lively music. They are also probably happier than most."

The kicker caught my eye. Compared with some of the BEIC's other findings ("The average boiled egg-eater[s] . . . have a tendency to be more disorganised, careless and impulsive. They may also run a greater risk of getting divorced") the "eggs factor" for poached fans was downright cheerful. It makes sense, the bit about happiness and a preference for things upbeat. The poached egg is an inherently hopeful preparation: It requires quite a few more steps than, say, a soft scramble (see page 60) and relies on technique and expertise to produce an evenly cooked, silky result.

I am not an optimist (my "eggs factor" is that I have an eggsiety disorder), so learning to poach perfectly without the little compartments of my youth has been an uncomfortable, decades-long process that only really became easy over the last few months of testing, with a trick unearthed from Mia Glickman, who helped me to test portions of the book. Despite my newfound confidence and the findings from BEIC, I'm still completely silent while the poaching's going down, a disposition Jorêt and co. could perhaps explain in the next study.

SALT IN COOKING WATER: This one's contentious! Most people aggressively warn you away from it, in the same tone reserved for discussions of whether you should wear white to a wedding. But—but—there are others. The authors of *Joy of Cooking* recorded that "contrary to popular belief," exposing eggs to salt before cooking does not cause them to become rubbery and tough—in fact, salt produces more tender eggs, by "encouraging egg proteins to bond less tightly."[3] And those others recommend salt in the water to increase the overall water temperature, causing the white to cook more quickly and sparing the yolk from prolonged exposure to heat.[4] Harold McGee also notes that salt increases the density of the cooking liquid, which aids in causing the poached egg to float when it's ready for lift-out.[5] However, perhaps for the same reason—the pushing of the uncooked egg up and toward the surface—the salted water resulted in wispier, ghostlier whites, so I prefer to **exclude salt from the water, and salt the poached egg after it's cooked**.

VINEGAR IN COOKING WATER, OR AS A PRE-SOAK: Acids like vinegar, the authors of *Joy of Cooking* note, allow egg proteins to unravel and bond enough to become thick and firm, but prevent a hard, clenched binding that would produce a stiff egg white.[6] The point of adding vinegar to your cooking water, according to Tasting Table, is to "reduce the pH of the water to speed up the denaturing of the proteins and reduce the cooking time" and "has the additional benefit of helping the poached egg to better hold its shape."[7] A teaspoon or two of **white vinegar in the cooking water consistently produced neater whites** without imparting a particularly strong flavor—but it had nothing on its cousin, **the vinegar soak**. This is a method I've seen attributed to Thomas Keller, after *Bon Appétit* published his recipe[8] in 2012, though I've heard it's been around professional kitchens for ages. The basic idea is to **crack your egg or eggs into white vinegar and let them hang out for about 5 to 10 minutes *before* you poach**, which sets up the outer layers of their whites so that when they make it into the simmering water, there's far less of a chance they'll splay into a million wisps. (Of note, I recorded that using vinegar at either phase in the poach produced duller whites, but to me, this visual concession is fully worth it for the tautness.)

WHITES STRAINED: Many cheffy poached egg recipes[9] will tell you to strain your eggs through a fine-mesh sieve to remove the loose part of the whites for a better shape. This advice is meant to mitigate the thin, loose whites that surround the thicker intact ones, and which develop over time as the egg sits in your fridge. This works and is a good tip, though McGee's version—**let the white drip through a large slotted spoon**[10] instead of a sieve—was actually much more manageable. In a few trials, my egg clung to the inside of the sieve and the white then either disconnected from the yolk or lost extra mass in the transfer to the hot water. (The sieve is a decent backup, though, if you don't have a large perforated spoon.)

I tested a few **methods for containing the egg whites without added ingredients**. The **whirlpool** (aka creating a swirling vortex in the simmering water) worked well, but—as its critics love to say—it **means you can poach only one egg at a time**. I still recommend its use for beginner poachers. Using plastic wrap as a sort of egg-shaped sous vide bag, which is called the **Arzak egg** after Spanish chef Juan Mari Arzak, was more trouble than it was worth for a plain poached egg, though I understood the appeal for professional production. I could see its use-case if you wanted to subtly infuse a poached egg with a specific flavor, like that of a fresh herb, since you could add it to the plastic wrap pocket along with the egg. But I'd rather add flavor by using a poaching liquid other than water (see page 35 for more details).

TEMPERATURE: Room-temperature eggs will, in theory, produce a more evenly poached final specimen, but the advantages of the poached egg whites I observed relative to **eggs straight from the refrigerator** were minimal. Also, the straight-from-the-fridge eggs had the benefit of colder yolks, which provided some **extra cushion against overcooking the center**. In other words, don't stress if you forget to take out your eggs before you poach to bring them to room temperature, and if you're a beginner poacher, plan to poach straight from the fridge.

POT SIZE: Here is where Mia's advice saved this chapter. Mia, who has poached more eggs than any of us as a line cook at a brunch restaurant, pointed out that they always, *always* used a tall stockpot, to preserve the pear shape of the egg. In trials, the **tall pot produced a consistently egg-shaped poached egg,** rather than the lopsided Frisbee I frequently got when using a shallow skillet or saucepan. This isn't just about aesthetics; the more symmetrical shape of the poached egg meant **more evenly cooked whites,** and less risk of overcooked yolk.

COOKING METHOD: A rolling boil (around 210°F or more) actually made for very solid poached eggs, which was surprising given the . . . whole point (using gentle heat to delicately coagulate the whites into a texture somewhere between pastry cream and baked soufflé core). While the eggs "poached" at a rolling boil were perceptibly a bit tougher, and visibly less regular—some looked perfect, others had rims of crazy bedhead-like whites—I definitely would not sweat water temperature if you're a beginner. Ninety-nine percent of your brunch guests will not notice the slight toughness. That said, **a rolling simmer produces more tender whites**, and you do not need a thermometer to achieve a rolling simmer; **just look for less than a dozen small-to-medium bubbles, rotating in their bursts on the surface every few seconds**. It's your surest bet for evenly shaped eggs with tender, creamy whites and uncooked yolks. The **residual heat method** (turning off the heat when a rolling boil is achieved, dropping in the raw eggs, and covering the pan for 4 or so minutes) also worked well for a **silky texture, though the shape of the egg was less regular** and thus the cook was less even. The microwaved egg was not ideal, despite my high hopes (I regularly use my microwave to make chawanmushi); its whites were the toughest of the bunch. The "poached" eggs baked in water within a muffin tin were also a disappointment, with a bizarre shape, textural unevenness, and whites that were tougher on the bottom but barely cooked on top.

POACHING LIQUID: If you take one thing away from this book, let it be the virtue of poaching eggs in anything other than water. This is an old technique, observable around the world in soups like changua con huevo. As poaching liquids, I tested **milk, cream, and chicken stock**. All three produced delicate poached eggs with exceptional flavor; the dairy-poached eggs had a richer, creamier mouthfeel and the stock-poached eggs were savory. See pages 38 and 39 for more tips on employing these methods at home, and do experiment with infusing herbs, ginger, and spices into your poaching liquid.

POST-TRIAL OMISSIONS: I've omitted both the sous vide egg[11] and David Chang's onsen-inspired egg[12] (also cooked in a sous vide around 145°F) after testing, as both require cooking inside of a shell. They are mind-bendingly melty, though, and I look forward to reporting back when I do soft-boiled egg tests.

THE BEST METHODS

BEST MAINSTAY METHOD: Crack your egg into a perforated spoon, soak it in vinegar for 5 to 10 minutes, and poach it at a rolling simmer, using the whirlpool method if you're a beginner. See page 36 for my technique.

FOR EXTRA YOLK INSURANCE: There are two things you can do to ensure that you don't accidentally cook through your yolk. Both might yield a slightly wonkier shape, but depending on your priorities, it may be worth it. The first is to use eggs straight from the refrigerator and the second is to poach eggs using the residual heat method (described at left) instead of at a rolling simmer.

BEST UPGRADES: Poach in stock. Or poach in milk and make a ricotta-ish cheese from the poaching liquid, to serve as a downy comforter on which to rest your egg. See page 39 for my technique.

MOTHER RECIPE

TALL POT PERFECT POACH

("The Mia")

LEVEL

Anyone can execute

TIME

15 minutes

MAKES

1 poached egg (but you can double, triple, quadruple . . .)

Mia Glickman, one of my recipe testers, might not like that I'm calling this "The Mia," because it's a little fussy—she is one of those intuitive cooks at whom Marcella Hazan would have nodded approvingly. Here is where Mia's advice saved my life (if you call me dramatic, you'll simply make it worse): the most consistently shaped egg white can be achieved by poaching in a tall stockpot rather than a shallow one. The former allows for a deep sea of water in which an egg can more or less begin to coagulate in its natural shape. The latter means a lower water level and, often, poached eggs shaped like Frisbees, occasionally with the dreaded ring of cooked yolk. I bring slightly less to the table than Mia on this one, but here's my two cents: The whirlpool method of swirling water before dropping in your egg is the rare low effort–high reward tweak that I'm going to recommend you do 100 percent of the time if you're a beginner. This recipe uses vinegar to encourage firm, consistently creamy whites. The vinegar is a quick soak for the strained eggs before they poach. As for salt, add it after you poach for the most cohesive whites.

1 or more eggs (straight from the refrigerator if you're a beginner; see my notes on temperature on page 34)

Several tablespoons white vinegar, or more if you're poaching multiple eggs

Diamond Crystal kosher salt

Freshly cracked black pepper

1. Bring a covered stockpot filled with roughly 4 to 6 quarts of unsalted water to a rolling boil. If you don't plan on serving your poached eggs immediately upon cooking, prepare an ice bath.

2. Grab a large slotted spoon and hold it over a bowl. Crack the egg into the spoon and let the teaspoon or so of old watery runny whites drip away from the firmer, intact whites. Discard the watery runny bits that dripped away. Transfer the egg to the bowl and cover in vinegar. (If you're working with multiple eggs at once, you can put them in the same bowl.) Let sit for 5 to 10 minutes, until the outer part of the egg white has become opaque and ghostly.

3. When your water reaches a rolling boil, turn the heat down for a hearty simmer (about 185°F if you're into temps, or burbling edges with less than a dozen bubbles bursting in the center every few seconds if you're just a person trying to poach an egg and the phrase "into temps" was viscerally upsetting to read). It's time to poach. Create a gentle vortex of water in your pot by dipping in your slotted spoon and confidently swirling it in the shape of a black hole once, twice, three times.

continued

4. Gently use your slotted spoon to transfer the egg from the vinegar to the center of the vortex you've created, so it gets pulled into the current and spins into itself. Let it poach for 2½ to 3½ minutes, until when you airlift it with the spoon, the whites are consistently opaque, and a gentle poke with your pointer finger reveals a center that feels fully gelatinous. Remove the egg, and if you're not planning to use it immediately, plunge it into the ice bath. Repeat to poach the rest of your eggs.

5. Sprinkle the egg with salt and black pepper before serving. (If you're entering him in a beauty pageant, you can use a sharp paring knife to cut off any remaining wisps.)

UPGRADE: *If you dare to treat yourself, poaching an egg in chicken or beef stock will not only delicately flavor the egg (go on, add fresh ginger, you coward), it will also yield a little mug of sippable soup once you've finished up business. Think of it as a super-pared-down relative of sopa de ajo, or of the instant ramen I ate nearly every day as a kid with an egg poached into the broth before serving, or don't think of it at all!!! I'm not the mind police. Strain out any weird wispy bits after you poach the eggs.*

MILK-POACHED EGGS ON WARM RICOTTA-ISH TOAST

LEVEL

A bit of skill required

TIME

15 minutes

MAKES

Breakfast for 2

I was so excited to write a headnote about how this is the sexiest recipe of all time—the drip of the yolk, the creamy curds of warm homemade cheese—and then I made it for my family, and my dad said, "Wow, it's so recursive." If there's a less sensual food-word than "recursive," I certainly haven't heard it. He wasn't wrong; there's a satisfying neatness to using up the poaching liquid as a ricotta-ish (or perhaps more accurately, a cottage cheese-ish) spread, which goes between the toasted bread and the milk-poached egg. But he also wasn't focusing on the thing I wanted him to focus on: that this is the sort of recipe you make on a weekend morning while Wolf Parade plays and you dance around in a tee shirt and underwear with unbrushed hair that's somehow still really good. So when you make this, try to focus on that part. By the way, when you're done making this, could I trouble you for your hair routine . . . ?

½ gallon whole milk

2 slices milk bread or sourdough, sliced Sunday-thick

2 eggs

½ cup white vinegar

Diamond Crystal kosher salt

Freshly cracked black pepper

Extra virgin olive oil

1. Fill a stockpot with the milk and set it over a medium-low heat. Stir frequently as it heats, scraping at the bottom of the pan. Watch carefully and lower the temperature to avoid that annoying thing where milk foams up and runs over the top and sides of the pan, forever making your burner smell strange.

2. Meanwhile, toast the bread slices until golden.

3. Hold a large slotted spoon over the sink. Crack each egg into the spoon and let the teaspoon or so of old watery, runny whites drip away from the firmer, intact whites. Discard the watery runny bits that dripped away. Transfer the eggs to the bowl and cover in the vinegar. Let sit for 5 to 10 minutes, until the translucent part of the egg whites has become opaque and ghostly.

4. When the milk reaches a simmer (about 185°F if you're into temps), get ready to poach. You want the milk to be steaming with little bubbles gathering around the sides. If you're a beginner, I recommend poaching one egg at a time, so you can use the whirlpool method to eliminate wisps. Create a gentle vortex of water in the pot by dipping in the slotted spoon and confidently swirling it in the shape of a black hole once, twice, three times (you don't want to go overboard, because too much movement will actually draw your whites into a wispy tail), then transfer an egg into the center of the vortex with the slotted spoon. If you're a pro, disregard and simply transfer each egg very gently into one side of the hot milk. (Reserve the soaking vinegar.)

continued

5. Let poach for about 3 minutes, until the whites are consistently set and the egg has bobbed to the surface; since the milk isn't transparent, you'll have to gently airlift it using the perforated spoon and give it a poke with your pointer finger. It should feel consistently set but still fully gelatinous in the center.

6. Sprinkle the poached eggs with salt and black pepper and set aside for a sec.

7. Meanwhile, cut the heat on the milk and add a few tablespoons of the reserved soaking vinegar. Let sit for about 1 minute, untouched—curds should form, separating the contents into a cottage cheese–like mixture and a cloudy solution. (If they don't, add more vinegar and repeat.) Let sit for a few minutes, then pour this mixture through a fine-mesh sieve lined with a clean kitchen towel set over the sink. Use a spatula to press the curds to release excess liquid.

8. Spread each piece of toast with warm ricotta, top with a poached egg, drizzle with olive oil, season with more salt and pepper, and serve.

NOTE: *If you don't use all the ricotta, you can save it in a sealed container in the fridge for up to a week; I suggest covering it in cream or milk. When you're ready to revive it, mix in the dairy and break up any clumps.*

4

Fluffy PANCAKES

MISSION

Pancakes with deep flavor, a degree of fluffiness that feels celebratory, and crispy edges.

WHAT I TESTED

Leaveners • Flours
Liquids • Additions • Cooking fats
Pancake thickness and composition

CAKE FLOUR
WHOLE WHEAT
CORNMEAL
BUCKWHEAT + SORGHUM
BAKING POWDER
BAKING SODA
COTTAGE CHEESE
MILK
LEMON + RICOTTA
RICE FLOUR SHELL
THIN + CRISPY
SIFT
SELTZER
DRY YEAST
STARTER
WHIPPED EGG WHITE
SOUFFLÉ
BUTTER
CLARIFIED BUTTER
OLIVE OIL
NEUTRAL OIL
COCONUT OIL

A PERFECT PANCAKE CAN TURN ONE'S WHOLE WEEK AROUND.

Or so I was reminded at a 7-Eleven outside of the Tokyo Ramen Festival on an unseasonably warm November day, on four hours of sleep, sweating through my button-up. Nikole Herriott and Michael Graydon—the photographers who traveled around the world with me as I tried to understand what it is about "the best" that's quite so compelling—emerged from the drugstore in unwrinkled linen, brandishing a bag of snacks. (No matter how little sleep we got, or how impounded my rental car became in a locked parking garage in an unmanned corner of Italy, or how many dozen slices of prosciutto we were offered in a thirty-minute period, their linen always seemed to be unwrinkled.) Nikole wordlessly handed me a Dorayaki, two rounds of pancake swaddling whipped cream and red bean paste.

It wasn't the first time a pancake had fixed me. The rich, tender stacks at the Commerce Inn in Manhattan fully renewed my interest in brunch after a decade of claiming it's the worst way to spend money. (Their secret: tapioca flour and baking the pancakes in an oven after a quick stovetop browning.) The soufflé-style pancakes I tasted across Osaka and Tokyo quivered like living pillows as I doused them in syrup, forcing me to consider at what point food becomes too beautiful to consume. In Alabama, at Salem's Diner, a perfectly taupe seven-inch round that was neither thick nor fluffy made me wonder if I was overthinking the pancake entirely. The kanom krok at a Bangkok street market reversed my jet lag. The skillet-size Bisquick pancakes my older sister Zoe and I would construct breathlessly when our parents went out of town, adding as many chocolate chips and raspberries as we could while still having some hint of batter continuity, still make me laugh. (Left with an uncaptained house, most other high school kids threw ragers; we sat around daring one another to fill the bathtub—which was outfitted with water-jet tech that in the late 1990s seemed impossibly cutting edge—with heavy cream, to see if it would whip with us in it.) I'm not convinced there's a single prototype for a perfect pancake; there's a time and a place for thin and crispy, for soft and crepe-like, for stuffed yeasted pancakes, for buttermilk ones, and for soufflé-style. Here, I focus on enhancing flavor, maximizing fluff, and retaining crispy edges.

There are many ways to amplify the flavor of a pancake, from flour (buckwheat, cornmeal, sorghum, and whole wheat are all great additions), to an acidic dairy-fat

(I love buttermilk best, and ricotta for its addition of lumps for the batter to climb, but anything from sour cream to yogurt will help), to mix-ins (fruit, zest, chocolate, corn kernels). My final formula uses buttermilk, like so many pancake recipes before me, for tang and tenderness, and as with Edna Lewis's blend from *The Taste of Country Cooking*, I swap in some whole wheat flour for a bit more nuttiness and presence. I've also added ricotta, which is insane on top of everything else, but I love the way it becomes a trellis for rising batter. If you'd like to play around, swap the whole wheat flour for finely milled cornmeal (let the batter sit 10 minutes before using) or buckwheat.

Then there's fluffiness. Baking powder is ubiquitous in American-style pancakes, since it reliably produces carbon dioxide when heated, causing a batter to rise when it hits the pan. Whipping egg whites with sugar until stiff creates a soft foam when you fold it into the batter, as in a sponge cake. The result is a pancake lighter than your standard buttermilk specimen, but denser than a slice of angel food or chiffon cake. I found that whipped egg whites produced the most consistent fluffy pancakes, in terms of a symmetrical rise with a tender crumb—the meringue seemed to coerce the batter to fry into rounder cakes. Seltzer is not a bad backup if you don't have the wherewithal to whip egg whites, though the results are inconsistent (some of my pancakes fluffed up on only one side), and the batter needs to be used immediately. Sifting the dry ingredients actually backfired, because—as with ricotta in pancake batter—the lumps give the aerating batter something to scramble up when it hits the hot surface. (Here's your annual reminder to abstain from overmixing your pancake batter, for the same reason! Underline this! Highlight it! Okay, move on.)

Dry yeast can be found in a number of pancake recipes across the globe, from hotteok to racuszki, which range in chewiness, density, and crumb. Besides adding structure (via air bubbles; when you add yeast to water and flour, it consumes sugars in the flour and excretes gas), yeast adds savory depth. Think of the slight complexity of a slice of bread, even if it isn't sourdough. Speaking of, sourdough starter can be used in a similar way. Pastry chef Caroline Schiff makes a legendary sourdough starter pancake that's tangy, crisp, and soft inside. The obvious downside, to me, is that I simply cannot and will not keep a sourdough starter alive. I found a recipe in my great-grandmother's recipe box for a pancake with a starter created just the night before (a very gentle-tasting baby starter), which did add some tang to the final pancakes, but ultimately I preferred buttermilk, since it required no planning.

As for cooking fats, ghee and clarified butter worked best, imparting a buttery flavor and golden tone without burning. Less fat led to more evenly browned faces, and more cooking fat (my safe words) created crispy griddled edges with spots and stripes.

THE BEST METHOD

MAINSTAY METHOD: Maximalism, which means here whipped egg whites, baking powder, buttermilk, and ricotta! Plus a bit of whole wheat flour for depth (page 48).

ALTERNATIVES: Add dry yeast to the batter, or go the thin and lacy route (pages 50 and 51, respectively).

FLUFFY NO-SPECIAL-EQUIPMENT PANCAKES, PAGE 48

YEASTED PUMPKIN SPICE PANCAKES, PAGE 50

LACY CHOCOLATE CHIP HANDKERCHIEF PANCAKES, PAGE 51

MOTHER RECIPE

FLUFFY NO-SPECIAL-EQUIPMENT PANCAKES

LEVEL

Anyone can execute

TIME

35 minutes

MAKES

Pancakes for 4

I refuse to tell you to pull out a stand mixer for breakfast. But I adore the effect of egg whites folded into pancake batter. It works just as well with a whisk, and, to be transparent, 6 minutes of whisking is exactly what I need to wake myself up to make polite conversation. These aren't as soft or towering as the soufflé pancakes I tasted across Japan, but they have a velvety, uniform crumb that soaks up butter and syrup beautifully. One recipe tester compared them to a more flavorful (!) crumpet. If you're in the mood to pretend you own an ironic and chic diner, you could use this batter to make two giant pancakes in oven-safe nonstick pans (finish them at 350°F, then soak with honey-butter or maple syrup, love you:-). I prefer to make dozens of smaller pancakes right away and top them with an amount of butter and syrup that would make a doctor blush. These use buttermilk for tang and tenderness, whole wheat flour for nuttiness, and ricotta to give the rising batter something to cling onto. Try swapping the whole wheat flour for buckwheat, or finely milled cornmeal—but then remember to let the batter hydrate for 10 minutes.*

2 cups (284 g) all-purpose flour

½ cup (65 g) whole wheat flour

4 tablespoons (50 g) granulated sugar

3 teaspoons baking powder

1½ teaspoons Diamond Crystal kosher salt

5 large eggs (275 g), at room temperature, whites and yolks separated

2½ cups (610 g) buttermilk

3 tablespoons (42 g) unsalted butter, melted and briefly cooled

½ cup (117 g) ricotta

Clarified butter or ghee (or a mix of neutral oil and butter)

Pure maple syrup and butter

1. In a large bowl, whisk together the dry ingredients: all-purpose flour, whole wheat flour, 2 tablespoons of the sugar, baking powder, and salt.

2. In a separate medium bowl, whisk the egg whites vigorously for about 5 minutes, until soft opaque clouds form, thicker than the foam that washes up during a high tide. Add the remaining 2 tablespoons sugar one little spoonful at a time, vigorously whisking until integrated and the whites become quite thick and glossy, like warmed marshmallows, another 3 minutes or so. (The peaks won't get as stiff as with a stand mixer, and that's okay; there's baking powder and more than enough egg white in there for insurance, and the pancakes will still plump up in the pan.)

3. Make a well in the middle of the dry ingredients. Add the buttermilk, egg yolks, butter, and ricotta and whisk until just combined, with lumps. Fold in about a quarter of the egg white meringue mixture, to loosen the batter. Fold in the rest, just until no streaks of egg whites remain. Do not overmix. Lumps are critical for height!

4. Heat a large cast-iron skillet or griddle over medium heat for 1 minute. Add a generous few tablespoons of clarified butter. (Use less fat if you want perfectly consistent golden pancake faces.) When the butter has melted, add ¼-cup scoops of batter about 2 inches apart, very gently smooshing the edges

into circles if they're lopsided. Keep an eye on their bottoms, lowering the heat to keep them from burning . When the edges have just set, about 1 minute, add a large spoonful (roughly another 2 tablespoons) of batter to the center of each pancake. Then, when tiny bubbles begin to form on the surface of the batter (timing here can vary, but you want some bubbles a bit inward of the immediate outer edge; there likely won't be any in the center, though), very gently flip each pancake and cook until golden on the second side, about 2 to 3 minutes.

5. Serve hot in stacks topped with maple syrup and butter. In between every two batches or so, replenish your cooking fat to keep it close to the original level, so every pancake gets just as crispy.

UPGRADE: *Add fork-mashed ripe banana and chopped dark chocolate to the batter before you fold in the egg whites. I also love to add fresh raspberries, with or without the other two!*

NOTE: *The easiest way to make a big batch of clarified butter is to melt a pound of butter in a small saucepan over medium-high heat and, after the foam recedes, skim off the fluffy white fat along the surface. Pour through a cheesecloth or super-fine sieve and store covered in the fridge.*

YEASTED PUMPKIN SPICE PANCAKES

LEVEL

Anyone can execute

TIME

1 hour and 15 minutes, including a 1-hour rest

MAKES

Pancakes for 4 to 6

These have virtually nothing to do with gözleme—stuffed, often savory Turkish flatbread—or with oladi, or racuszki, or hotteok, except that yeasted pancakes like those led me to fall in love with a subtle tang. That whole crew, as well as a formula I found in my great-grandmother's recipe box for sourdough starter pancakes (which were thick and tangy and a little chewy), led me here. So now this is the method I use when I'm craving pancakes with a yeasty flavor and a denser body. You can make them savory by halving the sugar and swapping in roasted, roughly chopped or pureed vegetables (such as squash), or adding grated cheese.

1½ cups (341 g) whole milk

2¼ teaspoons (1 packet) active dry yeast

2 cups (284 g) all-purpose flour

2 large eggs (110 g)

½ cup (99 g) lightly packed dark or light brown sugar

¼ cup (½ stick/56 g) unsalted butter, melted but cooled so it's not hot to the touch

1 teaspoon Diamond Crystal kosher salt

½ teaspoon ground ginger

1 teaspoon ground cinnamon

¼ teaspoon ground cloves

One 15-ounce can pumpkin puree, preferably Libby's

Clarified butter (see page 49) or ghee (or a mix of neutral oil and butter)

Pure maple syrup (or honey)

Flaky salt

1. In a large saucepan set over low heat or in a large heatproof bowl in the microwave, warm the milk until it feels like a rich person's pool (if you love your thermometer, about 120°F). Sprinkle the yeast over the top. Let it sit for about 5 minutes, until you see some fizzy frothing. Add the flour and stir with a silicone spatula until you have a shaggy, loose dough. In a medium bowl, whisk together the eggs, brown sugar, butter, salt, ginger, cinnamon, cloves, and pumpkin puree. Add to the yeasted flour mixture and stir very well to combine.

2. Cover with a kitchen towel and let sit for about 1 hour, until the batter puffs up slightly and smells like it's alive.

3. Heat a large cast-iron skillet or griddle over medium heat. Add a generous few tablespoons of clarified butter. (Use less fat if you want those perfectly consistent golden pancake faces.) When the butter has melted, use a ¼-cup measure to portion out batter about 2 inches apart, gently pressing them with the back of the measure to flatten. Cook for 4 to 5 minutes, lowering the heat as needed to keep the pancakes from burning before they cook through. Flip and cook until golden on the second side, another 4 to 5 minutes.

4. Serve hot in stacks covered in maple syrup and sprinkled with flaky salt.

LACY CHOCOLATE CHIP HANDKERCHIEF PANCAKES

LEVEL

Anyone can execute

TIME

20 minutes, plus
30 minutes for resting

MAKES

Pancakes for 4

Not quite a crepe, not quite a pancake. These cook over medium heat with less fat than your usual buttermilk pancake, or else they soak up too much moisture and become rubbery. When you flip them, the lacy edges crisp and occasionally curl up. Here I use a trick from Alison Roman's recipe for Thin Maple Pancakes in Sweet Enough *and add syrup to the batter. I use two kinds of flour and buttermilk for a super-tender (nearly emotional) pancake. If you find these too sweet—are you my father?—you can substitute ripe blueberries or fresh corn kernels for the chocolate chips, or skip the extra maple for serving.*

1 cup (142 g) all-purpose flour

¼ cup (32 g) whole wheat flour

1 heaping tablespoon (14 g) granulated sugar

½ teaspoon Diamond Crystal kosher salt

¼ cup (½ stick/56 g) unsalted butter, melted but cooled to the touch

1¼ cup (305 g) buttermilk, at room temperature

½ cup (115 g) whole milk

¼ cup (77 g) pure maple syrup, plus more for serving

3 large eggs plus 1 large egg yolk

Clarified butter (see page 49) or ghee (or a mix of neutral oil and butter)

¾ cup (127 g) semisweet or dark chocolate chips

Flaky salt, for topping

1. In a large bowl, combine the flours, sugar, and salt. Whisk.

2. In a medium bowl, combine the butter, buttermilk, milk, maple syrup, and eggs. Whisk. Make a well in the bowl of dry ingredients and add the wet ingredients. Whisk to combine.

3. Let sit uncovered for about 30 minutes (otherwise, you'll end up with rubbery pancakes).

4. Heat two skillets (cast-iron, stainless steel, and carbon steel are all fine; so, too, are griddles) over medium heat for about 3 minutes. Add just a bit, say a tablespoon, of clarified butter to each. (If you use too much fat with these, they won't crisp.) Add roughly ⅓ cup of batter to each pan. Sprinkle a handful of chocolate chips over each, avoiding the very edges (the chocolate will burn). Cook for 1½ to 2 minutes on the first side, until clearly quite set and crisp around the edges. Flip and cook for 30 seconds to 1 minute on the second side. Finish cooking in batches until you've used all your batter. If any chocolate lingers and begins to burn between batches, wipe it out with a kitchen towel.

5. Serve topped with a bit more maple syrup and flaky salt.

MISO-BANANA PUDDING TRIFLE

LEVEL

Anyone can execute

TIME

1 hour (plus chilling time)

MAKES

1 large trifle (or 8 to 10 smaller ramekins—or cocktail glasses—full of trifle)

This used to be a jelly roll cake with the pancake as one large layer and the cream and banana inside. It looked adorable but critically, one day, I mashed it all up into a quart container to store leftovers and discovered that there is no single more satisfying sensation than using a spoon to pierce layers of fluffy buttermilk pancake–banana pudding to draw a bite back up. I took the idea of burnt miso from an apple cake Christina Tosi developed, one of the first recipes I wrote about after I left Wall Street to work at Food52. Here it adds a savory depth to an otherwise super-sweet trifle that you could serve at brunch to spoil guests or for a festive dessert.

FOR THE PANCAKES

3 tablespoons shiro miso

3 ripe bananas, peeled, each sliced lengthwise into 4 long strips

2 cups (284 g) all-purpose flour

½ cup (65 g) whole wheat flour

4 tablespoons (58 g) granulated sugar

3 teaspoons baking powder

1½ teaspoons Diamond Crystal kosher salt

5 large eggs (275 g), at room temperature, separated into whites and yolks

2¼ cups (549 g) buttermilk

3 tablespoons (42 g) melted unsalted butter, cooled so it's not hot to the touch

Clarified butter (see page 49) or ghee (or a mix of neutral oil and butter)

1. Heat the oven to 425°F.

2. Decide on the size of the cups, ramekins, or single large trifle dish you'll use to assemble the dessert; you'll want to size your pancakes accordingly. Line a quarter sheet pan with parchment paper. Spread the miso out on the parchment to about ⅓ inch thick and place the banana slices on either side (so they're closer to the edges of the sheet pan). Bake for 8 to 10 minutes, until the miso is toasty and deep brown around its circumference and the bananas are fragrant and spotted. On the sheet pan, smash the miso and roasted bananas with a fork, until well combined (you don't want any lumps of miso).

3. Meanwhile, in a large bowl, whisk together the dry ingredients: all-purpose flour, whole wheat flour, 2 tablespoons of the sugar, the baking powder, and salt.

4. In a separate medium bowl, whisk the egg whites vigorously for about 4 minutes, until soft opaque clouds form, thicker than the foam that washes up during a high tide. Add the remaining 2 tablespoons sugar one spoonful at a time, vigorously whisking until integrated and the whites become glossy like melted marshmallows, another 2 minutes or so. (If you're doing this by hand, the peaks won't get as stiff as with a stand mixer; that's okay . . . there's baking powder elsewhere in the recipe, and more than enough egg white in there for insurance, and they'll still plump up immensely in the pan.)

5. Make a well in the middle of the dry ingredients. Add the buttermilk, egg yolks, butter, and cooled banana-miso mixture. Whisk until just combined, with some lumps. Fold in about a quarter of the egg white–meringue mixture, to loosen the batter. Fold in the rest just until no lumps or streaks of egg whites remain.

continued

FOR THE FILLING AND ASSEMBLY

2½ cups (575 g) cold heavy cream

¼ cup (77 g) pure maple syrup

¼ to ½ teaspoon Diamond Crystal kosher salt

⅔ cup (160 g) buttermilk, at room temperature

2 tablespoons whole milk powder

4 ripe bananas

1 cup Nilla Wafer crumbs (take a big handful of the cookies and crush in a sealed zip-top bag)

6. Heat a large cast-iron skillet or griddle over medium heat for 1 minute. Add a generous few tablespoons of clarified butter. For most trifle vessel choices, about ¼ cup of batter per pancake will work, and you can always tear or layer or shingle the pancakes for a larger or smaller vessel. When the butter has melted, add the ¼-cup scoops of batter about 2 inches apart. Keep an eye on their bottoms, adjusting the heat down to keep the pancakes from burning before they cook through as need be. Then, when a school of bubbles begins to form on the surface of the batter, flip each pancake and cook until golden on the second side, about 2 minutes. In between every two batches or so, replenish your cooking fat to keep it close to the original level, so every pancake gets just as crispy.

7. To make the filling, in a stand mixer fitted with a balloon whisk, whip the cream to stiff peaks. With the mixer running on the lowest setting, add the maple syrup, salt, and buttermilk. Mix until fully combined. Add the milk powder, and mix on low just until smooth and stable enough to hold a soft peak when you remove the whisk from the cream.

8. Peel the bananas. Slice 2 into roughly ½-inch discs and mash the other 2 with a fork to make a banana jam with small lumps. Use a spoon to swirl the mashed banana jam roughly into the whipped cream (don't fully blend it; think of this as a rippled whipped cream).

9. When the pancakes have cooled, create a trifle (or trifles!) with layers of pancake, whipped cream, Nilla crumbs, and banana slices. Tear the pancakes by hand if you need to for a perfect fit.

10. Cover the dish or dishes with foil, plastic wrap, or whatever you have, and refrigerate for at least 2 hours before serving to let the cookies soften. (You can refrigerate, covered, for up to 2 days, though the whipped cream will gradually seep into the pancake and the trifle will lose some volume.)

CAKE FLOUR
WHOLE WHEAT
CORNMEAL
BUCKWHEAT + SORGHUM
BAKING POWDER
BAKING SODA
COTTAGE CHEESE
MILK
LEMON + RICOTTA
RICE FLOUR SHELL
THIN + CRISPY
BUTTER
CLARIFIED BUTTER
OLIVE OIL
NEUTRAL

5

Custardy Soft-Scrambled EGGS

MISSION

Evenly cooked, creamy soft-scrambled eggs that don't require a sous vide, a blow torch, a steamer wand, or a degree from culinary school.

WHAT I TESTED

Cooking method • Heat level
Timing and type of added fat • Timing of salting
Frequency of whisking or stirring • Egg temperature
Other additions (life is a beautiful mystery)

COLD PAN

LOW HEAT

HIGH HEAT

DOUBLE BOILER

CONTINUOUS WHISKING

SESAME OIL

BUTTER (AT START)

BUTTER (AT END)

CRÈME FRAÎCHE (AT START)

CRÈME FRAÎCHE (AT END)

LOW HEAT + SELTZER

BUTTER (AT START), CRÈME FRAÎCHE (AT END)

BROWNED BUTTER (AT START)

WATER (AT START)
SALT + CREAM + SIT 15 MIN

NO SALT

SALT + SIT 15 MIN

SALT, NO SIT

COLD EGGS

ROOM-TEMPERATURE EGGS

AERATED

CREAM AT START

CORNSTARCH SLURRY

OVEN SCRAMBLE

SAUCE SCRAMBLE

THERE IS NO SUCH THING AS A PERFECTLY SCRAMBLED EGG.

As intimated by the name, scrambled eggs are, basically, proteins coagulated by heat, and they're disturbed while they're coagulating to become a shaggy, ruffled mess. To create eggs so custardy that they were halfway to dessert, I looked for ways to manipulate that coagulation:

COOK TEMPERATURE: Lower heat produced meltier, more velvety eggs, closer to the texture of steamed pudding than a hard scramble from a diner. It also afforded the egg maker an opportunity to stop cooking well before the scramble turned parched, since the heat worked through the eggs at a slower speed. One drawback, though, was an uneven cook; it took too long to finish firming up the last dregs. For my workaround, I developed a high-low-medium heat sequence, as detailed on page 60.

INGREDIENT COMPOSITION: An additional fat up front in cold, solid form (ideally in many small pieces) helped to stop the eggs from clenching in the pan more effectively than stirring in fat at the end of the cook, after the eggs had already been scrambled. I found that cold eggs and cold fat created even more of a buffer, meaning it was harder to accidentally overcook. Before the fat melted into the eggs and the eggs cooked through, everything had to warm in the pan, sort of like when you're running late preparing for a dinner party so you ask your guests to stop and get wine on their way to buy time.

TIMING OF SALTING: Salting eggs before cooking has many detractors, as well as several notable supporters, like Julia Child. In my trials, letting the cracked eggs sit salted for 10 to

20 minutes before scrambling them produced a perceptibly (if subtly) creamier scramble. J. Kenji López-Alt reported for *The New York Times* that letting your eggs sit with salt (as opposed to salting them just before scrambling) keeps them from weeping moisture[1] later, just when you've sat down with the paper to eat. (His explanation: "In their more uninhibited state, salted egg proteins tend to glom on to one another before individual proteins have even had a chance to fully unravel. The result is a protein matrix that sets up faster and at a lower temperature but has a weaker overall structure.")

ADDITIONS: The addition of a cornstarch slurry (say 1½ teaspoons of cornstarch whisked into 1½ teaspoons of milk and water, added to 3 eggs before they're cooked) was a good workaround toward more custardy eggs, and I would recommend it if you're struggling to master the technique on page 60, though ultimately the curds tended toward fluffy and fleecy. Scrambling eggs into a liquid or sauce, as in the Turkish dish menemen or the Chinese dish jia chang cai, also produced delicate eggs full of moisture, reminiscent of a braised meat. Adding ingredients like soy sauce and sesame oil to the eggs as they scrambled had a similar effect: more flavor and more delicate curds, though not necessarily more custardy ones. To adapt the technique on page 62 for a saucier egg, let your cooking liquid first come to a simmer in the skillet before adding the whisked eggs and crème fraîche to cook directly in the shallow puddle.

CURD SIZE: For large curds, letting the outer rim of the eggs set before attempting to scramble—like the early stages of cooking a French omelet—worked best. For small curds, the Jean-Georges Vongerichten method of constantly whisking the eggs[2] produced opulent, ricotta-like eggs. The double boiler method was great for small curds, too, since the eggs never really set enough to form large curds, but ultimately presented unnecessary extra equipment when the same curds could be produced with a whisk.

THE BEST METHOD

A high-low-medium heating sequence, using cold eggs and cold fat added at the start.

MOTHER RECIPE

HIGH-LOW-MEDIUM SOFT-SCRAMBLED EGGS

LEVEL

Anyone can execute

TIME

15 minutes

MAKES

Eggs for 1

My preferred technique for buttery-tender soft-scrambled eggs is in the title: I use high heat to start setting the eggs upon landing, then low heat for gentle cooking, and then medium heat at the end to firm up that stubborn runny ring that seems to linger. I take advantage of the fridge; in my trials, I found that cold eggs better protect against overcooking (they offer a few more degrees of chilliness at the outset, aka a little more wiggle room), and that adding a cold, acidic fat like crème fraîche earlier helps much more than stirring that same fat in at the end. The fat slowly melts into the eggs as you heat them, keeping the curds from becoming tough. This technique forms large, buttery curds, which is my preferred size and texture. If you like small curds, use a whisk instead of a silicone spatula and instead of every 90 seconds, stir the eggs every 30 seconds.

3 eggs, cold from the refrigerator

½ teaspoon Diamond Crystal kosher salt

1 heaping tablespoon cold crème fraîche

1 tablespoon salted butter

Flaky salt

Freshly cracked black pepper

1. Crack the eggs into a small bowl. Add the kosher salt. Use a fork to break the yolks, then forcefully whisk the eggs together for 30 seconds, or until totally homogeneous. Add the crème fraîche to the eggs in 5 or so little pieces (so it's not all in one clump), but don't bother to try to whisk it in. Refrigerate the bowl for 10 minutes.

2. After you've chilled the eggs, set a small to medium nonstick or well-seasoned carbon steel skillet over high heat. Set a timer for 1 minute. Drop in the butter. After the minute is up, the butter should be foaming. Turn the heat to low and add the cold eggs. Do not touch them for 90 seconds! Seriously, I'll know. After 90 seconds, they should have begun to set up around the sides, like the very early stages of a French omelet. Rotate the pan 180 degrees, so its handle is facing the opposite way it was facing before. Use a silicone spatula to draw in the egg from the edges, almost to the middle, but off to one side by a few degrees, like the spatula is a pilot taking a plane just off course. As you scrape toward the middle, be sure to scrape under the set eggs you've just drawn inward before moving on to the next stroke.

3. Don't touch for another 90 seconds! I'll definitely know. Then repeat the spatula motion. Turn the heat up to medium and finish cooking any runny egg around the edges that has stubbornly refused to start firming up, 20 to 40 seconds. Pull the eggs from the heat while still glossy.

4. Slide the eggs onto a plate and serve topped with flaky salt and black pepper.

MAKE ME THIS BREAKFAST SANDWICH

LEVEL

Anyone can execute

TIME

20 minutes

MAKES

1 breakfast sandwich

I understand the theatrical appeal of a dripping yolk. But I prioritize custardy, buttery soft-scrambled egg in each bite over drama. I also prioritize the eggs not falling out, which is why I prefer to either make breakfast tacos, or construct a breakfast sandwich with a bread that moves and flexes with its contents. Until I had the breakfast sandwich at Thai Diner in New York City, this meant slices of milk bread (only lightly toasted), or a fresh English muffin. But the first time I ordered the Thai Diner Egg Sandwich—egg, a patty of sai ua sausage, cheese, scallions, and Thai basil, wrapped in griddled roti—I learned that no better vessel for the dish exists. Now I stock frozen Thai roti, or else frozen paratha or scallion pancakes. When I come across it, like at Bangkok Center Grocery on Mosco Street, I stock Thai basil, too. I've taken a few additional departures in my homage, so it's not a dupe as much as a derivative film; rather than serving the sandwich alongside a punchy, delicious chile dipping sauce, I spread a lazy combination of mayonnaise and Huy Fong chili garlic sauce on the inside and I use whatever sausage I have lying around, which is often uncased Italian sweet sausage formed into a patty with damp hands.

2 eggs, cold from the refrigerator

¼ teaspoon Diamond Crystal kosher salt

1 tablespoon cold crème fraîche

1 sausage patty or a link uncased, formed into a disc

1 large paratha or scallion pancake or Thai roti

1 tablespoon mayonnaise

2 teaspoons Huy Fong chili garlic sauce (or sriracha)

1 tablespoon salted butter

1 slice American cheese

Flaky salt

Freshly cracked black pepper

2 tablespoons finely chopped scallions, plus basil or minced chives

1. Crack the eggs into a small bowl. Add the kosher salt. Use a fork to break the yolks, then forcefully whisk the eggs together for 30 seconds, or until totally homogeneous. Add the crème fraîche to the eggs in 5 or so little pieces (so it's not all in one clump). Refrigerate the bowl for 10 minutes.

2. Meanwhile, set a small or medium skillet over medium-high heat. Cook the sausage for a few minutes on each side until browned and cooked through, taking care to adjust your heat to avoid the sausage burning. Set the sausage aside. Wipe out the skillet. In the remaining slick of sausage fat, over medium heat, griddle the paratha until translucent and soft with spots of brown on both sides. Lay flat on a plate and spread with the mayonnaise and chili garlic sauce. Wipe out the skillet again.

3. Set the same skillet over high heat. Set a timer for 1 minute. When the pan is hot, follow steps 2 and 3 on page 60 to cook the eggs.

4. Drape the slice of cheese over the middle of the eggs. Cover the pan for a few minutes until the cheese melts. Top the cheesy eggs with flaky salt and black pepper.

5. Transfer the cheesy eggs to the center of the paratha. Lay the sausage patty on top of the eggs (their heat will rewarm it). Top with scallions and other herbs. Fold the paratha in two. Flip and cut diagonally down the middle, like a grilled cheese. Eat while hot.

CARAMELIZED SHALLOT SOFT SCRAMBLE WITH COMTÉ

LEVEL

Anyone can execute

TIME

20 minutes

MAKES

Eggs for 1

This uses a very similar technique to my High-Low-Medium Soft-Scrambled Eggs on page 60, but because your skillet will already be hot from caramelizing the shallots up front, I adjust the initial heat. You can use this method to add any allium—yellow onion, leeks, a mixture—to your soft scramble. If you want to incorporate bacon or uncased sausage crumbles, I recommend rendering the meat first and discarding some of the fat (you can leave a few teaspoons for flavor) before proceeding with alliums to avoid a greasy, rather than custardy, soft scramble.

3 eggs, cold from the refrigerator

½ teaspoon Diamond Crystal kosher salt, plus a pinch for the shallots

1 heaping tablespoon cold crème fraîche

3 tablespoons salted butter

1 large or 2 medium shallots, peeled and finely diced

¼ cup grated Comté cheese

Flaky salt

Freshly cracked black pepper

1. Crack the eggs into a small bowl. Add the kosher salt. Use a fork to break the yolks, then forcefully whisk the eggs together for 30 seconds, or until totally homogeneous. Add the crème fraîche to the eggs in 5 or so little pieces (so it's not all in one clump). Refrigerate the bowl while you cook the shallots.

2. Set a small to medium nonstick or well-seasoned carbon steel skillet over high heat. Drop in 2 tablespoons of the butter. When it melts and foams, adjust the heat to medium-low and add the shallots with a pinch of kosher salt. Sauté, keeping the heat moderate to avoid burning the butter, for 8 to 10 minutes, until the shallots are translucent and browning around the edges and they taste sweet and concentrated. Turn the heat to low and push the shallots to the sides of the skillet. After about 1 minute, add the remaining 1 tablespoon butter. Add the cold eggs. Do not touch them for 90 seconds! Seriously, I'll know. After 90 seconds, the eggs should have begun to set up around the sides, like the very early stages of a French omelet. Rotate the pan 180 degrees, so its handle is facing the opposite way it was facing before. Use a silicone spatula to draw in the eggs and shallots from the edges, almost to the middle, but off to one side by a few degrees, like the spatula is a pilot taking a plane just off course. As you scrape toward the middle, be sure to scrape under the set eggs you've just drawn inward before moving on to the next stroke.

3. Don't touch for another 90 seconds! I'll definitely know. After 90 seconds, repeat this spatula motion. Sprinkle the grated Comté over the middle of the eggs, where the large, set curds are hanging out. Turn the heat up to medium and finish cooking for 20 to 40 seconds any runny egg around the edges that has stubbornly refused to start firming up. Pull the eggs from the heat while still glossy on top and slide onto a plate.

4. Serve topped with flaky salt and black pepper.

THE BEST DAD

The best pasta in the world can be found by the side of a surface road in a Japanese suburb called Kai, which is about ninety minutes by bullet train from Tokyo, and then four minutes by local train. As an American tourist, you're unlikely to have ever heard of Kai unless (1) you are such a devoted fan of *Super Smash Bros.* that you happen to know that photographs of the town's skyline served as temporary backdrops for the game when it was unfinished and called *Dragon King: The Fighting Game*; or (2) you are my unsuspecting travel companion and you let me design the whole itinerary.

I shepherded my dad to Kai in October of 2023 somewhat accidentally, for the Porktoberfest—an offshoot of the Blue Ribbon Bacon Festival I'd attended in Des Moines earlier that year. Brooks Reynolds, whom I privately called "Bacon Jesus" for his efforts to evangelize Iowa pork around the globe, put on the Porktoberfest as a sub-event within an annual festival dedicated to a feudal lord named Takeda Shingen. This took place in Kofu, a city an American tourist might have heard of even if they weren't a devoted fan of *Super Smash Bros.*, because Kofu is the capital of Japan's Yamanashi Prefecture. Kofu is less well known as the sister city of Des Moines, Iowa, and better known for hosting the fortress of Takeda Shingen in the sixteenth century. Among other gifts, including a military prowess that gives rise once annually to the Shingen-kō Festival, Takeda is remembered for constructing a system of flood-control levees, which would soon become relevant to my own visit. Having essentially nothing to do with Takeda, but pleasing to many of the attendees, Brooks and his fellow travelers fill a small fairground within the Shingen-kō Festival with booths that offer American bacon. (Incidentally, a Costco will soon open near Kofu.) By the time I learned of Porktoberfest, all the hotels in Kofu had been fully booked for the festival. So I found an Airbnb as close as possible, in the neighboring town Kai.

One night, after hours spent drinking highballs and eating maple syrup–saturated sandwiches of defrosted pancakes with sausage patties in between (which had been labeled "American breakfast") with Brooks and his pals while surrounded by thousands of attendees dressed in feudal attire, I returned home to our Airbnb. My dad and I performed the 2023 deep cultural immersion ritual known as "we each opened up Google Maps and searched the term 'dinner open now.'" Unlike what is intimated to devoted fans of *Super Smash Bros.* by the richly sketched set pieces, very little is actually going on in Kai, and so our options were limited to a place about two minutes by foot from our rental house or the drugstore a little farther down the road where earlier in the day a woman had pointed at my father and giggled as she said he was big as a bear. The place two minutes by foot it was.

The restaurant's name, トラットリア イタリアン シチリ菜, when input into Google Translate, spit out "Trattoria Italian Sicilian." I should disclose that despite the bevy of lauded Italian restaurants in Tokyo, my father and I had so far avoided any sort of trattoria. In fact, we hadn't planned to eat Italian food in Japan at all. We had ignored the dozens of impassioned recommendations we'd received to seek out wood-fired pizza; there was just too much ramen and sushi and fugu and onigiri and 7-Eleven sandwiches and katsu-don to get through. I should also disclose that another key reason for this dining decision was that not long before our trip to Japan, I'd spent some weeks traveling around Italy to learn to make fresh pasta by hand. At Le Sfogline in Bologna, Monica Venturi—who was obsessed with American basketball—showed me how to make proper tortellini, of which she and her sister sell a shocking number of pounds each year at Christmastime. In Modena, Bologna's rival pasta city (not to be confused with a sister city), at L'Angolo della Pasta, Tania Raimondi taught me how to make tortellini stand up pert, and explained the way its shape was meant to mimic the belly button of Venus. In the hills of Calestano, a young woman had taught me how to use squid ink to make my ravioli striped like gift-wrapping paper while her cat wove possessively between my legs. So I had had my fill of pasta for the year.

But perhaps most important, pasta was not on our agenda because my dad thinks Japanese food is the best food of all time.

My dad is effusive by nature. A sip of water after a jog "tastes like a milkshake." People he meets become, in his accounts, the most interesting ones alive. Recently, he very briefly encountered a woman named Madge who had left her career in law to make hats. "Madge is a true artist," he texted me, days later. His thick wraparound leather iPhone case, which he purchased on Amazon, and which has so many flaps and Velcro strips that it turns what should be a small, sleek computer into a binder crossed with a purse, is "the best model on the market" and "completely waterproof."

To him, everything great is the best, everything bad is grounds for excommunication, and he freely declares all that he encounters to be one of the two. (Recently, when I gently pushed back on his feedback to a piece of my writing, he said, "Great, good luck with your life then.")

Japan, to him, is the very best of the best. If you get him going on Japanese food, or culture, or the landscape, or those Pocari Sweat drinks available in the vending machines by the metro, you will encounter the true powers of a man who once went abroad to Tokyo in 1976. When I was a child, he called the show *South Park* "a manga from Colorado." Every few years he rediscovers the simple Japanese breakfast of sushi rice with an egg and furikake, and it becomes his entire personality until my mother eventually intervenes due to the way that his large sacks of rice overwhelm their kitchen.

This time, Kai intervened. And so we arrived at the apparently Sicilian restaurant on a Sunday. There were only two other people there, eating in complete silence. The menu turned out to be extensive and pan-regional. We had the best pasta I've ever had or will ever have, which was a surprise not because we weren't in Italy—by this point in the trip I'd seen more than enough examples of a stunning and modest mastery pervading most aspects of culinary culture—but because the sauced vegetables and pizza we'd started with had been limp and sweet. And yet, the spinach tagliatelle had the sort of chew that would have corrected my disdain for fresh pasta

l'Angolo della Pasta
dal 1985

decades ago if it had been available in Huntington, Long Island. The lamb ragu was rich and delicate, each shred so tender it was challenging to usher onto the tongs of a fork. I swore to go back before we left and ask for more information, maybe even the recipe. I had to know why it was so good—why it was the best pasta I'd ever tasted.

I never found out, though, because minutes after eating it, in the middle of describing it so effusively that he might have been using his hands to conduct a grand orchestra, my dad lost his balance and fell several feet into a drainage ditch by the side of the road.

That was a key feature of downtown Kai: coffin-width concrete-lined rivers that ran alongside the roads, perhaps thanks to the innovations of Takeda Shingen. And into one of them, in the pitch black, both of his hands still hanging in the air as they outlined the shape of an imagined strand of tagliatelle, my father tumbled face first.

It's funny now, but for fifteen seconds, after he flew through the air and landed nose-down, his arms pinned in weird positions, his face stuck beneath the running water, I was certain he had broken his neck. His phone must have flown out of his hands as he fell because as my brain raced to catch up to what had happened to the man who had been, a second before, gesticulating wildly about the best pasta he had ever consumed, a biblical beam lit up the narrow ditch from beneath the flowing water, creating a backlight as his thick leather iPhone case flapped open in the current. It's funny now because his iPhone case did indeed turn out to be waterproof. It's funny now, but I had never heard a grown man scream the way he screamed when he lifted his face out of the stream of water, or seen one shake quite as hard as he shook, blood seeping into his sneakers as we waited for an ambulance. And it's funny now but the next day, when I went back to climb down into the ditch to fish his credit card out from where it had lodged onto a bit of flotsam, the stream flowing like nothing had happened, I thought about drying off and going into that drugstore for breakfast since we'd both been up all night at the hospital, but I didn't want to leave him for any longer than I had to, and I didn't have the vocabulary to explain where he was if the lady who had called him a bear asked what had happened.

What had happened was this: In an instant, I had seen my dad age thirty years. I had seen the sturdy guy who had painted such a compelling Technicolor movie of a country I'd never even been to that when I was six, I ate instant ramen every day for breakfast—I had seen that guy become helpless. I had been forced to consider the most horrifying thing for a cynical person like myself to consider, which is that really, despite all of the little ways we try to gain some semblance of control (snarky essays about pasta, a flattering pair of pants), the drainage ditch will come for us all. It was the second time I had seen someone I love narrowly avoid death; the first time, my friend Tucker fell head-first down two flights of a marble staircase after a night at The Box. I could say we were at a charity event, but I wouldn't want to mislead you. When Tucker gained consciousness, he was alone, and he could move only his pointer finger, a digit that had surely charmed him hours before. He used it to stab at his recent call log until someone picked up. It was 8 a.m. on a Sunday. Eventually, I answered. Sitting next to him as he lay crooked, while surly EMTs figured out how to get a gurney up the staircase of his prewar walk-up, his wails created a soundtrack about powerlessness and the suspension of time in the face of pain and the way it engenders no comfort to be the Dependable One when you're in a brightly lit hospital but you could be in bed.

And as it played again in the Kofu hospital, I started to understand why my dad was so intent on classifying and dramatizing, on ranking and ordering. Why the rest of us do it, too.

It's not just that he's the best storyteller I know, or the man in my life who feels the most deeply. (Tucker, whose back healed, and who after many months of physical therapy still describes that night at The Box as "magical," is a close second.) It's not a gimmick or a ruse. It's that we have the (perhaps fortunate) fate of existing in a world where despite every privilege and turn of good luck, your circumstances can literally reverse in a moment. Everything that was once charming and amusing can become in retrospect portentous and ghoulish. You can be thrust into a sleepless night navigating a hospital system in a country where (despite what you've been boldly claiming since your study abroad semester at Waseda University) you don't totally know the language. And in a world like that, it's nice to give your experiences some order. A ranking. How better to find a little meaning?

I also began to understand something that had been percolating at the sides of my research for much of the year: that we qualify things as better or worse than they are based on our emotional experience not because we're limited or because we're controlled by neurochemicals—but because our experiences really matter.

It's the same reason that, even after I wheeled my father to the security line (he wouldn't let me fly home with him for X-rays), I never went back for that pasta recipe. On some level I didn't want to know—I didn't want to bring the science of comparison into this. I didn't want to re-create it beside the delicate stuff I'd learn to churn out in Modena. The actual noodles might not be as good as I remembered, and for the first time, I really did not need them to be. I was happy for my brain to play its tricks.

The day he left, on the way to the airport, we pulled into a rest stop for onigiri. I wondered abruptly if we would ever come back to Japan together. My dad corrected my pronunciation twice as I practiced ordering for us both in the car. Inside I only pointed. I returned with my spoils and buckled my seatbelt and handed him a triangle cloaked in nori. I unwrapped my own, biting into the tangy rice. Sitting beside the most lovable dad, I watched out the window as the trees of Yamanashi seemed to freeze mid-costume change from green to citrine and Cheez-It orange and deep ruby, an act of nature that had nothing to do with me. It was thrilling, and terrifying, and it was the best thing I had ever seen.

FROM *THE* GROUND *OR NEARBY*

6

Melty CABBAGE

MISSION

To unlock the inherent and transfixing quality of cabbage manipulated by heat, which produces a texture almost like hot cheese and a flavor richer than butter.

WHAT I TESTED

Cooking method • Shape
Cooking fat • Type of cabbage

BUTTER
OLIVE OIL
BUTTER + OLIVE OIL
SCHMALTZ
BLANCH + HIGH-HEAT ROAST
CONFIT
DEEP FRY
CREAM
AIR FRY
HIGH-HEAT ROAST
BLANCH
BROWN + SAUTÉ FOREVER
BROWN + BRAISE (STOVETOP)
BROWN + BRAISE (OVEN)
STIR FRY

IN THESE THREE HUNDRED WORDS I'VE BEEN ALLOTTED TO PEN A COMPELLING ARGUMENT

for you to consider cooking with cabbage, I could write about the vegetable as a great equalizer. It's hardy, easy to store, and affordable to purchase, which means that since antiquity, cabbage has appeared in nearly every cuisine, from kimchi in Korea to mahshi kromb in Egypt, bai cai juan in China to holishkes in my Ashkenazi household, charuto de repolho in Brazil to malfouf in Lebanon—I could filibuster by continuing to list its many bylines. Or I could write about cabbage as the recently anointed sexiest food in New York City, maybe the entire country. But I want to write about cabbage as a time travel portal to the very best moments of my childhood (they aren't hard to pick out from most of the rest, which involved a weirdly intimate friendship with an elderly neighborhood gossip who used me to gather intel on neighbors, since her eyesight was poor). A food that when tasted in a specific format is even more transportive than a whiff of Dove deodorant mingling with sweat, which never fails to make me feel like it's the first day of my freshman year and I'm about to realize that there's so much more to getting a boyfriend than wanting one. Fortunately, I'm nearly out of space, so I'll just say this about the former: A bite of cabbage prepared a certain way could convince me that time is flat, and it could convince me that that isn't a bad thing.

Most cabbage is more than 90 percent water. To achieve a melty texture when cooked, then, is just an exercise in landing on the technique that softens it in the ideal way to make it slouch but not disintegrate, while offering different textures throughout one wedge or leaf.

- For cabbage sundered into **wedges**, after an initial round of cooking methods, I zeroed in on **searing, then braising.** This combined some of the most delicious elements from various standalone techniques: The sear produced a **sweet, crisp, browned facade and the braise introduced liquid** that not only melded flavors with the buttery vegetal ones naturally present but also encouraged the cabbage to slacken. The **braise also encouraged a level of sweetness** that no other method produced, even when the braising liquid was unsweetened.
- For **shredded cabbage**, I loved that even when stir-fried to oblivion, the **ribbons** retained their general shape but became buttery, a more exciting version of zoodles. Then I found that I could have the best of both worlds if I **roasted the shreds at a high heat at the end for crispness**.
- I performed another round of trials to see **whether there was a difference between cabbage seared and braised all on the stovetop or seared and then braised in the oven**. I was blown away* by the degree to which the **oven braise improved the final texture**, through heat circulation that dried out the parts of the cabbage sticking out from the sauce as it reduced.
- **Butter and schmaltz** both paired beautifully with the flavor of multiple types of cabbage (I tested with green, purple, Savoy, and Caraflex), though **neutral oil was best for high heat–searing methods** because it has a higher smoke point.

THE BEST METHODS

BEST MAINSTAY METHOD: Sear cabbage wedges in a heavy Dutch oven, then braise with aromatics in a hot oven, as with the Braised Tomato-Butter Cabbage on page 80.

BEST SHREDDED METHOD: Sauté or stir-fry for ages on the stovetop, then finish under the broiler or in a hot oven for some crisp, as with the Twice-Cooked Cabbage with Anchovy and Bacon on page 84.

BEST SPECIAL OCCASION METHOD: For cabbage that maintains a bit of chew and body in its center, I love the butter-caramelization method I first encountered on one punishingly cold trip to France; my version on page 82 (Crispy Rice and Caramelized Cabbage) is served with crispy rice, which also toasts in the butter, though you could serve the cabbage on its own with a perky side sauce, like a roasted garlic aioli.

* *My neighbors were so sick of me trying to strike up conversations about it in the elevator.*

MOTHER RECIPE

BRAISED TOMATO-BUTTER CABBAGE

LEVEL

Anyone can execute

TIME

1 hour

MAKES

A side for 6

This technique exemplifies my favorite way to prepare for a dinner party. I call it You-Can't-Prove-That-I-Made-This-Pantsless Cooking. There is minimal prep work required. The Dutch oven and the heat do all of the hard stuff. You don't even have to hover over the pan; cabbage is forgiving and difficult to destroy. The planks of ginger, paired with tomato paste, produce a flavor profile similar to the stuffed cabbage I grew up requesting for my birthday (many of my friends were stuffed animals), and you could totally lean into that, serving this with rice and meatballs or short ribs. For the record, my great-grandmother made her stuffed cabbage with crumbled gingersnap cookies in the bottom, and would look at my fresh ginger planks with more than a bit of suspicion.

¼ cup neutral oil, like avocado or vegetable oil

1 head Savoy cabbage, core intact, sliced into 6 wedges

6 tablespoons unsalted butter

4 large or 6 medium shallots, sliced into thin rings (about ¼ inch thick; any thinner and they will burn)

3 teaspoons Diamond Crystal kosher salt

2 teaspoons dried chile flakes

5 garlic cloves, minced

One 2-inch piece fresh ginger, sliced into planks about ⅓ inch thick

One 4½-ounce tube double concentrated tomato paste (it's fine to use a 6-ounce can)

Juice of 1 lemon

1. Heat the oven to 425°F.

2. Heat a large Dutch oven over medium-high heat for 3 minutes. Add the oil. When it's shimmering hot, place the cabbage wedges in the pot, cut side down. (If your Dutch oven isn't large enough, you can do this in two batches.) Cook the wedges for 8 to 10 minutes, until they have a deeply golden sear all over the bottom side. If you're in no rush, do this again on the second cut side. Use tongs to transfer the cabbage wedges to a plate. Set aside.

3. Lower the heat to medium. Add the butter, shallots, and 2 teaspoons of the salt. Sauté the shallots, stirring occasionally, until they have started to become translucent and jammy with the occasional caramel-colored, frizzly edge, about 10 minutes. Add the chile flakes, garlic, and ginger planks. Make a well in the center and add the tomato paste. Fry the paste in the melted butter for 2 to 3 minutes, until it turns dark red, then combine into the rest of the ingredients. Deglaze the pan with 2 cups water and the lemon juice, using a wooden spoon to scrape up any browned bits freed by the liquid.

4. Nestle the cabbage wedges in the tomato paste mixture, caramelized sides up. Place the lid most of the way on, with a little gap, and transfer to the oven. Roast for about 40 minutes, until the cabbage has lost all will to remain structured and firm, then remove the lid and baste the wedges with the reduced sauce. Roast, uncovered, for another 5 to 10 minutes, until the wedges look like they're extremely spent after a taxing workweek. Fish out the ginger planks and toss.

5. Serve the cabbage wedges with the thickened pan sauce, sprinkled with the remaining 1 teaspoon salt.

CRISPY RICE AND CARAMELIZED CABBAGE

LEVEL

Anyone can execute

TIME

50 minutes

MAKES

Cabbage and rice for 6

Have you ever done that thing where you force your significant other to wait two hours to get seats at a seafood bar, and then you accidentally love an afterthought vegetable—one you could have found elsewhere—the most? (My husband refuses to go back to Clamato.) This is my attempt to re-create the tender, radioactive green spear of cabbage-and-citrus I had in Paris. It was served with aioli, which I've replaced with labneh for extra acid, though a garlicky mayo would also be nice. The crispy rice, which cooks alongside the cabbage in the pan, rounds it out into a full entree, so you don't have to pretend to want to focus on a fish collar to prove a point to your dining companion.

½ cup (1 stick) unsalted butter

2 tablespoons neutral oil

1 head Savoy cabbage, core intact, sliced into 6 wedges

2 cups cooked sushi rice (white will crisp best; brown is also nutty and delicious)

2 teaspoons Diamond Crystal kosher salt

1 small wedge Pecorino Romano cheese

Zest of 1 navel orange (or any great winter citrus)

1 cup labneh

1. Heat a large Dutch oven over medium-high heat for 3 minutes. Add the butter and oil. When the butter foams, place the cabbage wedges in the pot cut side down. (If your Dutch oven isn't large enough, you can do just as many wedges as you can fit without overlap and save the others for another use.) In the spaces between the wedges, press the cooked rice into the hot pan, compressing it into planks as you let it sear. Cook for about 10 minutes, until the rice has begun to turn golden on the bottom and the cabbage wedges have a brown sear. Sprinkle the salt all over the cabbage and rice and use tongs to flip the wedges.

2. Reduce the heat to medium-low and cook uncovered for 35 minutes, or until the rice has developed a stiff, chestnut-brown bottom and the cabbage is caramelized and tender on the pan side. Microplane or finely grate a layer of cheese all over the cabbage and rice. Gently flip the cabbage again and cook for another 5 minutes, or until it appears wilted all the way through. Sprinkle the orange zest over the cabbage and rice and cut the heat.

3. Serve each wedge of cabbage over a smear of labneh and a plank of crispy rice (crispy side up), with more cheese grated liberally over the top.

TWICE-COOKED CABBAGE WITH ANCHOVY AND BACON

LEVEL

Anyone can execute

TIME

1 hour

MAKES

Hearty cabbage for 4 to 6

Whenever I have pre-shredded cabbage that isn't begging to become a pert little fridge salad, I turn to this hybrid technique: stir-frying in oil for tenderness, then roasting without liquid for a bit of dry crispiness. With bacon and Gruyère, as prescribed below by Dr. Me, this surprisingly elegant dish can easily be a whole meal—toss it with egg noodles, serve it over a plank of rice, or pile it high on a thin slice of bread toasted and smeared with cream cheese.

8 ounces thick-cut bacon, cut into bite-size pieces (½-inch squares, roughly)

2 tablespoons olive oil

2 anchovies in oil, drained

6 large shallots, minced

2 teaspoons kosher salt

¾ teaspoon freshly cracked black pepper

¼ teaspoon freshly grated nutmeg

1 head Savoy cabbage, cored and shredded into roughly ½-inch strips (no need to be overly precise)

3 tablespoons sherry vinegar

2 cups tightly packed grated Gruyère cheese

1. Heat the oven to 475°F.

2. Set a large Dutch oven or oven-safe wok (not a cast-iron or reactive pan) over medium heat. Add the bacon pieces and cook until mostly crispy, with a bit of chew. Use a slotted spoon to remove the bacon and set it aside to drain. Pour out about half of the fat from the pan. To the remaining fat, still set over medium heat, add the olive oil and anchovies. Heat until the oil is shimmering, about 1 minute. Add the shallots, salt, pepper, and nutmeg. Sauté for 10 to 12 minutes, until the anchovies have dissolved and the shallots are beginning to caramelize. Add half of the cabbage and sauté for about 5 minutes, until it begins to shrink. Add the rest of the cabbage. Continue to sauté for about 25 minutes, until everything has golden color around the edges. Increase the heat to high and cook for another 5 minutes, to encourage more caramelization. Deglaze with the vinegar.

3. Cut the heat. Return most of the bacon to the pan (reserve a bit for topping). Add most of the grated cheese and stir to combine as it begins to melt from the residual heat. Press the contents flat and top with the reserved cheese and bacon bits.

4. Place the pan in the oven and bake for 8 to 10 minutes, until melty and browning. Finish under the broiler until the top is spotted with brown all over and the cheesy cabbage around the sides of the pan is bubbling. Serve hot.

TWICE COOKED CABBAGE

7

Crispy SMASHED POTATOES

MISSION

Smashed potatoes with chip-like edges and creamy—not leathery—sauce-absorbing cores.

WHAT I TESTED*

Potato type • Additions to cooking water
Roasting vessel • Roasting temperature
Potato shape • Peel status • Cooking fat
Cooking method tweaks

** I also taste-tested all batches plain, as well as dipped into mayonnaise, and dipped in mayo plus a sprinkle of Cholula; no one suggested this last series of trials would be helpful, but they can't take away my book contract for it, either.*

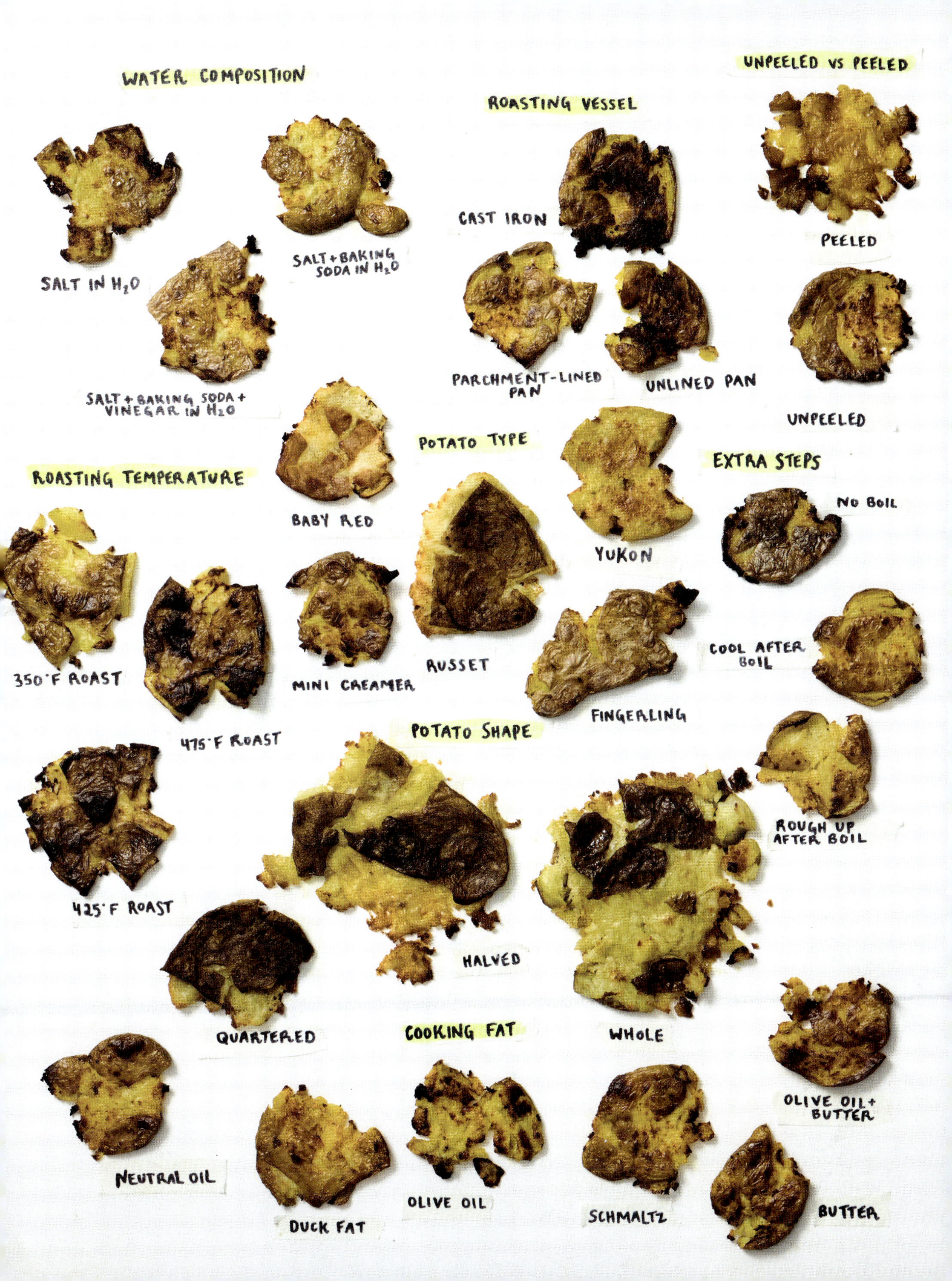

WATER COMPOSITION

SALT IN H_2O

SALT + BAKING SODA IN H_2O

SALT + BAKING SODA + VINEGAR IN H_2O

ROASTING VESSEL

CAST IRON

PARCHMENT-LINED PAN

UNLINED PAN

UNPEELED VS PEELED

PEELED

UNPEELED

ROASTING TEMPERATURE

350°F ROAST

475°F ROAST

425°F ROAST

POTATO TYPE

BABY RED

RUSSET

MINI CREAMER

YUKON

FINGERLING

EXTRA STEPS

NO BOIL

COOL AFTER BOIL

ROUGH UP AFTER BOIL

POTATO SHAPE

HALVED

QUARTERED

WHOLE

COOKING FAT

NEUTRAL OIL

DUCK FAT

OLIVE OIL

SCHMALTZ

OLIVE OIL + BUTTER

BUTTER

IF YOU EVER FIND YOURSELF WANTING TO THROW A GRENADE

into an otherwise placid Thanksgiving at my parents' home, then I suggest you clear your throat and say something like the following: There is a clear hierarchy of potato preparations, with mashed near, but not at, the top, and shoestring fries definitively at the bottom; roasted sweets rank in an entirely different category.

To weaponize the potato is one of the quickest ways to activate my family's latent urge to turn against one another. In case you aren't convinced, I lobbed this very potato hierarchy sentiment into our family text thread just last week. "Ew steak fries EW!!!!!," sent my sister Clementine, moments after another family member expressed them as a preference. "USE RUSSETS," said my mother ominously, before disappearing from the chat. "Mashed would rank at the bottom pour Moi [*sic*]," sent my dad, who had recently returned from a three-day work trip to Paris, and who knows that the rest of us would betray a spouse for a good mound of mashed. "Double-cooked fries are garbageeeeee," wrote my traitor husband, whom I would certainly betray for a good mound of mashed.

The only potato we can agree on as a group is a crispy smashed one. If you ever need to smooth over an emotional catastrophe you lobbed into an otherwise placid Thanksgiving at my parents' house, I suggest you make a tray of crispy smashed potatoes. I suspect they unite us because crispy smashed potatoes combine elements of the potato preparations that divide us: They emerge from the oven with glassy edges and soft centers ready to be doused in a condiment or topped with pats of cold butter. They are seasoned all the way through. They don't require twenty-four hours of prep, like a potato pavé might. They can be made with russets if you're my mother, or tiny creamer potatoes if you're one of my sisters, or fingerlings if you're mon père.

Boiling a potato before you roast it accomplishes several things. You might recognize the technique from recipes for French fries, which often call for a blanch and rest before the sliced potatoes go into the deep fryer, or from English roast potatoes. The initial hit of boiling water ensures that the centers are cooked all the way through no matter how long you roast them (which provides flexibility to cook at a higher heat for crispiness in a shorter amount of time). It also offers a first opportunity to season potatoes all the way through much like you would noodles.

Adding baking soda to the hot water, as noted[1] by J. Kenji López-Alt, makes it alkaline, which causes the potatoes' carapaces to break down a bit, leaving a fleecy, starchy layer that crisps up more than it otherwise would. And as with English roast potatoes, as López-Alt wrote about, tossing them quite roughly with their cooking fat before a high-heat roast helps to draw out as much of this soft, crumbly layer as possible, which leads to even more outer crunch.

I preferred crispy smashed potatoes that had been roasted on a parchment-lined pan to those roasted directly on a metal pan or cast-iron skillet—which goes against everything I've been taught—because their centers were creamier and fluffier. The potatoes roasted at high heat directly on a heat-conducting surface quickly became leathery, as though dehydrated too early into the roasting process. Last, I like to add a little bit of cheese to create a frico against the hot pan. Potatoes have a lot of variation, bag to bag (and even potato to potato), and once in a while you'll run into a batch that doesn't want to brown on top.

THE BEST METHOD

Boil in salty water with baking soda, toss roughly with fat, and roast at a high heat, as on page 90.

PICK YOUR POTATO

IF YOU WANT TO PRIORITIZE . . .	AND ACHIEVE AN INTERNAL TEXTURE THAT IS . . .	CHOOSE . . .
Crispy skin with fluffy insides, and spots of battered French fry texture	Fluffy and starchy	Russets, quartered
A battered French fry texture all over	Fluffy and starchy	Russets, peeled and quartered
Buttery, creamy internal texture with a decent skin-to-insides ratio	A mix of creamy, buttery, and waxy	Mini creamers (sometimes includes baby red potatoes)
Tender interiors	Waxy and tender	Baby reds
Buttery, creamy internal texture with bits of skin crisp	Creamy and buttery	Yukon Golds, halved
Buttery, creamy internal texture with more spots of browning but no skin crisp	Creamy and buttery	Yukon Golds, peeled and halved
Smashed potatoes that stay perfectly intact from boil to roast, with distinctive flavor	Creamy and waxy	Fingerlings

MOTHER RECIPE

CRISPY SMASHED POTATOES WITH INSURANCE CHEESE

LEVEL

Anyone can execute

TIME

45 minutes

MAKES

A side for 4

I have learned the hard way, again and again, to always get insurance. That's where the dusting of Microplaned cheese comes into play on these crispy smashed potatoes. Because the truth is, there's plenty you can do to maximize crispy edges and tender centers. The baking soda in the cooking water, the rough toss with cooking fat before the high heat roast, and the temperature all contribute texture. But every now and again, you'll come across a bag of potatoes that refuses to turn golden and crunchy.

About 1½ pounds (1 bag) mini creamer potatoes or fingerling potatoes or russet potatoes

About 5 teaspoons Diamond Crystal kosher salt

½ teaspoon baking soda

⅓ cup extra virgin olive oil

1 cup freshly grated or Microplaned Parmesan cheese

1. Line a sheet pan with parchment paper.

2. If using creamer potatoes, slice in two; leave any tiny ones whole. If using fingerlings, slice in half lengthwise. If using russet potatoes, quarter them.

3. Place the potatoes in a pot and cover with about 2 quarts of water. Set over high heat. Add 4 teaspoons of the salt and the baking soda to the water. Cover and bring to a rolling boil. Cook until you can easily pierce the largest potato all the way through with a butter knife—you're looking for it to feel like a super-ripe pear, not a firm apple, about 10 minutes after the water comes to a boil. Drain. Pat with a kitchen towel to remove any excess moisture from the exterior of the potatoes. Place them in a large bowl.

4. Heat the oven to 450°F.

5. Add the oil and the remaining 1 teaspoon salt to the potatoes and roughly toss and mix until the potatoes are coated in a downy layer of potato guts.

6. Transfer to the parchment-lined sheet pan. Separate the potatoes so no two overlap, with the cut sides facing down (if sliced). Use the flat bottom of a bowl or molcajete to swiftly, harshly smash each potato to about ⅓ inch flat. (If you have trouble with potato bits sticking to your smashing device, you can place another sheet of parchment over the potatoes before smashing.) The flatter the potato, the crispier its edges will get.

7. Roast for about 20 minutes, until the edges of the potatoes are turning golden. (If you really wanted gorgeous, cover-girl crispy potatoes, you would at this point—before the next instruction with the cheese—flip each one over, so its browned flesh is facing upward.) Sprinkle a few pinches of Parmesan over each potato, then roast for another 10 minutes, or until the Parmesan is browned and the edges of the potatoes are supremely crispy.

UPGRADE: *Roast in duck fat or schmaltz instead of olive oil.*

CRISPY SMASHED ONION DIP POTATOES
(aka California Potatoes)

LEVEL

Anyone can execute

TIME

1 hour

MAKES

A side for 4 to 6

Lipton Onion Dip was originally called "California Dip" when an unknown genius first popularized the combination in 1954. A subsequent squall of advertisements put out by Lipton used the California Dip as a synecdoche for the powdered mix's versatility: "Think how nice it would be to give everyday cookery a festive 'Continental' touch," read one ad, which featured the "festive California Dip" surrounded by a planetary ring of ridged chips.[2] Ostensibly the "California" part of its name came from the fact that whoever invented the dip hailed from my home state, though I like to think that "California" also represents something more thematic: a dish that's flexible, reliably satisfying, and spontaneous; a bowl of a Joan Didion character, captaining a convertible on a coastal road cut into a cliff. Here's the thing, though . . . I think that thematic "California" can and should describe the potato here, instead of just the dip. It's arguably even more flexible, satisfying, and spontaneous than a dip. I beg you to consider its range. When tossed with a rich, homemade version of onion dip, these crispy smashed potatoes are downright opulent.

About 1½ pounds (1 bag) mini creamer potatoes

2 yellow onions, halved and cut into ¼-inch-thick slices

1 garlic head, top trimmed

¼ cup plus 3 tablespoons extra virgin olive oil

6½ teaspoons Diamond Crystal kosher salt, plus more as needed (lol)

½ teaspoon baking soda

2 tablespoons unsalted butter, softened

1 cup sour cream or labneh

1 tablespoon freshly squeezed lemon juice, plus more if needed

A few chives, finely chopped

1. Heat the oven to 450°F. Line two sheet pans with parchment. Slice larger potatoes in two; leave any tiny ones whole.

2. Place the sliced onions and garlic head on one prepared sheet pan. Coat in the ¼ cup of oil (pour a little directly into the trimmed top of the garlic since it won't readily coat itself in there) and 1½ teaspoons of the salt and fan everything out across the pan. Roast, stirring the onions occasionally, until browning around edges, 30 to 45 minutes. If the onions around the edges start to get too brown before the others take on color, you can shift them to the center and pile them beneath the others to insulate them from too much direct heat.

3. Meanwhile, add the potatoes to a pot and cover with about 2 quarts of water. Set over high heat. Add 4 teaspoons of the remaining salt and the baking soda. Bring to a rolling boil. Cook until you can easily pierce the largest potato half all the way through with a butter knife. You're looking for it to feel like a super-ripe pear, not a firm apple. Drain. Pat with a kitchen towel to remove any excess moisture from the exterior of the potatoes. Place them in a large bowl.

continued

4. Roughly toss the potatoes with the butter until it melts and the potatoes begin to develop some fleecy matter on their outsides. Add the remaining 3 tablespoons oil and 1 teaspoon salt and toss again.

5. Transfer the potatoes to the second prepared sheet pan. Separate them and turn them as needed so the cut sides are facing down. Use the flat bottom of a bowl or molcajete to swiftly, harshly smash each potato to about ¼ inch flat. (If you have trouble with potato bits sticking to your smashing device, you can place a sheet of parchment over the potatoes before smashing.) The flatter the potato, the crispier its edges will get.

6. Place the potato pan on the top rack of the oven, while the onions and garlic roast below. Let the potatoes roast for 25 to 30 minutes, until supremely crispy, mahogany brown around the edges, and beginning to turn golden in the centers. (If the onions finish before the potatoes are done, or vice versa, you can pull them from the oven first and move the potatoes to the middle rack. You can also turn the temperature down if the potatoes are burning around the edges before they crisp on top, or adjust the pan to the bottom rack. You're the boss of your oven, no matter how much she taunts you.)

7. Make the onion dip. Squeeze the garlic cloves out of the head, then either chop the just-caramelized onion and garlic cloves on a cutting board until a rough paste forms or pulse them in a food processor. If using a food processor, pulse in the labneh and lemon juice and scrape down the sides; if chopping by hand, combine the garlic-onion paste with labneh and lemon juice in a bowl. Taste and, if needed, add more salt and lemon juice.

8. Either spread the dip on a platter and pile the potatoes on top, or pile the potatoes and top with the dip, or toss the warm, crispy smashed potatoes in the onion dip to serve. Garnish with chives.

STUFFED SMASHED POTATOES

LEVEL

A bit of skill required

TIME

1 hour

MAKES

6 potatoes

Some recipes solve a big problem ("It'd be great to be able to make sourdough without a three-day fermentation") and others, like this one, are simply extraneous. I don't mean that in a bad way. Extraneity is one of my favorite categories of delights; I'm all about a pretty watch that doesn't even work, or a marathon of Grey's Anatomy *once every two years even though I couldn't forget a single plot twist if it was the only thing I had to do to avoid sudden torture. And these whole stuffed smashed potatoes are, indeed, a delight. They're a cross between twice-baked and smashed. They're a special-occasion potato, even if the occasion is just you, wearing a watch that looks pretty but doesn't even work, watching a television show you've seen so many times you could rewrite the script from memory.*

6 Yukon Gold potatoes (about 2½ pounds), scrubbed

Diamond Crystal kosher salt

3 tablespoons unsalted butter, softened

½ cup labneh

3 large or 6 small shallots, finely diced

1 cup grated Gruyère cheese (use the medium side of a box grater)

1 tablespoon extra virgin olive oil

1. Place the potatoes in a large pot and cover with cold water. Add a good amount of salt (2-ish heaping teaspoons per quart) and bring to a boil. Boil until the potatoes are just tender enough to piece with a butter knife all the way through, 25 to 30 minutes. Drain.

2. Meanwhile, heat the oven to 450°F. Line a sheet pan with parchment paper.

3. When the potatoes have cooled enough to handle, slice off the bottom ¼ inch, so they sit flat. Save the bottoms!

4. Use a paring knife and a spoon to scrape out the insides of the potatoes and transfer the fluff to a bowl, so that each potato turns into a vessel with ½ inch of potato and skin around the sides and bottom. If you mess up and pierce a shell, no big deal—it's all getting smashed anyway. To the bowl with the flesh, add the butter, labneh, 1½ teaspoons salt, the shallots, and cheese. Mash it together.

5. Gently (!!!) rub the shells with the oil. Place them on the sheet pan with the cut side down. Refill each hollowed-out potato shell with the mashed mixture. Top with reserved potato slices you took from the bottoms to make the potatoes balance flat on the sheet tray, like jaunty hats! Drizzle with any remaining oil. Sprinkle with salt.

6. Use the bottom of a molcajete or heavy bowl to smash each stuffed, boiled potato to about ½ inch flat. The flatter the potato, the crispier its edges will get; the more interior stuffing you smash out, the more varying texture in the final product.

7. Roast for about 25 minutes, until the exteriors are golden and the insides are oozing, with some cheerful bubbling.

8

Dramatic CARROTS

MISSION

Stew-tender, flavorful carrots that can be achieved without too much fuss.

WHAT I TESTED

Brine • Cooking method
Carrot shape • Cooking fat

CONFIT
STIR FRY (COINS)
BUTTER
BUTTER + OLIVE OIL
SCHMALTZ
HIGH-HEAT ROAST
BRAISE
BOIL + SMASH + ROAST
STEAM + ROAST
OLIVE OIL
DUCK FAT
HIGH-HEAT ROAST (GRATED)
LOW-HEAT ROAST + BROIL
BUTTER-POACH
HALVES
FETA-BRINE + BRAISE
LONG SAUTÉ (GRATED)
LOW-HEAT ROAST
COINS
MATCHSTICKS

THERE ARE PLENTY OF THINGS I *COULD* DO TO A CARROT.

I could lacto-ferment it for weeks. I could bread it and shallow-fry it in duck fat. But there are only a few things I *would* actually do. Maybe this is a me problem—but when I approach a bunch of carrots, my instinct is simplicity. Perhaps it's because even a raw carrot is already spectacularly good, with a high water content for turgid crunch and lots of sweet earthiness.

In a world where a person could pickle, steam, smash, fry, and reshape a carrot a million different ways, I tried to set some parameters. Ultimately, I wanted my carrots to be completely saturated with flavor, and ready in less than 90 minutes. And I knew that I wanted carrots so tender that it was a wonder they hadn't disintegrated. The carrot, after all, is occasionally dangled from the end of a stick, spurring a lagging subject onward. An early mention of the phrase describes it as a metaphor for using the promise of positive reinforcement in place of negative reinforcement. In the 1849 *Narrative of the Late Expedition to the Dead Sea,* Edward P. Montague recalls a caricature he'd seen of a donkey race; the riders who incentivized their donkeys with a persuasive bunch of carrots tied to a stick and suspended overhead fared better than those who hit their animals with blackthorn twigs.[1] No word on whether those donkeys actually got their snack in the end, but you can!

There is a moment during cooking when carrots completely surrender themselves, becoming essentially structured baby food; here, I was trying to pinpoint the most efficient way to reach that moment while also suffusing the carrot with the sort of flavors that evoke flickering candles and hunks of tender beef. Carrots are roughly 88 percent water, which bodes well for raw preparations but means that concentrating the vegetal sweetness requires some fiddling and time.

- I found that in situations where time is too tight to braise for ages, poaching or braising the carrots in between a high heat sear and a lower heat sauté slightly concentrates flavor, massively improves tenderness, and removes some bitterness. (When tasted side by side, carrots that received a hard sear and a lower heat sauté with no steam in between tasted more of turnips than a sweeter, softer batch that got steamed before the lower heat sauté.) This steam-step also works if you're going to roast carrots; just steam them for a few minutes before tossing with fat. Harold McGee writes that a precooking also helps the carrots retain their shape, even when they've gone totally soft, as in a stew.[2]

- Because carrots are thicker on top and thinner on the bottom, if you're going to use a high-heat roast method (say hotter than 400°F), slice them into more evenly sized pieces first, to avoid fully burning some parts while undercooking others.
- Carrots were originally cultivated for their leaves and seeds; the root—the part we focus on now—was an afterthought; a sixth-century copy of Dioscorides's *De Materia Medica* notes, glibly, "the root can be cooked and eaten."[3] I love to keep at least a portion of the greens attached when braising, since they get tender and soak up sauce. You'll want to remove the greens for higher-heat roasting methods, because they'll burn.
- Any fat works here—unlike potatoes, the carrots won't absorb as much of it, but a slick on exteriors will help with flavor and browning. For that reason, I eliminated the butter braise (a two-ish-hour technique long-used and then widely popularized by the restaurant Noma[4]); it produced tender carrots but ones that weren't as suffused with flavor as they should have been after so long. I prefer either just olive oil, or, for decent browning and a bit more flavor, olive oil and butter together. Animal fats like duck fat won't penetrate the carrot as deeply as they would something starchier, and the result is an incongruent meaty flavor next to a more vegetal one. Which is fine in the case of something like a roasted chicken with schmaltz carrots below it, since the dishes go with one another, but when isolating the carrots, I prefer to leave out the animal fats.

THE BEST METHODS

BEST MAINSTAY METHOD: Sear your carrots like a piece of meat, sliced lengthwise, then give them a quick steam in the pan, then braise in an acidic liquid.

BEST SPECIAL-OCCASION METHOD: Treat your carrots like creamer potatoes: boil in baking soda and salt water, then smash them and toss with a cooking fat and salt and roast them at a high heat for tender interiors and crispy edges.

EAT THEM RAW! As has been noted in a number of places, including by Christopher Kimball in *The Milk Street Cookbook*,[5] **shredding raw carrots releases sugars** and increases their sweetness. I love to take advantage of this sweetness in a salty-sweet hot feta–grated carrot salad (see page 106). It doesn't satisfy the tender part of my equation as well as the cooking methods, but it's one of my favorite recipes in the book all the same. A few more uncooked preparations I love—try them all: the Salsa de Zanahoria y Habanero in Rick Martinez's *Mi Cocina,*[6] Deb Perelman's Carrot Salad with Harissa, Feta, and Mint,[7] and Samin Nosrat's Shaved Carrot Salad with Ginger and Lime in *Salt, Fat, Acid, Heat.*[8]

MOTHER RECIPE

QUICK-BRAISED CARROTS

LEVEL

Anyone can execute

TIME

45 minutes

MAKES

Carrots for 4

These are a stripped-down version of the melty-sweet carrot chunks that you—the brave and virtuous host—love to pluck from a stew before plating it for guests (I've seen you do it). I behave like that, too; a soft carrot is irresistible. Which is why I wanted to develop a method that produces a similar result. I treat the carrots like a tough cut of meat, browning them deeply on one side before letting a flavorful liquid break down their sturdiness, until they're basically baby food. I keep their natural shape intact for an elegant presentation that's less "supporting player in a bourguignon," and more, "did I meet her decades ago at a party? How does she still look so . . . good?" Once you master the technique, you may want to bring in alliums, or swap out the doenjang and tomato paste for other flavors you love, like curry paste, or miso, or a finely chopped blend of ginger-garlic-herb. The water could be coconut milk or chicken stock; the honey could be maple syrup. The important thing is that you let the braising liquid simmer until it's super-thick and sticky, like a glaze, and the carrots are no firmer than butter.

1 bunch (roughly 1¼ pounds) small to medium rainbow carrots or other organic carrots, scrubbed

3 tablespoons neutral oil, like avocado or canola

½ teaspoon Diamond Crystal kosher salt, plus more as needed

1 tablespoon doenjang

5 tablespoons double-concentrated tomato paste

1 teaspoon honey

1. Slice each carrot lengthwise, into two long strips, each with a flat side. Trim the greens to about 1 inch. If the carrots won't lie flat on their cut sides, trim off any gnarled tips.

2. Choose a Dutch oven or braising pan that will hold all the carrots in a single layer. Set it over high heat for 3 minutes, then add the oil. When it's shimmering, use tongs to place each carrot half flat side down in the hot oil. Sprinkle with salt. Sear for about 5 minutes, until the carrots are mostly evenly browned on the bottom. Flip the carrots with tongs and push them to the sides of the pot.

3. Add the doenjang and tomato paste to the center of the pot and sauté in the oil for 2 to 3 minutes, gradually mixing into the carrots to start to coat them. When the pastes are fragrant and a few shades darker in tone, add the honey and enough water to cover the carrots by 1 inch. Stir to combine with the pastes to make a broth (a few little lumps here and there are fine).

4. Turn the heat to medium and cook at a rolling simmer, half covered, for 25 to 35 minutes (it'll depend on the thickness of your carrots), until most of the liquid has evaporated to leave a thick, ketchup-textured sauce just coating the carrots. Stir occasionally to avoid burning. When they're done, the thickest part of the biggest carrot should be extremely fork-tender, i.e. even a baby could easily smash it. If the liquid evaporates before the carrots are tender, add a splash more water and continue to cook. Season to taste and serve.

BOIL-SMASH-ROAST CARROTS

LEVEL

A bit of skill required

TIME

1 hour

MAKES

A side for 4 to 6

Boil. Smash. Roast. That's all you need to remember. While in pursuit of the most tender carrots, I discovered that I liked the contrast of crisp exterior next to a stewed, dense interior. So I applied my Crispy Smashed Potato technique here. The result isn't exactly the same; even the sweetest of carrots won't crisp like a white potato. But by using baking soda and a pre-boil to develop a roughened-up sluice of carroty matter, you'll get enough crispy edges to make the effort worth it. Plus, the roasted garlic–shallot labneh is worth making even on its own. Because carrots don't naturally want to crisp as readily as a starchier vegetable, I recommend roasting right on the sheet pan, with no parchment paper; the carrots naturally retain enough moisture to not turn to leather. (If you hate to scrub your pans, you can use parchment here; just don't expect as much browning.)

Diamond Crystal kosher salt

1 teaspoon baking soda

1 bunch (about 1¼ pounds) medium to large rainbow carrots or other organic carrots, rinsed, greens removed and reserved for another use

6 medium or 4 large shallots, peeled and sliced into rings about ⅓ inch thick

8 garlic cloves, peeled and roughly smashed with your knife

⅓ cup extra virgin olive oil

⅔ cup labneh (you can swap in Greek yogurt or sour cream)

Juice of 1 lemon

Freshly cracked black pepper

1. Fill a large pot with 4 quarts of water and add 1 heaping tablespoon of salt and the baking soda. Bring the water to a rolling boil. Heat the oven to 450°F.

2. Slice thicker carrots once lengthwise. You can keep any finger-width or thinner carrots whole. Chop all the carrots into roughly 3-inch chunks. When the water reaches a boil, add the pieces. Cook until the carrots are floating and easily pierced all the way through with a butter knife, 8 to 10 minutes.

3. Drain the carrots and pat dry. Transfer to an unlined sheet pan (if the pan is even remotely new, rub it with a little oil first to prevent sticking). Cover the carrots with a sheet of parchment paper and use the pot or another heavy item (like a molcajete, or a large liquid cup measurer) to firmly smash them to about ¼ inch thick. You don't need to be overly precise here! Think smashed potatoes. Peel away the top layer of parchment. In between the carrots, add the sliced shallots and garlic cloves. Drizzle the olive oil all over the exposed carrots and alliums, and season with about 1½ teaspoons salt.

4. Roast for about 25 minutes, turning the pan if needed midway through for even browning, until the carrots are deeply crispy in the thinnest spots, with brown crime scene–style outlines, and the shallots and garlic are crisp and browned.

5. To serve, blend the labneh with the roasted garlic and about half of the roasted shallots, plus the lemon juice and a few pinches of salt and freshly cracked pepper. (Or just chop the alliums into a paste and stir into the labneh.) Spread the labneh on a platter and pile the crispy carrots and the rest of the shallots on top.

SUNTORY
EST. 1899
JAPAN
43% ALC/VOL (86PROOF)

HOT FETA CARROT SALAD

LEVEL

Anyone can execute

TIME

30 minutes

MAKES

A side for 4 to 6, or a lunch for 2

This is the absolute most delicious thing you can do with a couple of carrots, and that's all I have to say about that. Actually, I have one more thing to say: If you buy pre-grated carrots, this can become a ten-minute recipe, a silver bullet that will upgrade your hosting acuity by approximately five times. (Okay, two more things. The first is that this is obviously a riff on classic French carrot salad, but trust me on the hot cheese. The second is that you should heed the note about making the dressing in an eight-ounce—aka the shortest—Tupperware; it's somehow perfect for emulsifying a vinaigrette and perhaps the only thing that has made me less hostile toward my collection of old, warped takeout containers.)

One 8-ounce package feta in brine

Neutral oil for the pan

8 ounces small to medium rainbow carrots or other organic carrots, peeled and grated (with a food processor or the medium side of a box grater); you can use pre-grated carrots here, but avoid pre-shredded, which won't be as sweet or absorb the brine as well

Honey

1 medium shallot, peeled and finely diced

2 garlic cloves, finely diced

1 tablespoon Dijon mustard

4 teaspoons freshly squeezed lemon juice

2 tablespoons olive oil

1. Remove the feta from the brine (reserve the brine in the package) and pat dry. Turn on the broiler to heat. Rub or spray a sheet pan with a thin coating of oil, so the cheese doesn't stick.

2. Add the grated carrots directly to the feta brine. Let soak while you finish the recipe. (For a stronger flavor, you can brine the carrots covered overnight in the refrigerator or up to 12 hours in advance.)

3. Slice the feta into roughly ½-inch cubes, like croutons. (It's okay if you get some crumbles; they'll lose their form later anyway.) Transfer to the prepared sheet pan and drizzle with a few teaspoons of honey. Broil for about 5 minutes (watch carefully toward the end!), until the tops and corners of the feta begin to turn golden.

4. Meanwhile, combine the shallot, garlic, mustard, lemon juice, olive oil, 2 tablespoons of the feta brine (you can take it right from the soaking carrots), and 2 teaspoons honey in a small plastic container with a tight-fitting lid. Shake until well combined, creamy, and emulsified.

5. Drain the shredded carrots through a sieve, pressing out any extra brine. (If your carrots taste unpalatably salty, you can rinse them and pat dry, but with most feta brines, you won't need to.) Toss the carrots with the dressing and the hot feta and toss again. Serve warm, though it's also great cold the next day.

EXPLODING DOUBLE-ROASTED CARROT CAKE WITH CARROT CARAMEL, PAGE 110

EXPLODING DOUBLE-ROASTED CARROT CAKE WITH CARROT CARAMEL

LEVEL

A bit of skill required

TIME

2 hours, including resting

MAKES

A two-layer cake, to serve 10 to 12

I call this "exploding" double-roasted carrot cake because when you remove the first slice, the caramel in the center of the frosting on both layers will gush dramatically toward the core, creating a lava flow spectacle. You could avoid this by slicing each of the cake layers in two horizontally and using the caramel between them as a glue, with the cream cheese whipped cream on top and around the sides. Just don't invite me.

FOR THE CAKE

1½ pounds grated carrots (scrubbed but fine to leave the peels on)

1¼ cups extra virgin olive oil

One 3-inch ginger knob, peeled, Microplaned into 2 tablespoons grated ginger

4 teaspoons ground cinnamon (I'm crazy!)

¼ cup (49 g) plus 1¾ cups (346 g) lightly packed dark brown sugar

Butter or oil, for the pans

2½ cups (355 g) all-purpose flour

2½ teaspoons baking powder

2 teaspoons Diamond Crystal kosher salt

4 large eggs, at room temperature

1¼ cups labneh, at room temperature

½ cup (75 g) raisins (I prefer golden raisins; dried sour cherries are also great here)

1. To make the cake: Start by setting aside about 1 cup tightly packed grated raw carrots (we'll add these back to the batter later, for flavor and texture variety). Place the rest of the carrots and ½ cup of the oil in a large skillet and sauté over medium heat for 25 to 30 minutes, until reduced by about two-thirds, shrunken, browned, and beginning to crisp. Add the ginger and cinnamon and sauté for another 2 minutes. Deglaze the pan with ¼ cup water and add the ¼ cup (49 g) brown sugar. Stir as the sugar dissolves and continue to cook for another minute or two, until the sugar-syrup bubbles and becomes sticky. Cut the heat.

2. While the carrots cook, line the bottoms of two 8- or 9-inch cake pans with parchment. (Eight-inch pans will yield a smaller, taller cake.) Butter or spray the pans with cooking oil.

3. Heat the oven to 350°F.

4. In a medium bowl, whisk together the flour, baking powder, and salt.

5. In the bowl of a stand mixer fitted with the paddle attachment, beat together the eggs and remaining 1¾ cups (346 g) brown sugar on medium speed until the mixture is nearly doubled in volume and has turned light taupe in color, about 5 minutes. Stream in the remaining ¾ cup oil, then add the labneh and beat to combine. Add the dry mixture in three additions, mixing about 90 percent before adding the next, and with the last one, add the raisins, the 1 cup reserved raw carrot, and two-thirds of the sticky, sugar-coated carrots (save the rest for the caramel). Beat just until evenly integrated.

FOR THE CARROT CARAMEL

1 cup (198 g) lightly packed dark brown sugar

⅛ teaspoon cream of tartar

½ teaspoon Diamond Crystal kosher salt

¼ cup (½ stick) unsalted butter, at room temperature, cut into tablespoon chunks

½ cup heavy cream

FOR THE FROSTING

One 8-ounce package cream cheese, at room temperature

½ cup (99 g) lightly packed dark brown sugar

1½ cups heavy cream

1 tablespoon vanilla bean paste (or extract, though I really prefer paste here)

Diamond Crystal kosher salt

6. Divide the batter between the two pans and bake until the centers are set when you gently poke them with a finger, about 32 minutes for 9-inch pans and closer to 36 minutes for 8-inch pans. Invert the cakes onto cooling racks.

7. While the cake layers are in the oven, make the caramel. Chop the reserved cooked carrots into a rough paste. Place the 1 cup (198 g) dark brown sugar in a small, dry saucepan with the cream of tartar, salt, and 2 tablespoons room-temperature water. Heat over medium heat, picking up the pan and swirling it (rather than stirring—this helps avoid crystallization) every minute or so. When the mixture comes to a simmer, continue to swirl for another 2 to 3 minutes, until it's thickened and sticky. Remove from the heat and use a silicone spatula to stir in the butter in two additions—it will foam wildly!—and then the cream and chopped cooked carrot paste. Stir until combined and set aside to cool to room temperature.

8. Make the cream cheese whipped cream frosting. Combine the cream cheese and the ½ cup (99 g) dark brown sugar in the bowl of a stand mixer fitted with the balloon whisk attachment. Beat on medium speed, then medium-high, for 4 to 6 minutes, until loosened and fluffy, stopping to scrape down the sides every few minutes. Beat until the sugar has mostly dissolved (you can rub some of the cream cheese between your fingers to check). With the mixer running on medium-low, slowly stream in the heavy cream, then scrape down the sides of the bowl. Add the vanilla bean paste and salt. Continue to beat on medium until the cream aerates and integrates with the cream cheese for a whipped butter texture. Set in the refrigerator until the cake layers are ready.

9. When the layers have cooled to the touch, frost one layer with half of the frosting, using an offset spatula or spoon to create a (roughly 6-inch) well in the center. Pour half of the room-temperature carrot caramel into the well, so it doesn't run down the sides of the cake. Stack the second layer on top and repeat.

9

Buttery BROCCOLI STEMS

MISSION

Rich and appealing broccoli stems that call to the home cook like peak springtime asparagus.

WHAT I TESTED

Cooking method • Cooking fat
Prep method

LOW-HEAT ROAST
HIGH-HEAT ROAST
SAUTÉ
STEAM + ROAST
BLANCH + ROAST
STEAM + SAUTÉ

BREAD + FRY
QUICK PICKLE
MISO PICKLE
STEAM + SAUTÉ (DICED)
SAUTÉ + CREAM (DICED)
RAW

JUST SAUTÉ (DICED)
BUTTER
OLIVE OIL
BUTTER + OLIVE OIL
NEUTRAL OIL
SCHMALTZ

I DON'T MEAN TO GET ALL SANCTIMONIOUS HERE, SINCE I USE PAPER TOWELS ON OCCASION.

(Like, every occasion.) But taking on a project like this means I can't help but think about food waste—and those in need of food—pretty constantly. Whether I'm shepherding eleven different quart containers full of macaroni and cheese to my neighbors, or performing strange calculations in spreadsheets to determine minimum batch sizes for a cookie variation, I am always hoping to minimize the amount of waste piling up as a result of my whims. So it was my absolute pleasure to give thought to an item like the broccoli stem, which I've seen end up in the American compost bin more often than on the dinner plate. That's all wrong! Broccoli stems, prepared properly, are more deeply flavored and tender than the florets. There are a number of ways to achieve this, including uncooked preparations like pickling or tossing julienned slides with a vinaigrette. Here I focused on methods with heat, to concentrate flavor and eliminate any stringiness that might otherwise dissuade you. Or me.

- If you have time, peel the thick skin layer before dicing or grating or slicing, to eliminate any fibrous thready bits.
- Quickly blanching or steaming the stem before cooking pre-softens it so it becomes more tender more quickly but also maintains bite.
- Broccoli stems cooked for a while in lots of oil take on a luxurious texture, somewhere

between cauliflower rice and butter, with a flavor like broccoli-cheddar soup.

- The best fat for broccoli stems cooked all the way until tender on the stovetop or in the oven is a cooking fat that can withstand a prolonged heat exposure at varying temperatures, like olive oil, or oil with butter added later, or a neutral oil (though the latter contributes less flavor). I found schmaltz to be discordant with the stems, perhaps because they don't suck up the fat as readily as a potato (or a broccoli crown), and thus the flavors didn't meld.
- Roasting with high heat produced the most concentrated flavor, but with more dehydrated firmness than I ultimately wanted; that said, if you're roasting florets, you should add the stems, peeled and sliced.

THE BEST METHODS

BEST MAINSTAY METHOD: Severely overcooked broccoli stems are just as analgesic as mashed potatoes. I first came across this technique for dealing mainly with larger pieces of broccoli in a Roy Finamore recipe featured by Kristen Miglore, in her genius Genius column on Food52.[1] My technique on page 116 uses a similar approach, with a few modifications for simplicity, and to expedite the process of turning the stems melty.

BEST SPECIAL-OCCASION METHOD: Creamed broccoli stems with cheddar will make you forget about spinach. See page 120.

MAKE IT CALAMARI! Kind of. Honor the natural crunch of broccoli stems by turning them into a sort of fry, engineered for dipping into briny tonnato, detailed on page 118.

MOTHER RECIPE

BROCCOLI STEMS THAT HAVE LET THEMSELVES GO

LEVEL

Anyone can execute

TIME

45 minutes

MAKES

A side for 6

Overcooked broccoli has a bad reputation. But severely overcooked broccoli, well, no one really talks about that. Here, I use a method adapted from a Roy Finamore recipe, with a few modifications for simplicity's sake. The first is that I cut my broccoli into smaller gravel-size pieces. The second modification I use is, rather than blanching the broccoli in a separate pot of salted water before it cooks down, I let it take a quick blanch-steam right in the covered pan, then lift the lid and cover it with the rest of the oil. This is because I'm lazy!

4 large heads of broccoli, stems peeled, bottom ½ inch and tough bits trimmed

⅓ cup extra virgin olive oil

2 large yellow onions, finely diced

2½ teaspoons Diamond Crystal kosher salt, plus more if needed

Freshly ground black pepper

Zest and juice of 1 lemon

1. Finely dice (or food process, in batches) the broccoli heads and stalks, until you have pieces about the size of a small chunk of gravel. (It's okay if the pieces are inconsistent, with some of them sized more like swollen rice grains and some more like gravel.)

2. Heat a large skillet over medium-high heat. Add half of the oil. When it's glistening, add the onions and sauté until lightly browned and soft, about 15 minutes.

3. Add the broccoli. Pour in about ⅔ cup water, enough to come up about ¼ inch on the sides of the skillet. Cover the skillet and let cook until the water sizzles away, about 5 minutes. Lift the lid and add the rest of the oil, plus the salt. Cook, stirring every 5 or so minutes, until the stem pieces are completely tender and no longer a vibrant green—they should be so slack that you can easily mash one with your cooking utensil. This will take about 30 minutes. (Deglaze with a few tablespoons of water every so often, to expedite the softening, if it's going slowly.)

4. Off the heat, season with pepper, more salt, and lemon zest and juice to taste.

VARIATION: BROCCOLI STEM CHOPPED CHEESE

Swap out roughly one-third of the broccoli for finely diced mushrooms. Give the mushrooms a sear, then add the stems and cook as directed above. Deglaze the pan with a few tablespoons each of Worcestershire sauce and soy sauce, then season with salt, pepper, and lemon. Spread a soft roll with mayo and ketchup, add some shredded lettuce and the broccoli-mushroom mixture, and serve topped with hot sauce and melted American cheese.

BROCCOLI CALAMARI WITH GREEN GODDESS TONNATO

LEVEL

A bit of skill required

TIME

45 minutes

MAKES

A hearty appetizer for 6 people

Technically I did not include tonnato in the book twice; technically, this is green goddess! With . . . tuna and capers and anchovies. Whatever, you're going to love it. Here I take a very different approach to broccoli stems than in my Mother Recipe on page 116; I lean into their natural crunch and vegetal flavor to create something like a green French fry, which pairs perfectly with an herby, briny dip.

FOR THE BROCCOLI

3 to 4 large heads of broccoli

1 cup all-purpose flour

1½ teaspoons Diamond Crystal kosher salt

½ teaspoon freshly ground black pepper

¾ cup mayonnaise, preferably Hellmann's

Neutral oil, for frying

FOR THE GREEN GODDESS

One 5-ounce jar olive oil–packed tuna, drained

2 oil-packed anchovy fillets, drained

2 garlic cloves, peeled

⅔ cup mayonnaise, preferably Hellmann's

2 tablespoons buttermilk

2 tablespoons freshly squeezed lemon juice, plus more to taste

2 tablespoons capers, drained and patted dry

3 tablespoons extra virgin olive oil

1 cup packed chives, basil, and/or arugula

1. Roughly chop the broccoli crowns into small-ish florets. Peel the broccoli stalks and slice them into "fries," matchsticks about ½ inch thick and the length of the stalk. Pat very dry with a kitchen towel.

2. In a large bowl, whisk together the flour, 1 teaspoon of the salt, and the pepper. Place the mayonnaise in a separate large bowl. Add all the broccoli florets and stems to the mayonnaise and toss until fully coated. Scrape off any large globs of mayo—let it be a thin jacket—and then roll the broccoli pieces in the seasoned flour. You want to really press the broccoli pieces into the flour so they're breaded on every side.

3. Let rest for 10 minutes, then repeat with any remaining mayo and seasoned flour. (You don't have to, but more coats = more crunch.)

4. To make the green goddess tonnato: Pulse the drained tuna, anchovies, and garlic in a food processor until any large pieces are broken up. Add the mayonnaise, buttermilk, lemon juice, capers, olive oil, and greens. Run the food processor until a paste similar in texture to onion dip has formed. Taste and adjust the seasoning if needed with more lemon juice and capers; it should be briny and bright and difficult to stop eating. Set aside in the refrigerator as you work on the broccoli.

5. Add neutral oil to a large cast-iron skillet until it comes up to about ½ inch on the sides. Heat over medium-high heat until it produces tiny aggressive bubbles around the tip of a wooden spoon when it is inserted into the oil. Add just the flour-coated broccoli floret pieces (not the fries) and shallow-fry until crisp and tender, 4 to 7 minutes, gently turning over with a slotted spoon or tongs to get an even cook. Remove from the oil and let drain on a rimmed rack or paper towel–lined plate. Sprinkle with salt. Repeat to fry the broccoli fries for 5 to 8 minutes, until golden, then let drain.

6. Serve the broccoli on a platter with the green goddess tonnato, to dip.

CREAMED BROCCOLI STEMS AND CHEDDAR

LEVEL

Anyone can execute

TIME

40 minutes

MAKES

A rich side for 6 to 8

I don't envy Sue Li, who had to style the photo for this recipe. It's . . . not a looker! Consider it an incredibly rustic cousin of aligot, the stretchy French potato dish that's half cheese, half starch. It's reminiscent, too, of broccoli-cheddar soup, a distinctly Americana creation launched into our pantries by Campbell's in the 1990s as a contender in the "Get President George Bush to Eat Broccoli" recipe contest. (No word on whether it worked.) The thing it does have going for it is that I once ate half of the total recipe by accident in ten minutes. It's rich, vegetal, cozy, and just pert enough from the labneh and Aleppo pepper to beat out the creamed spinach your mom won't stop pitching as a Thanksgiving side. Like the Broccoli Stems That Have Let Themselves Go on page 116, this is just as good with only stems, no florets, if you have them left over.

4 large heads of broccoli, stems peeled, bottom ¼ inch and tough bits trimmed

3 tablespoons olive oil

1 large yellow onion, finely diced

2½ teaspoons Diamond Crystal kosher salt, plus more as needed

1 teaspoon Aleppo pepper flakes (or 2 teaspoons dried red pepper flakes)

1⅓ cups heavy cream

8 ounces cheddar cheese, grated into about 2 cups

¾ cup labneh

1. Finely dice or, in batches, food process the broccoli until you have pieces about the size of gravel. It's okay if the pieces are inconsistent, some of them sized more like swollen rice grains and some more like gravel.

2. Heat a large cast-iron skillet over medium-high heat. Add 2 tablespoons of the oil. When it's glistening, add the onion and sauté until lightly browned and soft, about 15 minutes. Add the remaining 1 tablespoon oil, the broccoli, and salt and cook, stirring every few minutes, until the broccoli stems are completely tender, to the point where you could almost mash one with your cooking utensil easily, about 20 minutes. Deglaze with a few tablespoons of water midway through to expedite the softening if needed.

3. Smash up all the broccoli and onion bits so you're left with a chunky paste that's not fully smooth (leave a small amount of textural variety).

4. Make a well in the center and add the pepper flakes. Let them cook for 1 minute, then mix in with the broccoli paste. Adjust the heat to low. Add the cream and stir to combine. Let the cream come to a simmer around the edges and stir as it bubbles for 30 seconds. Add the cheese and cut the heat. Mix the cheese into the creamed broccoli as it melts. Add the labneh and stir to combine. Taste and adjust the seasoning with more salt as needed.

BROCCOLI STEM SOUP WITH CRISPY FLORETS ON TOP

LEVEL

Anyone can execute

TIME

1 hour

MAKES

Soup for 3

I know I have a tendency to anthropomorphize vegetables, and we hate that about me, but . . . don't broccoli florets sort of seem like they would bully their stems? This soup reverses that classic, oft-discussed power dynamic by giving the stems a full spotlight and using the florets as a crispy afterthought of a topping (but don't skip it). The bulk of the flavor comes from the stems, which we can all feel good about. This is more of a blueprint for a simple method, and it beckons creativity; add miso to your sheet pan and let it get nice and burnt, then use that to flavor your soup. Add quartered onions, or shallots, or swap out the parsley for chives. Whatever you do, just don't compliment the florets.

3 large heads of broccoli, stems peeled, bottom ½ inch and tough bits trimmed

6 garlic cloves, peeled

⅓ cup extra virgin olive oil

2½ teaspoons Diamond Crystal kosher salt

½ teaspoon freshly ground black pepper

1½ cups freshly Microplaned Pecorino Romano cheese, plus more for topping

2 cups vegetable or chicken broth, warmed to a simmer, plus more as needed

1 tightly packed cup parsley leaves (some stem is fine)

½ cup crème fraîche

Zest and juice of 1 lemon

Toasted breadcrumbs, crushed croutons, or crushed Ritz crackers, for topping

1. Heat the oven to 425°F. Line a sheet pan with parchment paper.

2. Chop off and set aside about 1½ cups broccoli florets. Finely dice—or in batches, food process—the rest of the broccoli heads and stalks until you have pieces about the size of gravel. It's okay if the pieces are inconsistent, with some of them sized more like swollen rice grains and some more like gravel. Don't bother cleaning your food processor—we'll use it again shortly.

3. Transfer all the broccoli—the gravel-size pieces and larger florets—and the garlic to the prepared pan and toss with the oil, salt, and pepper. Spread the gravel out across the center of the pan (it's fine if it overlaps a bit) and place the larger florets around the edges of the pan, where they'll cook faster and get more color. If any of the florets are larger than a standard s'mores marshmallow, slice them in two.

4. Roast for 25 to 30 minutes, until the gravel- and rice-size pieces are darker green and duller than they were when you checked a few minutes ago, wondering if they were done. Sprinkle one-third of the cheese over the florets and return to the oven for another 10 minutes or so, until the cheese has crisped and there are brown leopard spots all over the surface of the smaller broccoli pieces.

5. Remove from the oven and set aside the crispy florets for topping the soup. Use the parchment paper to airlift the smaller broccoli bits, plus the garlic, back into the food processor. Add the warmed broth, the rest of the cheese, the parsley, and the crème fraîche and blend for about 2 minutes, until a thick, smooth soup forms. Add more warmed broth if needed to reach a soup-like consistency. Season to taste with lemon juice, zest, and more salt.

6. Serve topped with the crispy florets and breadcrumbs, plus more cheese.

BROCCOLI STEM SOUP

10

Toasted NUTS

MISSION

Toasted nuts with boosted flavor and a more intense crunch.

WHAT I TESTED

Cooking method • Length of toasting time
Shape for toasting • Timing of cooking fat and other additions

STOVETOP TOAST
OVEN ROAST
LOW-HEAT OVEN ROAST
5 MINUTES
10 MINUTES
15 MINUTES
PARCHMENT-LINED ROAST
DRY
DRY + BUTTER AT END
WHOLE
CHOPPED
GROUND
BROWN SUGAR
AIR FRYER
MICROWAVE
UNLINED ROAST
20 MINUTES
DRY + BROWN SUGAR AT END
DRY + OLIVE OIL AT END
OLIVE OIL
BUTTER

FOR . . .	USE . . .	KEEP IN MIND . . .
The most even toast with the least risk of burning	A low oven temperature (between 275°F and 325°F); roast the nuts on a parchment paper–lined metal pan	Stir every few minutes to bring the nuts on the outside in and the central nuts to the edges, for the most even flavor
The most even toast with maximal efficiency	A higher-heat oven (around 400°F), and roast the nuts directly on a metal pan	Stir often (bring the nuts on the outside in and the central nuts to the edges, for the most even flavor) and pull about 1 minute before you think you should, since they'll continue to cook in direct contact with the hot metal
The most efficient and easy-to-clean method with reliably solid even toasting, aka my favorite	Roast dry in a cast-iron skillet over medium-low heat for 10 to 20 minutes (depending on your burner strength), and add any fat or flavoring agents (or ingredients to caramelize, such as on page 129) when the nuts are deeply toasted and super fragrant	Stir often (bring the nuts on the outside in and the central nuts to the edges for the most even flavor); for even more intense flavor, coarsely grind the nuts (i.e. pulse in a food processor but don't let them turn to a paste) before toasting—but aim for a roughly even chop and watch them closely to avoid the smaller bits burning

MOTHER RECIPE

MAPLE-SESAME CARAMELIZED CASHEWS

LEVEL

Anyone can execute

TIME

10 minutes

MAKES

Enough nuts for 4 to snack on, or to chop and toss into a few large salads

While I found that oven toasting produced the nuttiest, most even flavor (thanks, I think, to heat approaching from multiple sides), you can make these in a skillet or Dutch oven on the stovetop and still get a deeply flavored nut—in this case, coated in salty caramel. I have you toast them in two stages, to develop flavor before coating the cashews. I love to let them cool and eat them as a snack, but they're also fantastic chopped and tossed into granola or cereal, or a large salad, or sprinkled into a sandwich.

2 cups raw cashews

1 tablespoon extra virgin olive oil

2 tablespoons unsalted butter

2 tablespoons packed dark or light brown sugar

1 teaspoon Diamond Crystal kosher salt, plus more as needed

3 tablespoons pure maple syrup

1 teaspoon soy sauce

2 tablespoons sesame seeds

1. Line a sheet pan with parchment paper and set aside. Grab a large (not cast-iron) skillet or a Dutch oven and set it over medium heat for 2 minutes. Reduce the heat to medium-low. Add the nuts and toast dry for 12 to 20 minutes (timing will vary depending on your burner strength), frequently jostling the pan or using a spatula to move the nuts around, until they're extremely fragrant and golden with a few spots of browning (adjust your heat as needed to encourage toasting and discourage burning; if you turn up the heat, watch the nuts *verrrrrry* closely).

2. Add the oil, butter, brown sugar, salt, maple syrup, and soy sauce. Stir until the sugar and salt have dissolved, the liquid is smooth, and the nuts are completely coated. Cook, stirring occasionally, for 4 to 6 minutes more, until the bubbling slows and the sauce is thickened and beginning to reduce. When the coating has reduced enough that no loose puddle lingers when you move the nuts from one side of the pan to another, add the sesame seeds and stir to combine. Cook for 1 to 2 minutes, just until the seeds have gotten a chance to toast.

3. Transfer to the prepared sheet pan as evenly as you can. Let cool, uncovered. After about 10 minutes, when the nuts are cool, you can break apart the clusters with your hands or chop the nuts if desired. Store covered.

TOMATO-BREAD DINNER

LEVEL

Anyone can execute

TIME

1 hour

MAKES

Dinner for a few tired people; halve the tomatoes and use a quarter sheet pan if you aren't starving

If you have access to a halfway-decent grocer, you can make me dinner while I watch reality TV and catch up on texts. Relatedly, this simple sheet pan dinner is one of the only things my husband knows how to make (though, per page 225, I'm optimistic about pasta). I don't even mind, since this particular dinner is my favorite. It's obviously excellent in the summer, but it works during shoulder season, too, when the tomatoes need a boost. It's a You-Can't-Prove-I-Made-This-Pantsless version of my Warm Sub Salad on page 134, with just the essentials. You could turn the oven temperature even lower, say to 300°F, and roast for up to 2 hours, but in my home—I'm already halfway through the season one finale of the worst brainrot you could imagine—we're impatient.

1 pint cherry tomatoes, stems plucked off

2 large bunches ripe Roma or Campari tomatoes, stems removed, quartered or cut into sixths if larger

1 garlic head, top ⅓ inch trimmed (or a big handful of peeled garlic cloves)

½ cup extra virgin olive oil, plus more as needed

2 teaspoons Diamond Crystal kosher salt, plus more as needed

½ cup raw walnuts (or any other nut you already have)

¾ cup packed freshly Microplaned or finely grated Parmesan cheese

3 cups fresh basil leaves

1 baguette or focaccia loaf

1. Heat the oven to 325°F. Line a sheet pan with parchment paper for easier cleanup, or leave it bare for more browning.

2. Place the cherry tomatoes and quartered tomatoes on the sheet pan. Add the garlic head. Toss everything with the oil and salt, making sure to drizzle oil into the cut parts of the garlic. Roast, uncovered, for 40 to 50 minutes, until the tomatoes are beginning to brown in places and burst. Raise the temperature to 375°F. Make a well in the middle of the pan—to keep everything separated—and add the walnuts, all in one place. (Don't toss.) Roast for another 6 to 8 minutes, until the nuts are fragrant and a shade darker.

3. Remove the pan from the oven and transfer the nuts to the bowl of a food processor or blender (or molcajete or mortar); leave the tomatoes on the pan. Squeeze out the roasted garlic cloves into the bowl of the food processor, too. Add the cheese, a few pinches of salt, and the basil. Pulse as you stream in more oil to combine into a pesto-like consistency.

4. Rip off hunks of the bread, drag them across the tomato-y, oily pan, and dip in the pesto to craft perfect bites.

FETA BRINE SALAD WITH TOASTED CASHEW–SHALLOT VINAIGRETTE

LEVEL

Anyone can execute

TIME

15 minutes, plus 45 minutes to 2 hours for resting

MAKES

Salad for 3 or 4

These cashews toast in shallot oil to form the body of a dressing for a pile of endive. Each leaf can be used like a Tostitos scoop. The shallots have two functions: Half of them are flavored with feta brine and the other half become a deep savory-sweet background flavor in the dressing.

1 bunch radishes, scrubbed, greens trimmed, sliced into thin shingles

4 large or 6 medium shallots, peeled and sliced into thin rings

One 8-ounce block feta in brine

¼ cup olive oil

1 cup raw cashews, whole or pieces

1 tablespoon pure maple syrup

2 tablespoons packed brown sugar

1½ teaspoons Diamond Crystal kosher salt

3 tablespoons unseasoned rice wine vinegar

Warm water

4 small (or 2 to 3 large) heads endive, washed and dried, cores trimmed and leaves separated

1. Place the sliced radishes in a medium bowl. Add half the sliced shallots and reserve the other half. Drizzle with all the brine from the cheese (set aside the actual cheese to use in the salad assembly). Toss together, separating out the little shallot rings, and let marinate for 45 minutes to 2 hours at room temperature.

2. Meanwhile, make the toasted cashew–shallot vinaigrette: Heat the oil in a large (not cast-iron) skillet over medium-high heat until shimmering, about 1 minute. Add the remaining shallots and reduce the heat to medium. Sauté for 4 to 7 minutes, until beginning to brown. Reduce the heat to medium-low. Add the cashews and toast, stirring intermittently, until fragrant and beginning to turn golden, 4 to 7 minutes. Add the maple syrup, brown sugar, and salt. Stir until the sugar dissolves and the nuts and shallots become sticky and caramelized, 4 to 6 minutes, then immediately cut the heat. Reserve 3 tablespoons of the mixture as a garnish, then add the vinegar and scrape with a fish spatula to deglaze, aka pull any sticky bits from the bottom and sides of the pan into the nut and shallot mixture.

3. Transfer the contents of the pan to a food processor. Pulse to combine. Add 6 tablespoons warm water and pulse until smooth, scraping down the sides as you go, until you have a cohesive, wildly delicious dressing the consistency of Thanksgiving gravy. (Add more water as needed to achieve a gravy-like texture; it should be pourable, or pipable with a squeeze bottle if you're more committed than I am to gorgeous presentation.)

4. Fan out the endive on a serving platter, the scoop facing upward. Drizzle with the vinaigrette. Spoon the marinated radishes and shallots onto the salad, including some but not most of the brining liquid. (Add the remaining liquid to a future martini.) Crumble the cheese over the top.

5. Chop the reserved nuts and shallots. Sprinkle over the top and serve.

FETA BRINE SALAD WITH TOASTED CASHEW-SHALLOT VINAIGRETTE, PAGE 131

WARM SUB SALAD,
PAGE 134

WARM SUB SALAD

LEVEL

Anyone can execute

TIME

1 hour

MAKES

Salad for 4

One of several good things to come out of TikTok—another that comes to mind is videos of dirty rugs being power-washed—is the reconceptualization of salads as deconstructed sandwiches. Consider this my contribution to the canon. It's sort of like the sub I order at Faicco's, except here those fillings are tossed with arugula while warm until the cheese begins to slump. The basil dressing is a thicker, supercharged acidic pesto, made with tomato-oil roasted walnuts. If you hate to mise before you cook, you can do most of the prep and chopping while the tomatoes roast.

3 pints cherry tomatoes, stems plucked off

1 garlic head, top ⅓ inch trimmed

¾ cup extra virgin olive oil, plus more as needed

2 teaspoons Diamond Crystal kosher salt, plus more for the dressing

3 cups cubed bread, like ciabatta or sandwich rolls

¾ cup raw walnuts

1 large (12-ounce) container arugula

¾ cup pitted Castelvetrano olives, roughly chopped, plus 2 tablespoons of their brine

One 8-ounce ball fresh mozzarella cheese, cut into roughly ¼-inch dice

6 ounces salami, roughly chopped (feel free to swap fresh or crisped prosciutto)

3 ounces Pecorino Romano cheese, Microplaned or finely grated (about ¾ cup)

3 tablespoons red wine vinegar

3 cups very tightly packed fresh basil leaves

1. Heat the oven to 325°F. Line a sheet pan with parchment paper.

2. Place the cherry tomatoes on the sheet pan and add the garlic head. Toss everything with the oil and salt. Roast, uncovered, for 45 to 50 minutes, until the tomatoes are a duller orange-red and beginning to burst and brown. Raise the temperature to 400°F. Add the bread and toss with the oil and tomatoes. Make a well in the middle of the pan and add the walnuts, all in one place; don't toss them in with the tomatoes or bread. Roast for 7 to 10 minutes, until the bread cubes are a bit toasty but still soft.

3. Meanwhile, in your largest salad bowl (your party bowl!), combine the arugula, olives, mozzarella cheese, and salami.

4. Remove the pan from the oven and use a slotted spoon to transfer the walnuts to the bowl of a food processor or blender. Transfer the tomatoes and bread cubes to the salad bowl. Toss now so that the cherry tomatoes transfer their flavor and heat as they cool.

5. Squeeze out the roasted garlic cloves into the bowl of the food processor with the walnuts. Pour the residual oil from the sheet pan—you should have about 3 tablespoons (but if you don't, you can supplement with fresh oil)—into the food processor bowl. Add the Pecorino cheese, vinegar, olive brine, a few pinches of salt, and the basil and pulse as you drizzle in more oil until you achieve a pesto-like consistency. Use about half of the nut mixture to dress the salad; toss well. Add more gradually, as you toss, until the salad is fully dressed, then reserve any extra for another use.

6. Serve the salad immediately, while warm.

HAZELNUT-COCOA TOAST

LEVEL

Anyone can execute

TIME

45 minutes

MAKES

Toast for 2, plus a bit of extra chocolate-nut butter for the fridge

I make this roasted nut and cocoa spread with brown sugar, for a just-perceptible glassy-sandy sugar texture in the final product. For a perfectly smooth nut butter, use maple syrup instead. (And for something closer to peanut butter, swap in honey for the maple and skip the cocoa powder.) In the summer, when stone fruits are in season, I pair this with jam, which I make by simmering macerated peaches with lemon juice, zest, a bit of sugar, and salt.

2 cups raw hazelnuts (or a mix of hazelnuts and cashews)

3 heaping tablespoons neutral oil or refined coconut oil, plus more if needed

¼ cup packed brown sugar, pure maple syrup, honey, or granulated sugar

½ teaspoon Diamond Crystal kosher salt

¼ cup Dutch-process cocoa powder

1 tablespoon unsalted butter, at room temperature

2 thick slices brioche or milk bread (or any bread you like; soft with some crust or structure is better here)

2 tablespoons peach jam (optional)

1. Set the nuts on a large cutting board. Use a chef's knife to coarsely chop them into gravel-size pieces. (You can also use a food processor fitted with an S-blade for this; if you go too fine, though, it'll be hard to rub off any large pieces of hazelnut skin later.)

2. In a dry skillet over medium or medium-low heat (modulate the heat based on the amount of browning you see), toast the nut pieces for anywhere from 10 to 15 minutes, stirring and jostling until they're covered in golden and mahogany spots and much of their skin has fallen off. Transfer the hot nuts to a kitchen towel and use it to vigorously rub the nuts for a minute; a lot of any remaining skin will flake right off. It's fine if some remains on the nuts. Discard any skin that falls off.

3. Transfer the nuts to a food processor fitted with the S-blade. Process for about 1 minute, until they're in tiny, sand grain–size pieces and starting to release a bit of moisture. Scrape down the sides and bottom of the bowl with a silicone spatula. Keep running the food processor as you drizzle in the oil. Add the brown sugar, salt, and cocoa powder and continue to run, stopping to scrape every 2 minutes or so, for 8 to 12 minutes, until super glossy, smooth, and shiny. (If that's just not happening, add more oil, but be judicious and scrape down the sides and bottom in between.) Taste and adjust with more salt if needed.

4. Meanwhile, wipe out the skillet and heat over medium-low heat. Add the butter. When it melts, add the bread and toast for a few minutes on each side.

5. Slather both slices with the nut spread. Top with dollops or swirls of jam (if using) and serve. Store any extra spread covered in the refrigerator and let it come to room temperature before using.

HAZELNUT-COCOA TOAST,
PAGE 135

11

Extra-Flavorful LATKES

MISSION

Latkes with deep flavor, creamy hash brown–evoking centers, and frizzled, lacy edges.

WHAT I TESTED

Potato type • Cooking method • Allium
Binder • Cooking fat • Squeezing technique
Moment of salting • Length of rest before cooking

YUKON
CREAMER
IDAHO
FINGERLINGS
SALT PRE-REST
SALT POST-REST
YELLOW ONION
SHALLOT
COLANDER
CHEESECLOTH
NO SQUEEZE
MATZO MEAL
OLIVE OIL
NEUTRAL OIL
SCHMALTZ
DUCK FAT
GIANT PAN LATKE
COOKED ONION
STAINLESS STEEL
NONSTICK
CAST IRON
BAKE
BAKE + BROIL
PANKO
NO REST
10-MIN REST
1-HOUR REST
OVERNIGHT REST
ALL-PURPOSE FLOUR

CONSTRUCTING THIS CHAPTER

felt how I imagine filming a provocative sex scene feels for an actor: As much as I wanted to throw my back into it, I couldn't help but think of all the ways it would scandalize my parents. They have only ever used one latke recipe, developed by their friend David Firestone, whom food writer Molly O'Neill called "the Latke King" in her 1992 *New York Cookbook*.[1] It's a seriously good recipe, one that had me doubting I could innovate on a canonical potato pancake formula. Most of the best latke recipes are simple; Claudia Roden's recipe for Potato Latkes in *The Book of Jewish Food* calls for just potatoes, eggs, salt, and oil for frying.

I do get it—why try to fix an unbroken thing? Here is where I clarify that absolutely nothing in this book was broken to begin with. Just like latkes, a lot of the subjects of my tests have deeply entrenched cultural legacies, and I wouldn't want to imply otherwise with my harebrained attempts to explore technique variations. I would, however, like to share my findings in case you, too, are always looking for a refinement; not a fix, and certainly not an absolutist statement about what's good. Unless we're talking about shoestring fries, which are, I regret to say for the thirteenth time in the book, my nightmare.

The most surprising intel I uncovered across all my trials came from a variation I hadn't even planned to test. Only after I'd finished my first round of head-to-heads did I accidentally drop a bit of cooked latke into leftover batter. While picking it out, one single shred of sautéed onion eluded my fingertips, sinking into the murky potato water beginning to gather in the bowl. It was then I realized: It makes *sense* to **caramelize, or half-caramelize, alliums before adding them to latke batter**. We cook our onions before guiding them with a silicone spatula into velvety scrambled eggs; we let them brown in butter before stir-frying in matzo brei. And latkes cook quickly, meaning there's scant time for the onion to reach its potential. As for the other tests, I found that:

- **Russet potatoes** are nonnegotiable for their high starch content, which means crispy edges and fluffy (not creamy) centers.
- Always **squeeze your grated potatoes and alliums** before making the batter—do so by hand through a colander atop a bowl for easier collection of residual starch, which will cling to the vessel beneath.

- Use a **cast-iron pan** for the crispiest edges; a Dutch oven will do the trick, too. Stainless steel is also fine, but be sure to heat the pan before adding the oil to avoid the batter sticking before you have a chance to flip, and to avoid crispy rings of browning around the edges of the latkes paired with undercooked centers. (I generally don't recommend a nonstick pan for latkes, which beckon a high initial heat.)
- You can't go wrong with yellow onion and parsley in a classic latke batter, though in my Mother Recipe, I'm recommending a slightly sweeter, funkier, precooked twist.
- Use **matzo meal (aka ground matzo) as your binder**, along with egg, for that brittle-tender texture. All-purpose flour and panko are decent swaps if you're making last-minute latkes, but in trials, both hydrated fairly quickly, resulting in mushier centers. The flour trials also had a denser, less appetizing texture, like those latkes that used to sit out at your neighbor's Hanukkah party until the very end of the night. You know the ones.
- **Rest your batter for about 10 minutes** before you begin to fry. While you can rest it longer, you'll get less textural contrast between the edges and the centers. Drop the batter into the pan with a cup measurer or spoon, then use its back to flatten so you get extra-lacy, crisp edges, rather than thick and consistent pucks.
- As for fat, skip vegetable oil, which imparts no flavor, and instead **use olive oil**, or if you're brazen, use an animal fat like schmaltz or duck fat for a luxurious latke.

THE BEST METHODS

BEST MAINSTAY METHOD AND BEST SHOWSTOPPER UPGRADE

- Fry your latkes on the stovetop in ⅓ inch of olive oil in a cast-iron pan. Before you make your batter—stay with me for a second—you should precook your alliums for a sweeter, deeper flavor; see my technique with shallots in the Mother Recipe on page 143.
- Fry in schmaltz or duck fat. I know! It's heresy!

HONORARY MENTIONS

- Many skillet latkes—giant, single, skillet-size potato pancakes—are more trouble than they're worth for a latke party, because they require a daunting inversion. Mine, on page 145, does not, expressly because I am uncoordinated and have only a middling amount of upper body strength. While a skillet-size latke won't get as damningly crisp as a single pan-fried one, it has its merits: It's festive for a crowd, and it's far less hands-on than individually portioned and fried pancakes.
- Baking latkes, as the brilliant recipe developer Rebecca Firkser suggests,[2] is a fabulous way to minimize splatter and stovetop chaos; plus, all your latkes will be done at the same time, which is otherwise tough to pull off unless you own several skillets. Just be sure to watch them closely toward the end and pull them out of the oven as soon as they're golden.

MOTHER RECIPE

SHALLOT AND CHIVE SILVER DOLLAR LATKES

LEVEL

A bit of skill required

TIME

1 hour 20 minutes

MAKES

Latkes for 4 to 6

Integrating cooked shallots into the latke batter, instead of raw ones, is so delicious that I'm willing to risk estranging family and friends over the recommendation. I've written this recipe to produce silver dollar latkes, because I love a French fry–crispy edge, and predictably, I like a heavy topping-to-latke ratio. But these can totally become normal-size; use the same recipe but scoop out latkes in ¼-cup increments, then flatten them with the back of the measuring device. If you're a traditionalist, shallot can be swapped for yellow onion; just be sure to cook the onion longer than called for in step 1 to ensure it reaches that point of In-N-Out meltiness. For an easy, luxurious upgrade, fry your latkes in schmaltz or duck fat. I know. Trust me.

3 tablespoons olive oil, plus more for frying

6 large or 9 medium shallots, finely diced

Diamond Crystal kosher salt

2½ pounds russet potatoes (roughly 2 large and 1 small-medium potato), unpeeled

2 eggs, lightly beaten

¼ cup matzo meal

¼ cup finely chopped fresh chives

¼ teaspoon freshly ground black pepper

1. Sauté the shallots: Set a large cast-iron skillet over medium heat. Add 3 tablespoons oil, the shallots, and a few pinches of salt and cook for about 5 minutes, until they begin to soften. Adjust the heat to medium-low and cook for 15 to 20 minutes, occasionally deglazing with a scant splash of water, until the shallots are caramel-brown, sweet, and melty. (You want them nearly caramelized but not 100 percent of the way there, because the ones that end up around the edges of the latkes will cook a little more in the hot oil.) Set aside to cool. (You can leave the oily pan on the stovetop to fry the latkes; wipe out any lingering shallot bits.)

2. While you cook and cool the shallots, prep the potatoes: Fit a food processor with the shredding disc. Scrub the potatoes and cut them into thick string cheese–size pieces to fit into the feed tube. Turn the food processor on and begin feeding in the potato sticks. (You can shred the potatoes with a box grater if you don't have a food processor; use the side that gives you medium-thick shreds, about twice as thick and long as bagged grocery store cheddar shreds.)

3. Place the shreds in a colander set over a large bowl. Squeeze out the moisture as hard as you can. You really want to spend the extra few minutes wringing out your shreds for a crispy final product that sticks together.

4. Lift the colander of shreds and set it aside for a moment; gently tip the bowl over the sink to pour the liquid out and discard it but leave the starch

continued

that clings to the bottom and sides of the bowl. Dump the shredded potatoes into the bowl with the potato starch. Add the eggs, matzo meal, cooled caramelized shallots, chives, pepper, and 1½ teaspoons salt. Stir the mixture briskly, then let it sit for 10 minutes.

5. Pour oil into the cast-iron skillet to about ⅓ inch high. Over high heat, let the oil get fairly hot, about 5 minutes—test its temperature by dipping the handle of a wooden spoon beneath the surface; it should attract tiny rapid bubbles. (If you're using an instant-read thermometer, aim for somewhere in the 350 to 380°F range; any higher will cause the olive oil to taste acrid by the end.)

6. Use a spoon with a long handle to scoop out roughly 2 tablespoons (⅛ cup) of batter and place it in the skillet; flatten the pancake from the center with the back of your spoon (this will give you those frizzled edges). Add more pancakes to the pan, keeping at least ¼ inch of space between them. Reduce the heat to medium and cook until golden brown on each side, about 5 minutes per side. Sprinkle with salt and drain on paper towels as you fry the rest of the batter in batches.

UPGRADE: *For a latke grilled cheese, use this batter for full-size (¼-cup) latkes and slightly undercook a pair of them on one side only. Sandwich two slices of American cheese between the golden brown sides, then finish browning the undercooked sides as the cheese melts. Add a scoop of tuna for a tuna melt–latke grilled cheese.*

GIANT PARTY LATKES

LEVEL

A bit of skill required

TIME

1 hour 30 minutes

MAKES

Two sliceable latkes, each for 4 to 6 people

Inverting heavy skillets with delicate contents is . . . not my strong suit. (My dog, however, loves when I do it.) I developed this Giant Party Latke so that neither you nor I would need to attempt that on a holiday. Turn to these big guys when you want a hands-off potato pancake. You'll need two well-seasoned 10-inch cast-iron skillets; do not attempt the recipe with a new pan, or your giant potato pancake will stick to the bottom with devastating strength. You can halve the batter and make just one Giant Party Latke if you please.

1 cup olive oil

6 large or 10 medium shallots, finely diced

1 large yellow onion, finely diced

Diamond Crystal kosher salt

4 large or 5 medium russet potatoes (3¾ pounds or so), unpeeled

3 eggs, lightly beaten

½ cup matzo meal

Heaping ⅓ cup finely chopped fresh parsley and chives

½ teaspoon freshly ground black pepper

1. To sauté the alliums: Set one of your cast-iron skillets over medium heat. Add ¼ cup of the oil, the shallots, onion, and 1 teaspoon salt. Cook for about 5 minutes, until the alliums begin to soften, then adjust the heat to medium-low and cook for 20 minutes or so, occasionally deglazing with a scant splash of water, until they're caramel-brown, sweet, and melty. (You want them nearly caramelized but not 100 percent of the way there, because the ones that end up around the edges of the latkes will cook a little more in the hot oil.) Set aside to cool. Leave the oily pan on the stovetop; wipe out any lingering shallot bits.

2. While you cook and cool the alliums, prep the potatoes: Fit a food processor with the shredding disc. Scrub the potatoes and cut into thick string cheese–size pieces to fit into the feed tube. Turn the food processor on and begin feeding in the potato sticks. (You can shred the potatoes with a box grater if you don't have a food processor; use the side that gives you medium-thick shreds, about twice as thick and long as bagged grocery store cheddar shreds.)

3. When the potatoes are shredded, place the shreds in a colander set over a large bowl. With your hands, squeeze out the moisture as hard as you can. You really want to spend the extra few minutes wringing out your shreds for a crispy final product that sticks together.

4. Lift the colander of shreds and set it aside; gently tip the bowl over the sink to pour the liquid out and discard it but leave the starch that clings to the bottom and sides of the bowl. Dump the shredded potatoes into the bowl with the potato starch. Add the eggs, matzo meal, cooled caramelized shallots, parsley and chives, pepper, and 1 tablespoon salt. Stir the mixture briskly, then let sit for 10 minutes.

5. While the batter rests, heat the oven to 425°F. Place a second 10-inch skillet onto the stovetop along with the dirtied one.

continued

6. Drizzle some of the remaining ¾ cup oil between the two pans (reserve a few tablespoons) and heat over medium heat until the oil is shimmering and hot enough to sizzle angrily when you drop a little pinch of the potato mixture in as a test. Divide the latke batter between the two hot skillets and use a cup measurer or spatula to carefully press it into a ½-inch-thick layer that doesn't fully reach the sides of the pan, as the bottoms sizzle. Pat the tops of each giant latke with a paper towel or absorbent kitchen towel to get them super dry, then use a spoon or pastry brush to spread the remaining oil over the tops of the pancakes. Cook on the stovetop for 3 minutes (don't let it go longer, though you'll be tempted to).

7. Bake for about 20 minutes, until the tops start to brown and the sides are crisp. Turn on the broiler and finish for 2 to 6 minutes per latke, swapping the pans to fully crisp and brown each top (the timing will depend on the strength of your broiler, but go for browning!). Carefully slide out to slice, top, and serve.

THE BEST VALUE

I have many character flaws, but according to my brother-in-law Ray, the gravest among them is my devotion to filler. "Filler" is a term that Ray and his fellow buffet aficionados use to describe the lower-cost items on offer within the Americana-Bacchanalia that is all-you-can-eat dining in Las Vegas, Nevada. The chafing dishes of overcooked elbow noodles with melted Velveeta and Gruyère are filler, the great heaps of mashed potatoes are filler, and the contents of the ever-puffing rice cooker, sweating in the corner next to the delicate steam baskets of shu mai, are filler.

"You don't even want to *look* at the filler till you've had your fourth or fifth plate," he explained from across a four-top in a dude ranch–size buffet on the Las Vegas strip on one hot summer day. He paused to suck a string of crab meat from a spindly appendage he held to his lips as though it were a 1920s cigarette holder, before discarding the tricky limb with a shrug. "Not worth it," he said. "I'll just get another."

A good Las Vegas buffet is a Bolshoi ballet, and Ray is its highest-ranking principal. The man just knows his way around a steam table. He is the only person I've met in real life who has purchased the now defunct[1] Buffet of Buffets pass, which allowed him to hit six separate buffets within a twenty-four-hour period. "Never stayed so long in one that I've been asked to leave, though," he told me with some measure of regret. Ray has been hitting the strip since he was a child, when his family would travel to the city of sin from Fremont, California, once a year; his inauguration occurred at some point in the early 1990s at the buffet at the Excalibur, which was, to Ray's delight, the largest in Vegas at the time, with 1,300 seats. As an adult, Ray assumed the mantle of planning annual Vegas visits for his group of friends, often leading multiple trips in one calendar year. Every single time, he and his friends would "do a buffet." Today, he has a whole system for maximizing the value of each foray, which he once generously relayed to me over text message, likely after he ran the cost-benefit analysis of how inefficient it would be to speak by phone. It begins at the raw bar. "First, I try to do four or five plates full of legs. That's like twenty-five to fifty legs?" he wrote, at an odd hour. His buffet system even has sidebars: "Other important fact: you can tell how good a buffet is by the shrimp cocktail," he wrote, in a follow-up. "Good ones have pre-peeled shrimp cocktail so you can down them without wasting time peeling."

Ray was born only a half-century or so behind the earliest Vegas buffet pioneers. The city's all-you-can-eat scene emerged in the middle of the twentieth century with the "Buckaroo Buffet" at El Rancho Las Vegas, conceptualized to keep gamblers energized through the night. It was the quintessential loss leader, a bargain-gorge that would fuel hours of ham-fisted spending. There began the late-night buffet boom. Then came the daytime fare, which was affordable, accessible, and advertised as a fantastical maelstrom of abundance. A 1960s postcard[2] from the now shuttered Dunes Hotel describes the "World Famous" English hunt–themed weekend breakfast buffet, with text so small that it's nearly illegible to accommodate the long list of available items: "our own country sausage," "kidney and mushroom saute," "braised Swiss steaks," "lamb chops," "fried spring chicken," and so on. At the end of the list comes the price, in large, bold, unmissable font: $1.50. "As late as the mid-'70s, inflation was still an unknown on the chuck-wagon scene. The most opulent spread, at Caesars Palace, cost $2.75," reported the Las Vegas–based author Anthony Curtis.[3] Just in time for Ray's first visit, "continental" offerings emerged in the early 1990s with Rio's Carnival World Buffet. The Carnival World Buffet was, Curtis wrote in the *Los Angeles Times* in 1994, a "quantum leap forward in the Las Vegas buffet," with distinct stations for Mexican, Chinese, Italian, and "American" dishes; it was a "mini food city with something for every taste."[4] Soon, the Las Vegas buffet offered a promise even more voyeuristic than a single-subject smorgasbord: the kingly ability to jet-set between cuisines for an hour or two, for $7.25.

Not for long, though. To keep up with the rapid development of the strip and its new culture of the celebrity restaurant, the Las Vegas buffet went luxe in the early 2000s. The Cosmopolitan opened Wicked Spoon in 2010, kicking off a cascade of copycat displays of wild extravagance: prime rib, king crab, soufflé, brûlée.[5] Self-serve chafing dishes gave way to elegantly plated bites on individual plates.

The buffet was, of course, never endemic to Las Vegas. The Swedish smörgåsbord—butter, bread, cured fish, et cetera—gained steam in the mid-seventeenth century, and during the 1912 Summer Olympics in Stockholm, it became a premium restaurant offering. There's also Brazilian rodízio, perhaps best known in America through the steakhouse chain Fogo de Chão, and all-you-can-eat forms of Korean barbecue. There's tabehoudai in Japan, in which a diner can select a tier of tabletop-grilled meat and sides for a fixed price and eat an unlimited amount of A4 wagyu for a set period of time. There are all-you-can-eat forms of hotpot around the world, and there is a five-hundred-year-old history[6] of Indian buffets in America rooted in the Sikh tradition of community kitchens, called *langar*. There are iftar buffets for breaking the fast during Ramadan. There are buffets so widely attended across China that, in 2021, *The U.S. Sun* reported[7] that a new ban had been put in place to curb excessive food waste: "Some eateries have pledged to offer smaller portion options, and one restaurant has put a scale at the door and . . . gives food recommendations in accordance to the person's weight." There are breakfast buffets at hotels around the world, including one at the Grand Hotel Tremezzo at which men in white gloves ferry soft-boiled eggs to each diner's plate. Far preceding any hotel breakfast was the Roman Convivium, technically more of a banquet in that the spoils were not self-serve, but a buffet in spirit: guests reclined on triclinium,[8] basically giant class-dividing versions of the Restoration Hardware cloud couch, designed for lounging during a meal[9]; raw oysters, lobster, shellfish, wild boar, and peacock were served in a parade.[10]

The word "buffet" comes from the term for a French sideboard. Originally, it referenced a display of wealth, as within the fifteenth-century court of Burgundy when "buffet" was evoked to describe the nearby display of opulent serve ware. In a passage describing the 1454 Feast of the Pheasant—a banquet thrown by Philip the Good, Duke of Burgundy, to promote a crusade that never actually took place—historian Edmund Bowles[11] writes:

> *The doors to the banqueting hall were guarded by uniformed nobles and crossbowmen, and three long tables were set up inside. . . . The* buffet *was close by, with a gold service and crystal glassware encrusted with jewels. The tablecloths of silk damask touched the floor. . . . A naked woman with long, flowing hair leaned against one of the large supporting columns in the hall, guarded by a live chained lion.*

I encountered no such live beast at my first visit to the Bacchanal Buffet in Las Vegas, but I did see a teenage girl bring green-lipped mussels into the bathroom and continue to consume them until the line finally spit her out into a stall. Back at our table, I told Ray about it. He wasn't horrified; he was impressed. There must be a word for a buffet attendee like that teen, I mused—someone who maximizes the dollar value of their consumption in the amount of time allotted (ninety minutes, though Ray got us out of there in eighty-eight). There was a name for people like me, Ray pointed out—literally pointed, with another crab leg—and it was "total novice."

I wasn't a *total* novice. It was true that my parents had hid me away from all things indulgent and Americana-excessive, having been scarred by their parents' respective penchants for the sort of things David Foster Wallace might have skewered in narrative essays. (After they retired to Lake Havasu, Arizona, my grandparents on my mother's side invested in an also-retired Las Vegas slot machine as the design centerpiece to their living room, and when my parents left us there for a few days at a time, I would watch my grandmother's friends play as they sipped scotch.) I might be the only person in America born in 1991 who has never been to Disneyland. In high school, in the way other teens snuck behind our movie theater to snort cocaine, my older sister and I used to sneak off to frequent a North Indian buffet in a motel by the side of the highway in my California hometown, and before that, a cherished babysitter had brought me to a pan-Asian buffet called East on Long Island, from which I have fond memories of rainbow Jell-O cubes and an inset vat of whipped cream. But Ray was mostly correct. This was my first time in the big leagues, in this sprawling set piece of culture that was in some ways—with its infinite options, with its lack of even a performative hint at community, with its actual historic roots from another place, and importantly, filled as it was with individuals hot on the pursuit of the absolute best value—very American.

So, a few months later, I went back to investigate. I planned a thirty-six-hour visit during which I would attempt to milk every last bit of value I could from the last Las Vegas strip buffets. Las Vegas was still the epicenter of disparate and incongruous foodstuffs, even after the pandemic had threatened to end the American buffet for good. At the time, only ten buffets had survived the pandemic and the invasion of upscale food halls. But if you entered the Bacchanal Buffet on a Sunday evening, close to closing time, you might not have realized that the buffet was a dying breed.

I arrived on Father's Day in the evening, before the Vegas sun had begun to hint that it would eventually set. An Uber from the airport spit me out at a hotel across the street from Salt Bae's steakhouse, where a sign read NO SALT, NO LIFE while "P.I.M.P." played from concealed speakers into the open air. At Bacchanal an hour later, several blocks north of where the Bellagio fountains spurted water to the beat of Celine Dion's "My Heart Will Go On," plates whizzed by at eye-level, some impressively full of Impossible Burger stroganoff and shrimp har gow and Sonoran street dogs topped with jalapeño and spicy mayo. Others were impressively restrained, with just a single piece of the Bacchanal Roll (tempura shrimp and eel maki with avocado Kewpie), or a caviar vol au vent bite: smoked salmon mousse in a jaunty puff pastry cup.

In line, before I scored my table, I spoke to a man named Shervin who was "drunk and hungry as hell" and in town specifically for the crab. It was the best way, he explained, to get bang for his buck. He was one of hundreds whose eyes were trained on the section of countertop where fresh mounds of legs would appear and then, after a swarm of diners, quickly vanish. On long countertops, rows of bloody Mary deviled eggs mingled with pickled turnips and slices of beef steamship. The constant resetting of tables created a chorus of clanking silverware, as if to remind any lingering listeners that the venerable Las Vegas buffet was no more aware of its inhabitants than an ocean is of flotsam. A fly landed on my kimchi in the hermetically sealed room and I wondered where he could have come from.

The next day, at the Cosmopolitan's Wicked Spoon buffet, as a hostess manned hordes of hungry tourists who were clamoring to skip the hour-plus purgatory required of walk-ins, all eyes were again on the legs. Inside, the shellfish-heads were swimming in them; clarified butter glowed amber in a Champagne tower-style arrangement of plastic shot glasses. A muted chorus of "yay" rang out when the steam table guy replaced a dwindling platter of long extremities with an overflowing one; guests readied their shell-crackers. A man at a nearby table leaned across a plate of inch-thick asparagus so his wife could pop a bite of buttered lobster meat into his mouth. A man at a table near to my own methodically dismantled a pile of pizza and sushi with a skewer instead of a fork. Another strode past me, balancing on a single plate a tower of tacos and pork buns, with a lone burger on top. A child handed another child a slice of lox and the second child clapped merrily. There were families, groups of revelers drinking Champagne, and at least one table of women with suitcases consuming a binder-size banana crepe, waiting to come or to go. Farther north, between the Jadeite green entranceway columns of the Buffet at the Wynn, a hot dad in a gray hoodie flashed a red card and skipped a zoo of hungry hopefuls, who watched forlornly as he disappeared in the direction of the foot-and-a-half-high tower of peeled shrimp. The caviar bar had just been restocked and three men dining as a group assessed its contents before passing it by for sliders. I watched a woman in a delicate yellow blouse move through the room double fisting two plates of filler, one in each hand, a proud grin on her face, like she was carrying a pair of geese she'd just killed with a single bullet. Nobody displayed any interest in the somewhat expensive-looking display of "Strawberry Giggly," a Barbie-toned pudding dessert.

Here is an incomplete list of what I consumed during that thirty-six-hour period: a queso-birria taco, duck carnitas, three Diet Pepsis, two miniature gyros, a ladleful of mashed potatoes, a mound of kimchi, shumai, shrimp har gow, pickled ginger, a bowl of black garlic ramen made to order by a kind man named Jesus, Jonah crab, burnt ends, Broccolini, Gruyère cavatappi, roasted eggplant, prime rib with horseradish cream sauce, a slice of chocolate blackout cake covered in rainbow sprinkles with a decorative square of white chocolate stamped with an edible design of a pansy, chicken potstickers, another ladleful of mashed potatoes, two coffees with cream, a "Baby Loco Moco" (which contained a beef patty, onion, gravy, furikake, and a fried quail egg), British-style bangers (mostly because they justified another ladleful of mashed potatoes), Spam musubi sushi, tamago nigiri, and a plate of "petite pork shank."

More important, though, was the opportunity to observe my comrades' approaches to the spread. I sat with my (mostly) filler and watched how others approached the dance: Yes, they began with the shellfish, as many plates as they could stomach. But their plans of action soon devolved. Unlike Ray—who moves methodically from a pas seul of crab to a waltz of shrimp cocktail to a march of prime cuts of beef, before scouring the composed dishes for traces of truffle or caviar, and then chassés over to the meticulously folded dim sum before a coda of several gelato flavors—many of the diners I observed embraced a more intemperate chaos. A plate split exactly in the middle, one half overflowing with thickly sauced macaroni and cheese and the other a pyramid of cut sushi rolls. A single slice of pizza. Just three of "grandma's" meatballs and a smear of sauce. I watched a dozen diners walk past an entire pig, roasted and splayed on its stomach, without even nodding hello. Sipping from a crispy Diet Pepsi, I glimpsed the essence of freedom—a paradoxical blend of abundance and restraint, of indulgence and discernment, of a cheese-based roux and room-temperature raw fish.

And as I watched the pig lie there, I thought of the Feast of the Pheasant, where each display of grandiosity was meant to convey a different, clear message. The naked woman with long, flowing hair, who was guarded by a live chained lion? "She symbolized the city of Constantinople," wrote Bowles. A tableau involving a castle made of pastry, in which twenty-eight musicians cowered? Christendom and its challengers. It was a show full of propaganda, an ostentatious display of power meant to tempt and persuade, and primarily to distract, while the person in charge did what he wanted to do all along.

At Bacchanal, I watched a family of six for half an hour. No one took a bite from their picked-over plates or said a word or even stood to consider another round, but no one made a move to leave, either. I wondered if perhaps it had never been about maximalizing value, really, so much as it had been about a spectacle of choice. "Call them tacky, or repulsive, but buffets elicit a hopeful, almost juvenile feeling of possibility," wrote Lauren Collins in a story about a gourmand-attracting buffet in France.[12] Was the Las Vegas buffet designed like this, to affirm our sense of agency in a world where autonomy so often feels elusive? Or had we brought that to it? I was in a country systematically dismantling my rights to birth control and abortion, but for $75, I could taste fourteen flavors of gelato.

Meanwhile, there we were, revealing all sorts of intimate pieces of ourselves as we reacted to that spectacle of choice. The ways in which we fulfilled our wishes told an onlooker anything he might want to know about what those wishes were: that Ray grew up ambitious, wanting nice things (he was the type of kid who saved all his allowance until he could purchase a $300 crocodile leather belt), that I grew up craving control (mashed potatoes never run out).

Eventually, at the Feast of the Pheasant, a live bird was brought in, on which vows, which were never acted upon, were taken against the Turks.[13] Philip the Good threw a banquet with a buffet-centerpiece to announce a crusade and then, when everybody had gorged themselves and fallen asleep, quietly canceled the crusade.

Eventually, at Bacchanal, the soundtrack mellowed out to Al Green. One woman at a nearby table fell asleep. A crock of bang bang shrimp was as full as it had ever been, glistening beneath the lights, as an employee brought out an industrial-size roll of Sysco plastic wrap and began to cover the great trays of cured meat. Shervin, for his part, never did get in line for those crab legs. I watched as he had a plate of gyros and mortadella, and something on a tortilla, and he paused to watch the tide of diners ebbing toward the dim sum station and flowing back to their tables, where sweating buckets of Champagne awaited. He dabbed at his lips with a napkin, then took a call before polishing off a third plate. And then he was gone, all within an hour. Which was, perhaps, exactly as much as he wanted.

ATTENTION-SEEKERS

12

Juicy Roasted

CHICKEN

MISSION

Maximally crispy skin and juicy, just-cooked-through meat with flavor that goes beneath the surface.

WHAT I TESTED

Brines • Rubs • Cooking method
Spatchcock and truss status

NO BRINE
WET BRINE
DRY BRINE
FETA BRINE
BUTTERMILK BRINE
SPATCHCOCK
ROAST (300°F)
ROAST (425°F)
ROAST (475°F)
COLD OVEN-ROAST
BROWN THEN 400°F
TRUSS
MAYO OVER SKIN
MAYO UNDER SKIN
MUSHROOM POWDER OVER SKIN
WHOLE
BUTTER UNDER SKIN
GARLIC BUTTER UNDER SKIN
HERBS UNDER SKIN
HERBS IN MEAT
ROAST STEAM

MOST COOKS FEAR PETE WELLS. I FEAR LAUREN.

Lauren is, by all appearances, a nice lady. She's a lawyer who lives in Los Angeles and has no ties to professional food criticism. But Lauren has thoughts about chicken. Thoughts that you could sense if you lived with her for several years in a small apartment in the East Village where the topic of other peoples' chicken often arose. Quietly scathing thoughts that would keep you up at night. (If Lauren were on Bravo's *Real Housewives,* "prudishly dry chicken" would be in her opening credits catchphrase.)

Before Lauren was my roommate in our twenties, she was Cheryl's daughter. Cheryl, too, has thoughts on chicken. Namely that most people out there, from the chefs behind the pass at Michelin-starred restaurants to family friends known for their dinner party prowess, are severely overcooking their birds. (If Cheryl were on Bravo, her catchphrase would be a withering glance.)

Having sampled many of their herbaceous, lemon-stuffed chickens, which emerge from the oven with their meat a shade of ballet slipper pink, I have to agree with the general concept. (My own mother, meanwhile, is on the opposite side of this particular issue and raised me to shine a flashlight into the thigh meat to ensure it was fully white.) It's true that the line between juicy chicken and sawdust chicken is razor thin.

One day in the spring, as I raced to meet my manuscript deadline, Lauren called. She wanted me to visit her in Los Angeles. There is the normal and healthy way to deal with fear of a critic's visit (or in this case, a visit to the home of the critic). Cook as you normally would, from the heart, and maybe imagine that critic in her underwear. Then there is the path I chose: spending four weeks testing dozens of methods to perfectly roast a chicken.

Two methods I considered were more promising than any others. The first was a low-and-slow cook. Carla Lalli Music wrote about this technique in a recipe for *Bon Appétit* called Herbed Faux-tisserie Chicken.[1] The recipe title is accurate; roasting chicken at this low temperature until it's just cooked through results in buttery, almost brothy meat. Midway into my trials, I happened upon a half chicken that was so juicy that I accosted the server at the Commerce Inn for details, and it turned out to be the result of something similar: a 300°F roast, deboning, then a blast to crisp skin. A restaurant called Sol Food near where I grew up in the Bay Area produces superior chicken thighs with a similar method and tons of olive oil. The main issue with this low-heat technique is that it doesn't ensure crispy skin without other effort; the easiest way I found to combat that downside is a quick skin-down crisp before the roast.

The second winning method was the exact opposite: a high-heat roast. You'll likely recognize this technique from the legendary Zuni Café chicken from Judy Rodgers,[2] or from the Barbara Kafka method for turkey[3] that's been adapted for whole chickens. Even when I eliminated the flipping and jostling called for by some adaptations of this technique, the oven inferno produced a perfectly browned, super-juicy bird in a fraction of the time. But roasting the chicken whole still presented a major issue. I kept ending up with chicken that looked like a pin cushion from my hopeful thermometer poking, with either juicy breasts or thighs, and if the thighs were juicy, the breasts were dry. Spatchcocking—removing the spine—is slightly helpful for an even cook, but it still didn't fix the issue. My big breakthrough came, finally, when I heard another patron in the butcher shop asking for a quartered chicken. I raced home and tried the high-heat method with the quarters, and pulled the breasts far before I pulled the thighs for the juiciest final pieces.

Of course, I had to decide when to pull the meat from the oven, with Cheryl and Lauren on one shoulder and my mother on the other, wielding her still-functional Taylor meat thermometer from 1990. Writing for Serious Eats, J. Kenji López-Alt synthesized a bunch of information from the USDA into findings on this topic. "What the USDA is looking for is a 7.0 log10 relative reduction in salmonella bacteria in chicken. That is, a reduction that ensures that out of every 10,000,000 bacteria living on that piece of chicken to start, only one will survive," he wrote. His analysis? "Pasteurization Time for Chicken with 5% Fat Content"—aka how long it takes to kill harmful bacteria in meat at a certain temperature—for chicken held at 155°F was less than one minute.[4] In other words, pink is just a color.

Then, I began to dabble in prep, which was . . . eye opening. I don't fraternize with many conspiracy theorists as far as I know, but a great handful of my loved ones do align on questioning one particular piece of common chicken knowledge: that it helps to air dry a chicken in the refrigerator for 24 hours before use. (These people would not even entertain a wet brine, committed as they are to crispy skin. Yes, of course, *obviously* Lauren recently became one of them a few months back, when she dutifully air dried a chicken for a full 24 hours and then, upon learning of additional dinner guests just before hosting, had to pick up a second chicken, which she merely patted dry. She roasted both using the same methods and seasonings and found they were identical.)

So that was my first order of business: wet brine, dry brine, no brine, air dry, or just . . . pat it down really well? I wasn't only assessing skin crispiness, I was assessing whether the prep method imparted flavor into the meat. Buttermilk, a brine popularized by Samin Nosrat[5] in *Salt, Fat, Acid, Heat*, itself a riff on the common Southern marinade for fried chicken, produced burnished-brown skin that wasn't quite crackly, but which had a delicious tang; so, too, did its meat. Feta brine, popularized by Melissa Clark when she adapted the recipe from the restaurant Souvla for the *New York Times Cooking*[6] site, offered a subtle seasoning to the meat, and made for the most even, golden, crispy skin. The dry brine did not produce all that much crispier skin than no brine at all (I'm as shocked as you are, given its legions of fans) and its meat was marginally better seasoned, but blindfolded or under duress I'm not sure I could have properly pointed to it, and the wet brine produced underwhelming meat compared to the feta brine and the buttermilk brine.

From there I moved on to seasonings. For an unbrined chicken, I wanted to find another way to imbue the meat with flavor, and I refused to use one of those kitchen syringes to do so. I experimented with butter and herbs under the skin, with concentrated flavors like mushroom powder and fennel pollen, with rubbing the underside in an herby paste, and with cutting slits into the bird in strategic places to stuff it with more flavors. The best method I found for seasoning that penetrated beneath the skin without a brine was to slice tiny, narrow pockets into the meat beneath the skin and stuff them with aromatics.

And then there was the question of what to wedge into those little pockets. While you absolutely can and should cook a chicken with whatever flavors you like best, my most critical finding for my palate was this: Chicken doesn't want to be a steak. Here's what I mean: When I looked at a chicken as it naturally occurred (in particular, at its relative lack of grassy, thick fat), I saw it was a really neat feat of the universe. A clean protein that wanted to pair with herbaceous garden matter and citrus and celery and seeds. It didn't want to be jammed full of butter and covered in heavy cream, or breaded, or served au poivre. It wanted to be lifted and complemented more than it wanted to be coated and covered.

Finally, I arrived at Lauren's home in the hills of Los Angeles holding two raw chickens, a lot of citrus, and dried mushrooms to blend into powder minutes before I had to turn in the chicken recipes.

But as I cooked through both Mother Recipes with conviction, I realized the true power of facing my critic. The fear of Lauren had forced me to really wrestle with my own understanding of the roast chicken and arrive at a place of faith. And wasn't that a gift?

When it was time to serve the first method, I dropped two of the best pieces on the floor as I walked over to face my terrifying friend. She took a bite, and reported that it was so juicy, it would "make a chicken prude squirm." She took a bite of the second chicken, and said it was so juicy, it made the first chicken seem like rubber. I just shrugged, no longer invested—a new Bravo catchphrase of my own.

THE BEST METHODS

THE BEST PRESSED-FOR-TIME METHOD: High heat roast, using mushroom powder on the skin and stuffing the meat with herbs and garlic (page 162).

THE BEST LEISURELY METHOD: Feta-brine, then roast at a low temperature (page 164).

ROASTED CHICKEN
MY WAY, PAGE 162

MOTHER RECIPE #1

ROASTED CHICKEN MY WAY

LEVEL

A bit of skill required

TIME

1 hour

MAKES

Dinner for 4

This is my one-hour method. It comes out of the oven with mahogany-colored, evenly crisped skin and meat that tastes like herbs and citrus. There are a few ways to encourage even cooking on a roasted chicken, and most of them involve quite a bit of flipping and the sort of oven timer beeping that makes me want to lie down. I landed on a slightly different strategy: roasting the chicken in quarters, so I could pull the breasts from the oven 5 to 10 minutes before the hindquarters. Is this technically a whole roasted chicken???? I'm going to kick that over to my chicken conspiracy theorists on page 159. I call for mushroom powder, which will create the kind of skin that has people around your table sucking on their fork tongs. Because I'm making you speak with another human (your butcher) or else watch a video on quartering a chicken on YouTube, I keep the rest of the recipe simple. My method here calls for a high heat for super-crispy skin, and for the sake of efficiency. The baking powder helps with that, too. I have you turn down the heat midway through to avoid the one drawback to a high temperature (you can quickly overcook the bird toward the end). In a heavy-handed homage to my favorite high heat roasted chicken at Zuni Café, I have you serve these quarters with a bread salad that soaks up the pan drippings.

HOW TO MAKE MUSHROOM POWDER

You can buy a concentrated, finely ground mushroom powder online—I like shiitake powder. But I prefer to make my own by blending dried mushrooms until they're fine dust, then toasting that dust in a skillet for 5 to 10 minutes while you stir, until it's gone from pale beige to dark taupe and is super fragrant. Store it in your cupboard in a sealed container.

TIP: I love to use toasted mushroom powder to make an instant broth. I whisk 1 to 2 tablespoons into a large mug of boiled water along with ½ teaspoon granulated or brown sugar, 1 to 2 teaspoons soy sauce, and 1 teaspoon unseasoned rice wine vinegar. You could also make a stock with the back and wingtips from your quartered chicken, and stir these ingredients into that, or use it in the Triple-Secret Meatballs on page 175.

1 small chicken (about 3½ pounds), quartered by your butcher (or by you!!!)

10 garlic cloves, peeled and gently smashed with a knife

10 thyme sprigs

10 sage leaves on the stem (more than one leaf per stem is fine—great even)

2 teaspoons Diamond Crystal kosher salt, plus more as needed

1 lemon, cut into as many thin slices as you can get, seeds picked out

3 tablespoons mushroom powder (see sidebar)

Freshly cracked black pepper

½ teaspoon baking powder

6 medium shallots or 4 large shallots, peeled and cut into roughly ¼-inch-thick slices

3 tablespoons extra virgin olive oil

One 12-ounce container arugula

A small loaf of soft bread (such as focaccia or ciabatta), cut into about ½-inch dice (roughly 4 cups), tossed with oil and broiled a few minutes until there are spots of crisp

2 tablespoons sherry vinegar, plus more to taste

1. Pat the chicken quarters dry. Gently pull back the skin on each piece while keeping it attached on one end, like you're opening a steno pad. Use a sharp paring knife to cut 2 to 3 slits about 1 inch deep into the meat of each chicken piece. Stuff those slits with the garlic cloves and herb pieces (keep the long stems attached to easily pluck them out later). Distribute about ½ teaspoon salt over each quarter and top each with 1 to 2 lemon slices, depending on the size of the piece. Replace the skin to cover each piece of chicken. Pat the top of the skin dry *again*.

2. In a small bowl, whisk or fork together the mushroom powder, a few pinches each of salt and pepper, and the baking powder. Rub about two-thirds of the mixture all over the chicken skin, sides, and bottoms. (Note: If your chicken pieces are small, you don't need to use the whole rub; treat it like a dry rub on barbecued meat . . . you want a thin, dry layer, not a thick, caked-on one.)

3. Let the chicken sit for at least 20 minutes or up to 1 hour.

4. Heat the oven to 475°F. Pat the chicken skin one final time. Sprinkle a bit more of the powder blend onto the skin. Add the sliced shallots and olive oil to a large cast-iron skillet and toss to combine. Top with a few lemon slices. Place the chicken pieces on top of the lemon.

5. Roast for about 25 minutes, until the skin is super crackly and browned, then reduce the heat to 425°F and finish cooking, 5 to 15 minutes for the breasts and 10 to 20 minutes for the thighs and legs. You'll know the pieces are ready to pull when their juices run clear, but you can use an instant-read thermometer to check for 155°F or cut into the meat if you're unsure; when the breast pieces are done, remove them with tongs and set them aside.

6. Meanwhile, put the arugula in a large salad bowl along with the diced bread.

7. When all the chicken pieces are roasted, remove them to the platter. Pluck out as much of the herb matter as you can by the stem, but don't drive yourself crazy; it won't be unpleasant for diners to encounter. If any garlic fell out of the chicken while roasting, leave it in the skillet. Pluck out the lemon slices and transfer them to a cutting board, along with the slices from the pan.

8. Set the skillet full of drippings and shallots over medium heat and bring to a simmer. Cook for 4 minutes, until a bit reduced. Add the vinegar and whisk to combine. Cut the heat.

9. Roughly chop the lemon pieces and add them to the arugula and bread cubes. Taste the pan dressing and add more vinegar (or salt) if needed for a deep, acidic warm vinaigrette. Drizzle most of the dressing over the arugula and bread, reserving some to avoid a greasy salad. Toss. Taste and add more dressing or salt as needed.

10. Serve the salad with the roasted chicken.

MOTHER RECIPE #2

OPULENT ROASTED CHICKEN

LEVEL

A bit of skill required

TIME

2 hours, plus 1 to 2 days of brining

MAKES

Dinner for 4

This is the method to pull out for the first time you cook for your mother-in-law, or when consensus allows you to cook a chicken instead of turkey on Thanksgiving. There's a fair amount of fuss involved, from brining the bird to painstakingly patting it very dry to waiting patiently while it cooks through after a quick jaunt in a hot skillet to crisp its skin. If you favor succulent chicken with a savory flavor all the way through, and you're willing to read this recipe and get it started a day before the dinner, you'll be handsomely rewarded with chicken that could make a poultry hater's head turn. I call for feta brine, a trick I learned from Melissa Clark (see page 160); here the cheese will become part of the dinner spread, though if the brine's hard for you to come by, in her original recipe, Clark asks you to just blend 2 ounces feta, 2 teaspoons salt, and 4 cups water to make your own. You could also use buttermilk instead for equally nuanced meat—a ubiquitous, beloved technique from Samin Nosrat—but just be sure to wipe the buttermilk off before proceeding with the stovetop sear to avoid burning.

1 small chicken (about 3½ pounds), quartered by your butcher (or by you!!!)

One 16-ounce container feta in brine, yielding 2 to 3 cups of brine plus 8 ounces of feta; cut the feta into ½-inch dice

2 bunches scallions

Diamond Crystal kosher salt

Freshly cracked black pepper

3 tablespoons extra virgin olive oil, plus more as needed

2 large shallots, peeled and cut into ¼-inch-thick slices

A selection of salad-friendly citrus (like clementines, tangerines, grapefruits), enough to yield about 4 cups suprêmed citrus slices

2 tablespoons citrus juice

1 tablespoon sherry vinegar

2 cups cooked pearl couscous

1. Place the quartered chicken in a large zip-top bag and cover in feta brine (reserve the diced feta in the fridge). Squeeze out the air, seal, and chill in the refrigerator for 24 hours (or up to 36 hours).

2. Remove the chicken from the brine about an hour before you plan to cook it. Pat it dry all over and let sit out and continue to air dry as it comes to room temperature.

3. Meanwhile, heat the oven to 300°F.

4. Slice the roots off both bunches of scallions. Slice one bunch into roughly 1½-inch pieces, including the whites, and set aside on the cutting board. Slice the other bunch more finely and add its white parts to the first bunch.

5. Pat the chicken all over again (moisture is the enemy of crispy skin), and season liberally on the skin, sides, and bottom with salt and freshly cracked pepper, using a drizzle of oil if needed to get the seasoning to stick. Heat your largest (I use a 12-inch) cast-iron skillet over high heat for 2 minutes. Add the oil and swirl to coat the pan, so the entire surface is greased (if not, add a little more to keep the skin from sticking). Add the chicken pieces skin side down, turn the heat to medium, and cook for 7 to 10 minutes, using tongs to press various parts of the chicken skin down into the hot pan, until parts of the skin are golden and crisp. Don't go overboard! You want to avoid tough meat. Set

continued

aside on a plate (yes, I know, they're still raw!). To the schmaltz and oil in the skillet, add the 1½-inch scallion chunks (plus the extra whites you added to the pile), plus the shallots, and sauté over high heat for about 5 minutes, until there's apparent browning on most of the pieces in at least one spot. Return the chicken pieces to the skillet, setting them skin side up on top of the shallots and scallions.

6. Roast in the oven for 40 to 45 minutes, until the juices of the breast pieces run clear, or until they've reached 155°F on an instant-read thermometer. Pull the breast pieces carefully with tongs and set aside on a (clean) platter. Finish cooking the thigh and leg pieces until they reach the same markers, another 10 to 15 minutes.

7. Turn on the broiler. Transfer any remaining chicken pieces from the skillet to rest with the breasts. Add the feta cubes to the skillet of drippings, shallots, and scallions. Broil for 4 to 7 minutes (timing will vary depending on your broiler strength; keep a close eye on it), until the cubes are browned and spotted all over their tops. Remove from the oven.

8. In a large bowl, combine the citrus segments, citrus juice, vinegar, and pearl couscous. Use a perforated spoon or fish spatula to transfer all the scallions and shallots and feta to the bowl, plus only whatever pan drippings cling to them (don't add in all the pan drippings or it will get far too greasy). Toss the citrus salad. Add the reserved finely chopped scallions and a few pinches of salt and toss again; some of the feta will dissolve and crumble, which is not only fine, it's ideal. Taste and adjust the seasoning as needed.

9. Serve the chicken quarters atop piles of couscous-citrus salad.

AN UNDERRATED THING TO DO WHILE YOU ROAST A CHICKEN

While your chicken roasts, use the liver that your butcher lovingly tucked into the package to make a spread to serve with crackers or chips:

Pat the liver dry and season it with salt on all sides. Set a tiny saucepan over medium-high heat. Add 2 tablespoons olive oil and 1 tablespoon butter, and when the butter begins to foam, add the liver.

As it browns on its bottom side, finely (finely!!!) mince a large shallot. Add it to the saucepan with a few pinches of freshly cracked black pepper.

Flip the liver and brown it on the other side, as the shallots soften and begin to caramelize.

As soon as the liver feels stiff around its outside (but still a bit wiggly in the center) when you poke it with a wooden spoon or your finger, deglaze the pan with a tablespoon of sherry vinegar. Scrape up any browned bits and cut the heat.

Add about 2 tablespoons more softened butter and about ¼ cup heavy cream. Immersion blend everything until super smooth, and pour into a bowl. Cover with plastic wrap and let it chill in the refrigerator for at least 90 minutes, or up to a day before serving.

SPICY GINGERY CHICKEN AND CABBAGE SALAD

LEVEL

Anyone can execute

TIME

20 minutes

MAKES

Lunch for 3 or 4

Sometimes you want a roast chicken for everyone to focus on, as though you're a Laurie Colwin protagonist. Other times, it's the day after those times, and leftover roast chicken is ready to become a supporting character—a foil to a punchy, sippable dressing. This is what I make on those next days. You could easily use this same strategy with a store-bought rotisserie chicken, or with a few broth-poached chicken breasts. The dressing references both num choc (minus the fish sauce) and the ginger-carrot dressing I like to fill up on before sushi. Slicing or mandolining a cabbage into confetti is a personal matter, but my go-to strategy is rolling several leaves at once into a giant cigar, and slicing them into thin shreds, like basil into a chiffonade. For an elegant lunch, serve this alongside hot, fluffy sushi rice and mugs of broth made from the leftover chicken bones and back.

One 3-inch knob ginger, peeled with a spoon

¼ cup unseasoned rice wine vinegar

2 tablespoons freshly squeezed lime juice

2 tablespoons honey

2 tablespoons shiro miso

2 tablespoons olive oil

2 garlic cloves, peeled

2 small carrots, cut into chunks

1 small head green cabbage, sliced into ¼-inch-wide confetti shreds

½ Thai bird's-eye chile, seeds scraped out, thinly sliced

2 to 3 cups cooked chicken, shredded by hand

2 tablespoons sesame seeds (lightly toasted in a skillet if you're fancy)

1 bunch scallions, thinly sliced

1. Blend the ginger, vinegar, lime juice, honey, miso, oil, garlic, and carrots in a high-speed blender or a food processor fitted with the S-blade until smooth and thick, like a (pulpy) milkshake. As the blender runs, drizzle in enough water to get it to the thickness of tomato bisque, ¼ cup or a bit more. Taste and adjust the seasoning as needed, with more lime juice for tang, honey for sweetness, or miso for salt. You want it to be so balanced and intoxicating that you'd sip it.

2. In a large bowl, toss the dressing with the shredded cabbage, chile, chicken, and half the sesame seeds and scallions. Serve topped with the rest.

13

Plush MEATBALLS

MISSION

Meatballs so plush that they weep when pressed or cut.

WHAT I TESTED

Type of meat (or substitution)
Meat texture and grind • Additions and binders
Coating • Cooking method

PANKO
PANADE
PORK BEEF
BROWN+ SIMMER
GROUND+ HAND-CHOP
GRATE + SQUEEZE ONION
RICOTTA
BAKING SODA+LEMON
HALF-TOFU
HALF-MUSHROOM
FOOD PROCESSOR+ MIX
PAN FRY+ STEAM
NO COATING
CORNSTARCH
FOOD PROCESSOR + PULSE
COOK IN OVEN
FLOUR
BREADCRUMBS
COOK ON STOVE
NO SAUCE (IN OVEN)
SMASH+ PAN FRY

IN ROME, I WAS TOLD THAT YOU CAN WORK OUT WHICH GRANDCHILD A NONNA FAVORS

by the tweaks she makes to her meatballs. If a beloved grandson loves garlic, meatballs for a family feast will come to the table pungent and spicy, no matter how the other offspring feel about the allium. Having a grandchild is one of the only things I didn't incorporate into my testing of Italian-style meatballs. I did, however, soak various forms of carbohydrate in various liquids (I was later chastened into calling this a "panade"). I experimented with tenderizing ingredients and crisp coatings, and at one point, for reasons I can't completely remember, I took a meatball and smashed it into a skillet like I was an old-timey hamburger man. In the end, still with no grandchild, I landed on meatballs that were revealing all the same, in that they are perfectly tailored to my own whims. They're ridiculously juicy; be careful slicing into one while wearing a white shirt. They're seasoned scrupulously, with lots of fennel, a pinch of sugar, and parsley. They're tender from a panade (I'm doing it), from a mixture of higher fat meats, and from a trick I picked up in Rome and Tokyo. And each one is nearly the size of a tennis ball, because despite the other thing I was told again and again in Rome—that they are not a food for a special occasion but a humble way to use leftover meat—I strongly believe that a good meatball should feel like a celebration.

Across so many culinary traditions, the appeal of the meatball lies in its versatility: It can be made from almost anything, and often uses ingredients that might otherwise go to waste. In initial tests, I found that (unsurprisingly) there are a number of ingredients you can swap into meatballs to make them more tender, from higher-fat meats, to wetter dairy products and panades (there I go again), to crumbled tofu, to sautéed mushrooms, and so on. There's also a well-recorded trick to add baking soda and lemon juice, though for me, it didn't produce perceptibly more tender balls and left a faint flavor.

I traveled to Rome to observe as many chefs and home cooks make Italian-style meatballs as I could, and one morning, I broke into a meatball so tender that it seemed held together by sheer will. I was confused; I'd watched its creator make the mix and fry it, using the same high-quality ingredients and ratios as all the other meatballs around town. She'd employed great care and precision, but so had everyone else. So I interrogated her: What had she done differently? After about a hundred questions—what had she prepped before I'd arrived? What temperature was her refrigerator? Was she sure there hadn't been any steps I'd missed?—we arrived back in time at her butcher shop. What, I asked, had she purchased exactly? A pound of pork and a pound of beef, she said. Just like everyone else. Well, had she given any instructions? Just to double-grind the meat, she told me. There it was! A revelation that led to fleecy-soft interiors that percolated fat when you sliced them in two.

Back at home, and without a meat grinder for the last round of my head-to-head trials, I adapted this technique using my food processor. To avoid a texture like lunch meat or baby food, especially since occasionally some butcher beef in the United States is already double-ground, I add the meat in batches, so some becomes fine and almost pasty while the rest maintains a bit of textural diversity. This mimics a trick I learned from Jo Takasaki, a chef in Tokyo who showed me how he makes his pillowy tsukune with three different textures of chicken for an optimal mouthfeel.

I used another of Takasaki's tips in the final trials by grating and then squeezing the onion, to get as much of the flavor in the mix as possible while keeping the moisture under tight control. Sohla El-Waylly also suggests this method of onion integration into her Broiler Lamb Kofta in *Start Here*.[1] As for other levers for flavor, you should tweak meatballs to your liking with seasoning and meat type or any other ingredients. For my final product, like a few recipes I found for kofte that use the food processor, I employ its S-blade to mince in fresh parsley, and then I add Parmesan, fennel, and sugar. (An ingredient for meatballs that blew my mind with its depth of flavor was mushroom powder—see page 162—another tip from Takasaki, who incorporated ground dried mushrooms into his tsukune.)

I roll my meatballs in finely ground breadcrumbs for a super-crispy exterior. I found that this produced a longer-lasting crunch than flour or cornstarch. In a move that would likely upset most of the lovely nonnas who invited me into their homes for meatball school, I don't finish cooking them in a sauce, but instead recommend a pan steam. It's similar to the way lion's head meatballs are cooked through; I found it promotes extremely succulent centers that taste as though they've been fat-poached. In almost all my trials wherein I didn't brown the balls first, they were much more likely to fall apart as they cooked; the browning seemed to give them enough structure to hold together despite their moisture levels.

THE BEST METHOD

Double-grind most of the meat, grate and squeeze the onion, use a panade, and roll in breadcrumbs as on page 175.

MOTHER RECIPE

TRIPLE-SECRET MEATBALLS

LEVEL

Anyone can execute

TIME

45 minutes

MAKES

16 to 20 large meatballs

As discussed in great detail on page 173, I traveled to Italy to observe as many cooks as I could make Italian-style meatballs. One morning, I encountered on a hilltop in Rome a meatball that was so tender, it wept its own fat when forked in two. After lots of questions for its architect, Daniela del Balzo, I arrived at a clue: double-ground meat. To avoid a texture like paste, I add the pork and beef in batches, modeling the method after another technique I learned in Tokyo from Jo Takasaki, who uses a number of textures in his chicken tsukune. (These are great served with the Not Exactly Three-Ingredient Tomato-Butter Sauce on page 214.)

½ large yellow onion, peeled (keep the root intact so it doesn't fall apart while grating)

2 slices white bread, crusts removed, torn into halves

¼ cup whole milk

⅓ cup parsley leaves

2 garlic cloves, peeled

½ teaspoon fennel seeds

¼ teaspoon granulated sugar

2 ounces Parmesan cheese, grated or broken into chunks

2¼ teaspoons Diamond Crystal kosher salt, plus more as needed

Freshly cracked black pepper

2 eggs

1 pound ground pork

1 pound ground beef (75–25 fat content)

2 cups fine breadcrumbs

Neutral oil or olive oil, for frying

Sauce of your choice, for serving (optional)

1. Grate the onion half by hand on the medium side of a box grater. Gather the grated onion and, in a cheesecloth or thin kitchen towel or with your hands over a sieve, squeeze as much moisture as you can from the grated bits (discard the liquid), so you end up with about 3 heaping tablespoons of tightly packed pulp. If you don't have a box grater or if you prefer to simplify, you can also grate the onion in a food processor, which you're about to use for the rest of the recipe. (Then, as above, squeeze as much liquid as possible from the onion so you're just left with pulp.)

2. Set the bread slices in the bowl of a food processor fitted with the S-blade and cover in the milk. Let soak for about 5 minutes.

3. To the bowl of the food processor, add the parsley, garlic, fennel seeds, sugar, onion, cheese, salt, a few pinches of freshly cracked pepper, and the eggs. Pulse until finely minced and well mixed.

4. Add half of the pork and beef to the food processor. Pulse for 30 to 45 seconds, until well combined and the meat looks finely ground with some paste around the sides. Add the rest of the meat and pulse just four or five times to combine without overworking the meat. Use a spoon to finish mixing, just until the newly added meat is integrated. Microwave or fry off a tiny test piece and adjust with more salt if needed. Roll into roughly 16 medium-large meatballs, each bigger than a golf ball but smaller than a tennis ball.

5. Pour the breadcrumbs into a shallow bowl and season with a few pinches of salt. Roll each meatball in breadcrumbs to coat it.

6. Pour about ¼ inch of oil into a large skillet that has a tight-fitting lid or a Dutch oven and heat it over medium heat until shimmery but not smoking.

continued

Add as many meatballs as you can while leaving about an inch around each one (a large Dutch oven should fit half of the batch). Brown on all sides of each meatball, 14 to 16 minutes total—use a fish spatula or two spoons to gently flip them without breaking. (Wait until the first side of each meatball is deeply browned before trying to flip it, or else it will stick to the pan and break.) When they are brown all over, very carefully use a ladle or spoon to remove a few tablespoons of the excess oil, as much as you can without going too nuts. Then, also very carefully, pour in about 2 tablespoons water and immediately cover the pan (there will be a chaotic splattering!). Steam the balls for about 4 minutes, until the splatter sounds die back down to a sizzling. Uncover, cook for another minute or two, until the remaining water has sizzled off, cut into one to check for doneness, and transfer to a plate. Repeat as needed to cook any remaining balls.

7. Serve with sauce, or however you like.

UPGRADE: *Add 1 tablespoon toasted mushroom powder—see page 162—to the mix.*

TEENY TINY MEATBALLS

LEVEL

Anyone can execute

TIME

30 minutes

MAKES

Many dozen tiny meatballs

These are very similar to the Triple-Secret Meatballs on page 175, except that they're bite-size. If you found this recipe because of the Adult "Pasta Os" "Made of Spaghetti" on page 219, skip the pork and use beef for all 24 ounces, for more accuracy. These are delicious with just about any pasta or sauce, and most surprisingly perfect with a bastardized version of the Joshua McFadden kale sauce. Blanch a few rinsed broccoli stems, a roughly chopped bunch of kale, and a few handfuls of spinach in heavily salted water. Then, in a high-speed blender like a Vitamix, blend the blanched vegetables with a bunch of chives, a garlic clove, and 4 ounces of grated Pecorino Romano, plus a few whole peppercorns and a ladleful of cooking water, until extremely smooth and thick. Add more salt to taste, toss with al dente noodles, and top with tiny meatballs and more grated cheese.

2 slices white bread, crusts removed, torn into halves

¼ cup whole milk

½ large yellow onion, peeled

⅓ cup parsley leaves

2 garlic cloves, peeled

½ teaspoon fennel seeds

¼ teaspoon granulated sugar

½ cup Microplaned Parmesan cheese

2¼ teaspoons Diamond Crystal kosher salt, plus more

Freshly cracked black pepper

2 eggs

1 pound ground pork

1 pound ground beef (75–25 is ideal)

2 cups fine breadcrumbs

Neutral oil or olive oil

Sauce of your choice, for serving (optional)

1. Set the slices of bread in the bowl of a food processor fitted with the S-blade and cover in the milk. Let soak for about 5 minutes.

2. Grate the onion half. Gather the grated onion and, in a cheesecloth or thin kitchen towel or with your hands over a sieve, squeeze as much moisture as you can from the grated bits, so you end up with about 2 heaping tablespoons of pressed pulp tightly packed.

3. To the bowl of the food processor, add the parsley, garlic, fennel seeds, sugar, onion, cheese, salt, a few pinches of freshly cracked pepper, and the eggs. Pulse until finely minced and well mixed.

4. Add half of the pork and beef to the food processor. Pulse for 45 seconds, until well combined and the meat looks finely ground with some paste around the sides. Add the rest of the meat and pulse just four or five times to combine without overworking the meat. Use a spoon to finish mixing, just until the newly added meat is integrated. Fry off a tiny test piece and adjust the mixture with more salt if needed.

5. Pour the breadcrumbs into a bowl and season with a few pinches of salt.

6. Roll the tiny meatballs: Take about a teaspoon of the mixture, gently form a ½-inch ball with your palms, then very lightly roll the ball in the breadcrumbs just to coat. Set aside. Repeat with the remainder of the mixture. You should

continued

get about 60 to 65 meatballs. (I promise, this'll go more quickly than you'd think, and I also promise 60 to 65 tiny meatballs is the correct number of tiny meatballs.)

7. Pour about ¼ inch of oil into a large skillet that has a tight-fitting lid or a Dutch oven and heat it over medium heat until shimmery but not smoking. Add as many meatballs as you can without overcrowding the pan (a large Dutch oven should fit the whole batch) and brown them deeply, about 8 minutes total—use a fish spatula or two spoons to gently flip them without breaking. (Wait until the bottom side of each meatball is deeply browned before trying to flip it, or else it will stick to the pan and break.) Cut into one to check for doneness and transfer to a plate. Repeat to cook any remaining balls.

8. Serve with sauce, or however you like.

THE JUICIEST MEATLESS MEATBALLS

LEVEL

Anyone can execute

TIME

40 minutes

MAKES

About 20 to 24 medium meatballs

These meatless meatballs use many of the same techniques for flavor and optimal texture as the Triple-Secret Meatballs on page 175. Because the undrained tofu releases water as you sear them, you don't need to steam these after browning for a super-tender interior; they're self-saucing. I like to toss them with tomato sauce, or, if I'm in the mood for a sandwich, I'll shape them into patties and fry them as veggie burgers instead.

Olive oil

1 pound mushrooms, diced (Baby Bellas will work, but you can go fancier)

Diamond Crystal kosher salt

½ large yellow onion, peeled (keep the root intact so it doesn't fall apart while grating)

1 slice white bread, crust removed, torn into halves

2 tablespoons whole milk

⅓ cup parsley leaves

½ teaspoon fennel seeds

1 teaspoon dried red chile flakes

½ cup (tightly packed) Microplaned Parmesan cheese

Freshly cracked black pepper

2 eggs

2⅔ cups fine breadcrumbs

One 14-ounce package firm tofu, drained but not pressed, crumbled

Neutral oil (or more olive oil), for frying

1. Set a large skillet or a Dutch oven over medium heat for about 1 minute. Lower the heat to medium. Add ¼ cup olive oil, the mushrooms, and 1½ teaspoons salt. Cook for 12 to 15 minutes, until they're golden brown and beginning to crisp. Remove from the skillet and set aside. (Don't bother cleaning the skillet, just give it a wipe.)

2. Grate the onion half on the medium side of a box grater. Gather the grated onion and, in a cheesecloth or thin kitchen towel or with your hands over a sieve, squeeze as much moisture as you can from the grated bits, so you end up with about 2 heaping tablespoons of pressed pulp tightly packed. (If you prefer, you can grate in a food processor. Then, as above, squeeze out as much liquid as possible so you're just left with the pulp.)

3. Set the bread slice in the bowl of a food processor fitted with the S-blade, and cover in the milk. Let soak for about 5 minutes.

4. To the bowl of the food processor, add the parsley, onion, fennel seeds, red chile flakes, cheese, 1 teaspoon of salt, a few pinches of black pepper, the eggs, and ⅔ cup of the breadcrumbs. Pulse until finely minced.

5. Add half of the crumbled tofu and half of the cooked mushrooms. Pulse for about 45 seconds. Add the rest of the tofu and mushrooms and pulse just four or five times to combine, then finish mixing with a large spoon. Fry off a tiny test piece and adjust with more salt if needed. Roll into roughly 20 to 24 medium meatballs (if you roll these too large, they'll break in the pan).

6. Pour the remaining 2 cups breadcrumbs into a shallow bowl and season with a few pinches of salt. Roll each meatball in breadcrumbs to coat it.

7. In the same pan you used to cook the mushrooms, pour about ¼ inch of neutral oil and heat it over medium heat until shimmery. Add as many balls as you can without overcrowding the pan and brown them on all sides, very gently using tongs to cook all over, 12 to 15 minutes. (Note: Let them fully brown on a side before trying to flip or they will stick and crumble.)

14

Opulent SHRIMP

MISSION

Plump, tender shrimp suffused with flavor.

WHAT I TESTED

Shell and head status • Precook preparation
Cooking method

GRILL
SEAR
HIGH-HEAT ROAST
POACH IN BROTH
STEAM
BRINE
MARINATE
BAKING SODA-RUB
SOUS VIDE
AIR FRY
STEEP
SHALLOW STOVETOP SIMMER
BRAISE

WHEN THE SHRIMP TREE

gained internet fame around Christmas of 2023, I ascended to my final form: Woman Who Had Been Pinning Crustaceans to Kale-Covered Foam Cores Since Before You Were Born. I couldn't be as crabby as I wanted to be, though, because mostly in life, I just want people to eat more shrimp. I love shrimp on a tree, or cresting a dish of crushed ice with a lemon wedge and cocktail sauce; I love them with their shells intact, their heads filled with braising liquid, their meat sweet and tender. I love them raw in aguachile, grilled over direct heat, and sautéed in scampi. I could go on, but I'll cut myself off before my husband realizes this is longer and more detailed than my wedding vows.

PEEL-ON SHRIMP: Shrimp insulated by their heads and shells benefited from high heat methods, like the grill or a high-temperature roast, both because the shell took on flavor from the browning (I eat the shell) and because the heat was able to penetrate without overcooking the meat. The marinades didn't flavor the shell-protected shrimp nearly as perceptibly, so I used other ways to infuse extra liquid and flavor, as in the recipe on page 190, which has you treat the shrimp like escargot and stuff their shells with herby butter.

PEELED SHRIMP: For peeled shrimp, two methods produced superlative results: poaching the shrimp in liquid that was cold to begin with and steeping the shrimp in hot liquid like a tea bag. Both introduced supremely gentle heat that allowed each piece to cook through evenly before it became tough and clenched. And, since both are wet cooking methods, they didn't strip away moisture. While I would have loved to adopt the steeping method, since I initially came across it in a sprightly comment on an old article I wrote ("Pour boiling water over your uncooked shrimp and leave just as you would tea. When they change color they are done and NEVER more tender!"), and that's truly my favorite way to collect information, including bad news, I ultimately championed the cold poach because it offers more control than the steep. (With the cold poach, you can continue to apply heat until the shrimp are done; with the steep, there's a risk the liquid will cool too quickly.) I tested cooking the shrimp right in their marinade to infuse more flavor, which worked beautifully. I also added baking soda, which is commonly called for as a tenderizer. I offer a second method that pays homage to the technique you'd use for Louisiana barbecued shrimp, like the recipe Toni Tipton-Martin includes from B. Smith in *Jubilee,*[1] or in shrimp scampi like the kind Lidia Bastianich writes about in *Lidia's Italian-American Kitchen,*[2] in which you cook the crustaceans in a shallow braise, so they're flavored as they're gently heated.

THE BEST METHODS

FOR SHRIMP COCKTAIL: cold poach, page 186.

FOR A BUTTERY SHRIMP PASTA: make a hybrid scampi, as on page 188.

FOR SHELL-ON SHRIMP: roast stuffed with herb butter, as on page 190.

MOTHER RECIPE

LEMON-BUTTER COLD-POACHED SHRIMP

LEVEL

Anyone can execute

TIME

45 minutes

MAKES

Shrimp for 4

This is the recipe to use when you have really great shrimp and are using them to perform the feat of wizardry known as "preparing shrimp cocktail." (Leave out the lemon butter for shrimp cocktail if you want unadorned shrimp; serve chilled after draining.) Ultimately, the poach won my trials over the steep method, because even though it's fun to pretend you're making shrimp-flavored tea, poaching gives a cook more control. I settled on the cold poach in particular, and have you poach in the brining liquid for the most flavorful outcome. Feel free to nip and tuck my formula, to add spices, or herbs, or more heat to the brine-that-becomes-broth. You should also play around with the lemon butter; think of it as an invitation for flavor.

⅓ cup Diamond Crystal kosher salt, plus more to finish

⅓ cup granulated sugar

6 garlic cloves, smashed and peeled, and 3 garlic cloves, minced

½ teaspoon baking soda

Zest of 1 lemon

3 tablespoons unsalted butter, at room temperature

1 pound medium or large shrimp, deveined, peeled

1 tablespoon freshly squeezed lemon juice

1. Brine the shrimp. In a medium pot, prepare the brine: Dissolve the salt and sugar in 6 cups (1½ quarts) simmering water. Add the smashed garlic cloves and baking soda. Let the water come fully to room temperature so you don't accidentally cook the shrimp at this stage. When it's cool, add the shrimp. Cover and brine for about 30 minutes, or up to 1 hour.

2. Meanwhile, mash the zest and the rest of the garlic into the butter with a fork, and set aside.

3. Place the pot of shrimp and brine over medium-high heat, covered, and bring just to a bare simmer (i.e. when you peek, you'll see steam rising from the surface and a hint of bubbling around the sides; temp heads, you're looking for 170°F). When the liquid reaches a simmer, cook for about 1 minute more, just until the flesh of the shrimp turns perky pink and opaque. Keep the temperature at a bare simmer; don't let it boil—you may need to fuss with the heat level. Drain the shrimp and toss it while warm with the lemon butter, lemon juice, and a few pinches of salt.

BUTTER-BRAISED CHILE CRISP SHRIMP SCAMPI WITH BREADCRUMBS

LEVEL

Anyone can execute

TIME

30 minutes

MAKES

Pasta for 4 to 6

Some nights you just want scampi. This . . . isn't exactly that, but it's my version, with more liquid to meld a stovetop sauté with a sort of braise, to hedge against overcooked shrimp. Cooking the heads and the shells in the eventual sauce liquid adds a deep flavor, which is helpful since the actual meat of the shrimp cooks for only a minute. The chile crisp and spicy breadcrumbs add texture and dimension.

Diamond Crystal kosher salt

1 pound dried cavatappi or other fun noodle

1 pound medium or large shrimp, deveined, shells and heads removed and set aside (if you buy your shrimp peeled, ask the fishmonger for shells and heads)

4 garlic cloves, finely chopped, plus 4 garlic cloves, minced

1 tablespoon freshly squeezed lemon juice

Zest of ½ lemon, about ½ teaspoon

6 tablespoons unsalted butter, at room temperature

1 cup panko or breadcrumbs

2 tablespoons chile crisp, plus 2 tablespoons of just the oil, plus more for topping

2½ cups dry white wine

1½ cups heavy cream

6 ounces Parmigiano Reggiano cheese, Microplaned

1. Bring a pot of heavily salted water—about 2 heaping teaspoons salt per quart of water—to a boil on your best burner. The one that's so good it taunts the other burners when you leave the room. Add the noodles and set a timer for 3 minutes before the package says they'll be done.

2. Remove the shrimp tails and coarsely chop the meat into bite-size pieces.

3. In a small bowl, combine the finely chopped garlic, lemon juice, zest, 1 teaspoon salt, and 2 tablespoons of the softened butter. Mash together.

4. Make the breadcrumb topping: Melt 1 tablespoon of the remaining butter in a Dutch oven over medium heat. Add the panko or homemade breadcrumbs and toast until fragrant and golden, 3 to 6 minutes. Add the garlic-lemon paste and toss to combine as it melts. Remove from the heat. Transfer to a bowl and wipe out the Dutch oven, but leave it on the stove.

5. To the same Dutch oven over medium heat, add the remaining 3 tablespoons butter and the chile crisp and oil. Add the minced garlic and the reserved shrimp heads and shells and sauté until fragrant, about 1 minute. Add the wine, 1 teaspoon salt, the heavy cream, and 1 cup of the starchy pasta cooking water and let simmer until reduced by about half (closer to the viscosity of cream than of wine), 10 to 15 minutes. Remove the shells and heads (you can discard them).

6. Drain the cavatappi, add it to the liquid in the Dutch oven, and toss for 1 minute as the sauce simmers. Add the shrimp, toss, and let just cook through, 1 to 2 minutes. Turn off the heat, add the cheese, and toss; the residual heat will thicken the sauce as the Parm melts. (If things look too dry, add a splash more pasta water.) Taste and add more salt as needed.

7. Serve in bowls topped with breadcrumbs and more chile crisp.

HEAD-ON HERBY GARLIC PRAWNS WITH BAGUETTE

LEVEL

A bit of skill required

TIME

45 minutes

MAKES

An entree for 2 to 3, a side for 5

This is the best recipe in the book! I'm not supposed to say that, but if you made me these and served them alongside the Hot Feta Carrot Salad on page 106, with a cake frosted in the Brown Butter French-ish Buttercream on page 321 for dessert, I'd agree to do anything for you. It's funny to write that, because French cuisine is so not the type of food I crave. But these stuffed, roasted head-on prawns are an obvious play on escargot, and in fact, a search tells me there is "a Lutèce classic, Gambas au Beurre d'Escargot" that could be a cousin of my recipe. In any case, I absolutely love them. The only intimidating step is that I ask you to leave the prawns in their shells, but I have you snip a slit up their backs so you can remove the "vein." It's a fussy task that guarantees you won't have any grittiness. And you're cutting a slit anyway so you can pipe in the garlicky herb butter.

½ cup almonds or pine nuts

6 garlic cloves, peeled (swap green garlic when possible)

2 cups fresh basil leaves

1 cup fresh parsley leaves

1¼ teaspoons Diamond Crystal kosher salt, plus more if needed

2 tablespoons olive oil

1 cup freshly Microplaned Parmigiano Reggiano cheese

Zest and juice of 1 lemon

8 tablespoons butter, at room temperature

½ cup dry white wine

1 pound head-on prawns (about 10)

Baguette, for serving

1. Heat the oven to 450°F.

2. Make the herb-butter: In a food processor, pulse the nuts and garlic into rough crumbles. Add the basil, parsley, and salt and pulse until well chopped. Run the processor as you drizzle in the oil to bring the mixture to a thick salsa verde texture. Pulse in the cheese, then the lemon zest and juice, butter, and wine. You should have a soft, fluffy paste, like a compound butter. Adjust with more salt if needed.

3. Use kitchen shears to slice a slit up the backs of the prawns, then remove the black "vein" using tweezers or a precisely wielded fork.

4. Use a small spoon to gently make a few pockets between the shrimp and shell where you've snipped it open. Using a spoon or a plastic bag with one corner snipped off, pipe at least 1 tablespoon of herb butter into each prawn.

5. Lay the stuffed prawns spooning side by side in a shallow dish (it's okay if some overlap) and spread the rest of the herb butter over the top.

6. Roast until the shrimp are sizzling and pink but not tightly clamped toward themselves, 12 to 15 minutes.

7. Serve with a baguette torn in hunks, for dipping.

NOTE: *If you're making this when green garlic is in season, do swap it in! It's lovely and sweet. Use the bulb and white and light green parts of the whole bulb, up until you reach the not-tender part of the dark green stem.*

15

Silky VODKA SAUCE

MISSION

A vodka sauce that's maximally silky, hypnotically rich, and tangy, and which binds gracefully to noodles. Bonus points if it reheats well.

WHAT I TESTED

Cooking fat • Alliums • Spice
Ratio and timing of steps
Silkiness enhancers and other additions

HIGH TOMATO-TO-CREAM RATIO
MEDIUM TOMATO-TO-CREAM RATIO
LOW TOMATO-TO-CREAM RATIO
HIGH VODKA RATIO
SUGAR
WHITE VINEGAR
RICOTTA
CALABRIAN CHILI
MICROPLANED CHEESE
YELLOW ONION
SHALLOT
GARLIC
CORNSTARCH SLURRY
POTATO STARCH SLURRY
CRUSHED TOMATOES
CREAM ADDED LATER
OLIVE OIL
BUTTER
OLIVE OIL + BUTTER
GHEE
PASTA WATER ADDED EARLY
ROAST IN OVEN
RED PEPPER FLAKES
FANCY VODKA
ALLIUM BLEND

AS MUCH AS I HATE TO OVERINTELLECTUALIZE A CONDIMENT,

I feel strongly that vodka sauce provides the perfect allegory for the way that the modern internet functions: chewing up enduring relics of society and spitting out viral pop culture set pieces as though they are novel or shocking instead of merely accessible and gratifying in a way that pleases the algorithmic overlords. (If you never want to invite me to your dinner party again, I'll understand.) There's no denying that it's the Great Vodka Sauce Boom; we're just living through it. Every time a version of the glossy Cara Cara–colored potage enters the proverbial chat, slicked over rigatoni or paccheri or some other barely-safe-for-work tubular noodle, we lose our minds. We are sitting ducks for the stuff. It has transcended red sauce menus and cameos on Carmela Soprano's wraparound kitchen island to become social media catnip. In the last decade, vodka sauce has launched careers, jumped from restaurant tables to jars on supermarket shelves, and served as the centerpiece for at least one viral nepo baby's TikTok confessional about being grounded for trying to charter a helicopter from New York to Maryland on her father's credit card.

It's impossible to write about vodka sauce in America without mentioning Carbone, which was a key player in the leap it made from red-and-white checkered tablecloths to ubiquity. Though no one really knows who served it first, more than fifty years before that. Theories, which converge around the mid to late twentieth century, include the restaurant Taverna Flavia in Rome, the restaurant Dante in Bologna, the Italian actor Ugo Tognazzi's cookbook *L'Abbuffone,* and an Italian-born chef's "penne alla Russia," prepared tableside at New York City's Orsini's.

As far as I can tell, though, it took the advent of Instagram for vodka sauce to surpass subcultures (be they red sauce joints or breathless foodie reports of a curious peppered elixir) and become the American celebrity that it is today.

This isn't a cautionary tale about mass cultural porousness. I absolutely adore vodka sauce. It deserves every rave it's received. If anything, it's an allegory that exemplifies one of the internet's greatest strengths. The internet enables an amplification of unique relics that might have otherwise stayed right on the tables where they'd always been, and only there.

Switching gears for a sec, in the hopes that you'll forget about all of that and indeed invite me to a party . . . let's talk about the dish itself. A fair number of the ingredients or recipes tackled in these head-to-head tests—I won't beat around the bush, I'm talking specifically about broccoli stems—were ripe for improvement. Vodka sauce was not one of them. I would eat an old boot simmered in most home cooks' takes on vodka sauce. My friend Eric once researched how exactly vodka performs a sort of alchemy that takes tomato paste or sauce, plus cream, from a reliably delicious combination to an ambrosial sauce. He reported two key assists from the high-proof potato spirit. The first, he says, occurs during the deglaze: "A clean-tasting vodka has mostly water and ethanol (a solvent), which is excellent at carrying aromatic compounds—like those in tomatoes. In other words, the vodka in this dish can help you smell, and in turn taste, the sauce's flavors in a heightened way." The second has to do with the melding of flavor and texture. "According to the *Journal of Food Science,* the ethanol also helps more evenly disperse the fat, keeping the emulsified sauce bound, glossy and creamy," he wrote.[1] Vodka, in other words, does an essential job: It lifts and smooths.

Most of the tweaks you might make to vodka sauce are relatively self-explanatory. Swapping in shallot for yellow onion will add a subtle sweetness and reduce some of the pungency. Using a combination of alliums lends a nuanced grassiness that is both delicious and slightly overwhelming to the other flavors. Beginning with butter *and* oil imparts round flavors to the sauce; ghee is also nice for its nutty-buttery flavor and higher smoke point. A higher cream-to-tomato ratio will yield a milder sauce with a bisque-like flavor; a lower cream-to-tomato ratio will produce rich acidity. More vodka will yield a slightly bitter, sharper flavor. Fancy vodka doesn't necessarily improve your sauce, but vodkas with different flavors impart those varying nuances to your dish. Adding crushed tomatoes will give your sauce a looser body, which I don't prefer for a vodka sauce; if you're going to go this route anyway, I recommend roasting your canned tomatoes first (see page 204 for my Vodka Sauce Tomato Soup recipe, which has a similar technique) to concentrate flavor. Calabrian chiles add a background spice while dried chile flakes dispense a sharp upfront kick. Parmesan provides a deep cohesiveness, and Pecorino—as Pecorino does—offers strong saltiness.

As far as I found, there are two important factors to make any vodka sauce better, no matter what ratio or spice or additions you prefer—a vodka sauce with a richer, more nuanced flavor that clings readily to noodles. Those factors are: (1) length of cook and (2) when you integrate the starchy pasta water. As detailed on page 200, there are two vodka sauces on which I have a raw fixation: Dan Pelosi's "Sawce" and the Carbone vodka sauce. My research and trials revealed that these two factors were key elements to achieve a melded version of the two, with my own ingredient ratio for extra tomatoey pungency. The longer simmer, as in Pelosi's recipe, allowed for the earlier addition of starchy pasta water, which increased the silky clinginess. The richness and some of the sweetness I craved also came from that lengthier reduction, which really mellowed out the tomato paste and allowed its flavor to merge with the flavor of the vodka (added pretty early in the process). One last subtle tweak that enhanced my perception of sweetness and contributed a creamy mouthfeel was adding the cream later than the vodka, so it had a chance to reduce, but not too much.

THE BEST METHODS

BEST MAINSTAY METHOD: A slow(er) simmer, with tomato paste only (no canned tomatoes), starchy pasta water added early, and a trio of Calabrian chiles, vinegar, and sugar. See page 200 for the Vodka Sauce Mother Recipe, which combines all my findings.

SKIP: Adding either a cornstarch or potato starch slurry. While I totally get the impulse—I'm the one who had it—these slurries contributed more gumminess than silkiness to the final sauces, which did cling to noodles, but in a thick, stew-like way rather than in the velvety-slick way I wanted. A better way to enhance clinginess was by adding the starchy cooking water early into the sauce reduction, and by adding freshly Microplaned (not pre-grated) Parmesan with the pasta before tossing to melt.

FOR REHEATING: Save some cooking water from your pasta in a separate container in the fridge and add a few tablespoons to the sauce, or the sauced noodles, when you're ready to reheat, along with more freshly grated Parm or Pecorino. Toss over low heat.

VODKA SAUCE
PACCHERI,
PAGE 200

MOTHER RECIPE

VODKA SAUCE PACCHERI

LEVEL

Anyone can execute

TIME

1 hour

MAKES

Pasta for 4 hungry people, or 6 as a side

*I have an unbridled fixation on two vodka sauces. This recipe aims to meld them, plus amp up the tanginess. The first is of course the venerable Grossy Sawce, which its loyal architect Dan Pelosi accurately describes as "completely flawless," "inappropriately thick," and "illegally glossy." The second is the vodka sauce from Carbone. Internet "dupe" recipes abound, but it wasn't until Major Food Group released a jarred line that I was able to go full Carrie-from-*Homeland *on their true formula. A few things stand out. The first is that the primary ingredient listed is whole peeled tomatoes. This guided me toward adding more sweetness to the otherwise punchy, acidic tomato paste. The second thing is the term "slow cooked," which is rarely advertised in competitors' vodka sauce recipes. But "slow cooked" overlapped with a key finding from my trials, and something I've long admired about Pelosi's Sawce: there's a protracted reduction period after adding the starchy pasta water, which is "slow" relative to popular variations. I leaned into the sort-of-slow cook, with a dedicated 20 minutes of onion attention to get you to halfway-caramelized, and then a first reduction with starchy pasta water and vodka and tomato paste, and a second with cream. The third thing that stands out from the jar is that Carbone adds a Calabrian chile spread that includes vinegar. I'd long turned to these peppers in my sauce because I love the slow creep of background heat, but just the preserved kind in oil. So, to mimic the pickled spread, I added a bit of vinegar.*

Diamond Crystal kosher salt

1 pound paccheri or rigatoni

3 tablespoons olive oil

2 tablespoons unsalted butter, plus 1 tablespoon

1 large yellow onion, finely diced

4 garlic cloves, minced

1 tube (4½ ounces) double-concentrated tomato paste

1 to 2 Calabrian chiles in oil, drained and minced

1 teaspoon white vinegar

½ cup decent-quality vodka

1 teaspoon sugar

1⅓ cups heavy cream

1 cup freshly Microplaned Parmesan cheese

1. Bring a pot of heavily salted water—about 2 heaping teaspoons per quart of water—to a boil on your scariest burner. Add the noodles and cook for 3 minutes less than the package suggests. Before draining, reserve at least 1½ cups of starchy cooking water. Drain the pasta and set it aside.

2. Meanwhile, place a large, nonreactive pan (i.e. not cast iron—think a Dutch oven or stainless-steel skillet) over medium-low heat. Add the oil and 2 tablespoons of the butter. When the butter has melted, add the onion and garlic and 1½ teaspoons salt. Cook for about 20 minutes, stirring occasionally, until the onion is melty, fragrant, sweet, and beginning to turn caramel-brown around the edges.

3. Adjust the heat to medium. Add the tomato paste and cook for about 4 minutes, until darkened and sticking to the bottom and sides of the pan. Add the chiles and sauté into the paste and onion. Deglaze with the vinegar and vodka and scrape down the sides and bottom of the pan to incorporate the browned bits. Whisk to combine into the tomato paste. Add about ¾ cup of the reserved cooking water and the sugar and whisk again. Turn the heat to medium-low and cook at a simmer until reduced by one-third, about 15 minutes. Add the cream. Continue to cook for another 15 minutes or so, until thick, glossy, and rusty orange.

4. Add the reserved al dente noodles to the sauce over low heat, plus ⅔ cup of the cheese and the remaining 1 tablespoon butter, and toss to coat. You may need more pasta water to thin the sauce enough to coat and grip your noodles; the sauce should be thick and shiny but should cling for dear life to the pasta. I typically add about ⅓ cup more reserved cooking water at this point. Taste and add more salt if needed to bring out all the sour, spicy, and savory notes.

5. Top with the rest of the cheese to serve.

NOTE: *If you're making more sauce than you need, transfer the extra to an airtight container; it will keep in the refrigerator for about 5 days, and if you save and add some of that extra starchy water, it will come alive when tossed with hot noodles.*

RIGATONI ALLA VODKA "ALL'AMATRICIANA"

LEVEL

Anyone can execute

TIME

1 hour

MAKES

Pasta for 3 hangry people, or 6 as a side

I suspect any Roman would balk at this recipe, so I'm hoping you won't tell one about it! To me, a bowl of this hybrid sauce–amatriciana is even more analgesic than Google Map–searching "Italian courtyard" and using the little person icon to drop myself down into ruins, which I do regularly, and which is always why I'm late to your drinks-thing. "Crisped pig jowl," "spicy tomato sauce," "vodka for depth," and "cream to tamp down the sharper edges" are all phrases that reduce my cortisol levels. This Frankenstein pasta is the perfect thing to make when you arrive home at midnight recounting all the things you said that you're sure sounded dumb, or when an unrelenting stream of emails threatens to send you under the covers. If you can't be pressed to find guanciale—which you can source from Eataly—or if, like my mother, you find it "gamey," use thick-cut bacon instead. The vodka sauce that gets mashed up with the amatriciana here is a little different from the Mother Recipe on page 200. I've cut down on the initial fats added, in light of the rendered fat, which contributes flavor as well as a velvety-thick oil. I've cut the garlic and sugar and vinegar because we get dry heat from the chile, a kick from black pepper (a hallmark of all'amatriciana), and sweetness from the tomatoes.

Diamond Crystal kosher salt

1 pound dried rigatoni

12 ounces guanciale, in a ¼-inch dice (throw it in the freezer for 20 minutes first if you have trouble dicing)

2 tablespoons extra virgin olive oil

1 large yellow onion, diced

4 garlic cloves, minced

1 tube (4½ ounces) double-concentrated tomato paste

2 teaspoons red chile flakes

½ teaspoon freshly crushed black pepper

½ cup vodka

One (14-ounce) can crushed tomatoes

1 cup heavy cream

1 cup freshly Microplaned Parmesan cheese

1. Bring a pot of heavily salted water—about 2 heaping teaspoons per quart of water—to a boil on your scariest burner. When the water comes to a boil, add the noodles and cook for 3 minutes less than the package suggests. Before draining, reserve at least 1½ cups of starchy cooking water. Set the pasta aside.

2. Meanwhile, place a large, nonreactive pan (i.e. not cast iron—think a Dutch oven or stainless-steel skillet) over low heat. Add the guanciale and cook until browned and rendered, about 15 to 20 minutes. Lift the crispy guanciale bits out with a slotted spoon; set them aside on a paper towel–lined plate.

3. Drain most of the fat that has rendered from the guanciale, leaving a spoonful or two. Set the pan back over medium-low heat and add the oil, onion, and garlic. Cook for about 20 minutes, stirring occasionally, until the onion is soft, fragrant, sweet, and beginning to turn caramel-brown around the edges.

4. Adjust the heat to medium. Add the tomato paste and cook for 3 to 4 minutes, until darkened and fragrant and sticking to the bottom and sides of the pan. Add the dried chile flakes and black pepper and sauté into the paste and onion. Deglaze with the vodka, whisking to combine into the tomato paste. Add about ¾ cup of the reserved cooking water and the crushed tomatoes and whisk again. Cook at a simmer over medium-low heat until reduced by one-third, about 25 minutes. Add the cream. Continue to cook for another 6 to 8 minutes or so, until the sauce is the consistency of a chunky tomato bisque.

5. Add the reserved al dente noodles to the sauce over low heat, plus ⅔ cup of the cheese, and toss to coat. Add half of the reserved guanciale. Taste and add more salt if needed to bring out all the sour, spicy, savory notes. If needed, add more reserved cooking water in splashes—the sauce should be thick and shiny and should cling for dear life to the noodles.

6. Top with the rest of the cheese and guanciale to serve.

Recipe pictured on page ii.

VODKA SAUCE TOMATO SOUP

LEVEL

Anyone can execute

TIME

1 hour 45 minutes

MAKES

Soup for 6 to 8

This soup relies on a layering of flavor, from roasted fresh and canned tomatoes, which each produce different levels of sweetness, acidity, and tomato-to-water concentrations. Then, a sort of demi-vodka sauce enters the picture and contributes bisque-adjacent richness and spice. It's excellent with a grilled cheese sandwich (American between two soft slices of white bread or milk bread), on its own, or with crumbled crackers softening over the top as you eat.

One 28-ounce can (or roughly 3½ cups) crushed tomatoes and their juices

2 pints cherry tomatoes

¼ cup plus 2 tablespoons olive oil

2 teaspoons Diamond Crystal kosher salt, plus more as needed

½ teaspoon freshly cracked black pepper, plus more as needed

3 tablespoons unsalted butter

1 yellow onion, diced

4 garlic cloves, roughly smashed and peeled

1 tube (4½ ounces) double-concentrated tomato paste

3 Calabrian chiles, drained and diced

½ cup vodka

1 cup heavy cream

Fresh basil leaves

1. Heat the oven to 375°F. Spread the canned tomatoes and their juices and the cherry tomatoes in a high-sided roasting pan (say a 9 × 13-inch pan, or a sheet pan) with the ¼ cup oil, the salt, and the pepper. Roast for about 1 hour, until the cherry tomatoes are tender and sweet and the canned crushed tomatoes have gone jammy and dark red, with the oil floating at the top.

2. Meanwhile, heat the remaining 2 tablespoons oil in a Dutch oven over medium-low heat. Melt the butter in the oil, then add the onion and garlic and sauté for about 20 minutes, until softened and beginning to caramelize around the edges. Make a well in the center and add the tomato paste. Cook for about 4 minutes, until darkened and fragrant and sticking to the bottom and sides of the pan. Add the Calabrian chiles and deglaze the pan with the vodka.

3. Add the oven-roasted tomatoes and all their juices from the pan, scraping in any sticky bits. Add 3 cups water and the cream. Cook at a low but sprightly simmer for 25 to 30 minutes, until the soup is reduced and thick and deeply flavored. (You can cook it for longer if you like an extra-thick soup.)

4. Use an immersion blender to make it as smooth as you like, and season with more salt and pepper to taste.

5. Serve topped with basil cut in a chiffonade.

URBANI TARTUFI
S.ANATOLIA
WHITE TRUFFLE
FLAVORED
OLIVE OIL
MANUFACTURED FOR:
URBANI TRUFFLES USA
10 WEST END AVENUE
NEW YORK NY 10023
PRODUCT OF ITALY
TRUFFLES
URBANI

DEFINITELY-NOT-A-LASAGNA BAKED CABBAGE AND SHELLS

LEVEL

A bit of skill required

TIME

1 hour 45 minutes

MAKES

Dinner for 6

This is an unsanctioned riff on a Marcella Hazan recipe that once won me a lasagna cook-off against a friend's boyfriend. The winning Hazan dish was an elegant, subtle composition of blanched savoy cabbage, an amount of bechamel that demonstrated great restraint, cheese, and ground pork. It was layered and baked until browned on top, and it was creamy throughout, but it was definitely not a lasagna. My friend's ex spent a few days leading up to our contest making marinara from scratch and painstakingly forging homemade lasagna noodles out of flour and egg, and on the day of, he performed the impressive feat of turning milk into a bucket of ricotta, which he used in between his other components. I spent 30 minutes doing prep work for Hazan's cabbage dish and felt incredibly bad when I got every single guest's vote. I can't take credit for that victory, since I was just executing a recipe. But if you win a contest with this variation, I will definitely claim credit. So keep me posted!!! I like to lay down the cabbage in layers, like a sideways cabbage mille-feuille nabe, to simulate noodles. You'll need a super-sharp knife to cut out pieces, though in the event they fall apart anyway while you're serving the dish, the final shape does not matter. No problem! Not a lasagna.

Butter, for the baking dish

Diamond Crystal kosher salt

1 head Savoy cabbage, cored but intact

2 tablespoons olive oil

2 pounds sweet Italian sausages, uncased

1 double batch Vodka Sauce Paccheri (page 200), made with just 1 pound of a small shape, like shells (aka conchiglie)

1 cup freshly Microplaned Parmesan cheese

1. Heat the oven to 350°F. Butter a 9 × 13-inch baking dish.

2. In the same pot you'll eventually use to boil the pasta, bring a few heavily salted quarts of water—2 heaping teaspoons for each quart of water—to a boil. Add the cabbage and blanch for 5 to 6 minutes, until bright green and tender. Remove and set aside. Leave the salted water in the pot for the pasta.

3. Place a large, nonreactive pan (i.e. not cast iron—think a Dutch oven or stainless-steel skillet) over medium heat. Add the oil. Smash in the uncased sausages, season with a few pinches of salt, and let brown deeply, undisturbed, for 4 to 5 minutes, then break up the sausage into small pieces with a wooden spoon. When the sausage is browned and cooked through, set it aside and drain the fat from the pan.

4. In the same Dutch oven, make a double batch of vodka sauce on page 200 (as noted in the list of ingredients, you're doubling the sauce but not the noodles).

5. Combine any cheese you have left over from the vodka sauce with the 1 cup called for here.

6. In the prepared baking dish, lay down an overlapping layer of boiled cabbage leaves (about 6 to 7; cut out the core from any particularly thick ones to make it easier to slice later), like lasagna noodles. Cover with one-third of the cheese, one-third of the reserved sausage, and half of the sauced noodles. Repeat. Top with a final layer of overlapping cabbage leaves, the rest of the sausage, and the rest of the cheese.

7. Bake for about 25 minutes, until gently bubbling around the edges and the cheese is browned in spots all over the top. (If the cheese hasn't browned on top, you can use your broiler to finish briefly at the end, but don't let it linger—the cabbage will burn and the vodka sauce will break from the high heat.)

8. Let cool for about 10 minutes, then use a sharp knife to serve.

DEFINITELY-NOT-A-LASAGNA BAKED CABBAGE AND SHELLS, PAGE 206

16

Tweaked Tomato-Butter
SAUCE

MISSION

An homage to Marcella Hazan's Tomato Sauce
with Onion and Butter that explores the many tweaks made by its fans.

WHAT I TESTED

Types of tomatoes • Types of alliums
Allium composition • Cooking method
Other enhancements

RED ONION
SHALLOTS
GARLIC CLOVES
YELLOW ONION
ANCHOVY

ONION HALVED

ONION WHOLE

ONION, DICED + SAUTÉED

ONION, DICED + RAW

ONION, QUARTERED + LOW-SEARED

LOW-HEAT-ROASTED TOMATOES

HIGH-HEAT-ROASTED TOMATOES

STOVETOP

DUTCH OVEN

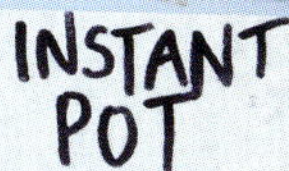
INSTANT POT

WHOLE PEELED CANNED TOMATOES-MILLED

FRESH TOMATOES-BLANCHED

FRESH TOMATOES-FROZEN + THAWED

FRESH TOMATOES-MILLED

CHERRY TOMATOES-MILLED

SHOULD YOU EVER WISH TO MAKE YOUR OWN COMMUNICATIONS FEEL LESS COMBATIVE,

spend some time in the comments section of *New York Times Cooking*. "At our house, we called this Train Wreck," wrote Anne, somewhat cryptically, under an otherwise positively reviewed recipe for a meat pasta. Often the commenters become sucked into a brawl. "Let's make this easy for everyone. If you don't already know how much spice/heat you prefer, you probably shouldn't be including spice/heat in anything you cook. This isn't difficult," wrote Mayor McCheese under one. "In the words of my 'eat anything' teen: 'this is very mid,'" said Martha elsewhere.

In particular, the comments under Marcella Hazan's lauded three-ingredient sauce provide enough material to offset many of your own couples' therapy sessions.[1] While most citizens of the world, myself included, adore this formula for tomato sauce, the *New York Times Cooking* comments section has detractors. "I did not like this. Too much fat," complains Emliza. "To me, it tasted like canned cream of tomato soup," laments Kathy. Lisa Trent calls it "greasy gross." Then there are the riffers, those who offer opportunities to improve on Hazan's formula. "Has anyone introduced a Parmesan rind? Or am I coming late to the party??" asks Bob D. Commenter Michael N., six years ago, added duck fat. "God help us all," he reports. Bill adds just a "hint of" fresh basil and oregano, but cooks it over low heat for "several hours" (!). Some suggest crushed red pepper, others note that shallots melt right in. Garlic, Pecorino, even a poached egg are mentioned. There is discussion of additional butter, and spirited talk of less.

Before I set out testing dozens of tweaks to Hazan's tomato-butter sauce, I knew I had to create some ground rules. I could not stray too far from the original, and I wanted to adhere to the spirit of the recipe. If everyone would be mad about my attempts to deconstruct this recipe anyway, I knew at least *I* had to feel good about wherever I ended up. So first, I went back to the source, *Essentials of Classic Italian Cooking*. In it, Hazan proposes a Renaissance for red sauce, writing that Italian tomato sauce had been mischaracterized abroad too crudely. She argues that in fact, tomato sauce, if executed properly, is the best expression of the "prodigious satisfactions of Italian cooking."[2]

Also of note, she firmly insists one toss the onion before eating. Hazan's other rules include a warning not to cook the sauce in a covered pan ("it will emerge with a bland, steamed, weakly formulated taste") and that the cook will know when it's finished by flavor and texture ("It should be neither too thick nor too watery, and for flavor the tomato must lose its raw taste, without losing sweetness or freshness.").

With those guidelines, I set out to experiment, with anchovies, with cherry tomatoes, with Calabrian chiles and many garlic cloves. In the words of Michael N., god help us all.

Ultimately, most tweaks either violated the sanctity of the original sauce, which is intended to be simple, highlight the tomato, and be so buttery and savory that it tempts you to finish it with a spoon before the pasta cooks. Butter, added in large enough quantities to an acidic sauce, will facilitate a perfect balance on the palate, as in chicken tikka makhani, or butter chicken. (In fact, the late, lauded chef Floyd Cardoz's recipe for butter chicken calls for even more butter-per-tomato than Hazan's red sauce.)

Butter aside, red onion contributed too much earthiness and changed the character of the dish. Shallot was delicious, but another sauce entirely. The Instant Pot produced something watery, disappointing, and virtually unrecognizable. The one allium-arena enhancement I found that didn't flout Hazan's core tenets was to caramelize several faces of the yellow onion before proceeding with the sauce, so that the fond of butter-sautéed onion got picked up by the canned tomato juice.

The upgrade detailed after the Mother Recipe on page 214, in which I suggest that you roast the tomatoes to concentrate flavor and add an anchovy to the onion-butter-fond situation, definitely alters the sauce fundamentally, but I still encourage you to try it. Keeping the juice of the canned tomatoes unroasted means that the final sauce doesn't taste overcooked, per Hazan's warnings, but the tomatoes themselves get super acidic and intense, halfway to a sun-dried to mato paste. The anchovy, meanwhile, adds a bit of meaty saltiness. And who could be mad about that? (The answer is Mayor McCheese.)

THE BEST METHODS

THE BEST MAINSTAY TWEAK: Caramelize the faces of your onion in butter.

THE BEST UPGRADE: Pre-roast your tomatoes to concentrate flavor, and add an anchovy to the fond.

MOTHER RECIPE

NOT EXACTLY THREE-INGREDIENT TOMATO-BUTTER SAUCE

LEVEL

Anyone can execute

TIME

1 hour

MAKES

A scant 3 cups sauce, resulting in 4 bowls of pasta

I spent many weeks trying to find my favorite version of a tomato-butter sauce, based on the prolific version from Marcella Hazan. I tried most of the additions commenters suggested—garlic! anchovy! shallots!—as well as several cautioned for and against by the enthusiastic community who live beneath the comments section on the New York Times Cooking *recipe for the Hazan sauce. Ultimately, most every tweak violated the sanctity of the original sauce. One change I could abide: Caramelize several faces of the onion to add another subtle layer of flavor and sweetness that doesn't overshadow the tomato, but which is, in all its faint brown buttery glory, magnificently* naughty. *I serve the tomato-butter pasta over a bed of cold ricotta, which is a trick my parents employed to make a meal of red sauce and noodles seem luxurious when I was a kid. It works perfectly here, so long as you keep the ricotta chilled to cut through the roundness of everything on top of it.*

FOR THE SAUCE

1 large yellow onion, peeled

7 tablespoons unsalted butter

3 heaping cups (i.e. a 28-ounce can) whole peeled tomatoes and juices

1 teaspoon Diamond Crystal kosher salt, plus more for the pasta water

TO SERVE

12 to 16 ounces bucatini, linguine, or other dried pasta

Freshly Microplaned Parmesan cheese

1⅓ cups cold whole-milk ricotta

1. Make the sauce. Cut the onion in quarters. Set a heavy-bottomed saucepan or small Dutch oven over medium heat. Add 3 tablespoons of the butter. When it foams, add the onion quarters. Don't move them for 8 to 10 minutes, adjusting the heat down to medium-low or low if it gets too hot (i.e. starts to brown deeply or threaten to blacken); you don't want it to burn, just to gently sizzle as the onion turns the color of toffee. Once the bottom side is browned, use tongs or a fork to flip and brown the second cut side of each quartered onion, another 8 to 10 minutes. Turn over the onion quarters so both of each piece's browned sides are facing upward.

2. Add the tomatoes and juices, the remaining 4 tablespoons butter, and the salt. Stir. Use kitchen shears to cut the tomatoes into quarters (or smaller) and cook, uncovered, at a slow, burbling simmer for about 40 minutes, until the liquid part of the sauce has reduced into a thicker bright-orange broth, the consistency of a chunky bisque. Stir occasionally to avoid scalding the tomato pieces on the bottom of the saucepan.

3. Meanwhile, bring a pot of well-salted water—2 heaping teaspoons per quart—to a boil over high heat. Add the noodles and cook for 2 minutes less than the pasta packaging says. Reserve 1 cup of cooking water, then drain the noodles.

4. When the sauce is done, remove the onion (reserve it for another use) and use an immersion blender to make the sauce relatively smooth, with a few chunks here and there.

5. To serve: Toss the noodles with the sauce and pinches of cheese and a bit of pasta water over low heat until the sauce wraps itself around every noodle. Spread about ⅓ cup of cold ricotta over the bottom of each plate or bowl and place a nest of saucy pasta on top, with more cheese on top of that.

UPGRADE: *About an hour before you're ready to make the sauce, roast just the tomatoes (plucked from their juices, which you'll reserve) in a parchment-lined metal baking dish at 350°F for 45 minutes. Then, after you sear the onion as directed, add a single anchovy (drained of oil) and break it up in the butter with a wooden spoon. Add the roasted tomatoes, reserved tomato juices, the 7 tablespoons butter, and about ¾ teaspoon salt instead of 1 teaspoon. Proceed with the recipe from the rest of step 2 to the end.*

l'Angolo della Pasta
dal 1985

NOT
EXACTLY
THREE
NGREDIENT
TOMATO
BUTTER
AUCE

ADULT "PASTA Os" "MADE OF SPAGHETTI"

LEVEL

Anyone can execute

TIME

1 hour

MAKES

Pasta for 4 (aka 2)

Like the "Pasta Os" "Made of Spaghetti" that I used to microwave every day after school, this recipe is meant to be a private ritual that helps you forget about the birthday party that a hot girl who plays volleyball didn't invite you to, but about which all the other fourth graders can't stop talking. Whatever, it probably wasn't that fun! Unlike my canned pasta ritual, which was sacred, even though it made the laundry room where my parents kept the microwave smell weird for years to follow.

1 batch Not Exactly Three-Ingredient Tomato-Butter Sauce (page 214)

1 batch Teeny Tiny Meatballs (page 177)

Diamond Crystal kosher salt

1 pound short pasta shape, anellini for the classic, or an incredibly fun one, like rotelle or lumache

Microplaned Parmesan cheese, for serving

1. Make one batch of the Not Exactly Three-Ingredient Sauce on page 214, without the ricotta or noodles—just the sauce.

2. Make one batch of the Teeny Tiny Meatballs on page 177. Note: For even more resemblance to actual you-know-whats (oh for god's sake I'm just going to do it—SpaghettiOs), use all beef—no pork—in the meatball mix.

3. Bring a pot of heavily salted water—about 2 teaspoons salt per quart of water—to a rolling boil. Add the noodles and cook for 2 minutes less than the package says. Reserve 1 cup of cooking water before draining. Return the noodles to the pot and, over low heat, toss with the sauce, pinches of cheese, and some pasta water to coat the noodles. Add the fried meatballs to the pot. Toss just to combine.

4. To serve, Microplane a little more cheese over each bowl.

CHICKEN PEC

LEVEL

A bit of skill required

TIME

1 hour

MAKES

Chicken for 4

The key to especially perfect chicken pec (aka chicken parm, but with Pecorino, for more tang) is to pound your cutlets as thin as you can get them, so by the time the breading has turned golden-caramel and crispy, they're just cooked through and super juicy. If you have a rolling pin, you can place the cutlets between two pieces of parchment, or one at a time in a plastic bag, and use that to achieve even thinness; a full wine bottle works, too. Otherwise, this recipe is pretty simple, so the sauce can take all the credit.

Four 3- to 4-ounce chicken breast cutlets, pounded to ¼ inch thick (see the headnote about getting them thin)

Juice of 2 lemons

4 garlic cloves, minced

Diamond Crystal kosher salt

1 batch Not Exactly Three-Ingredient Tomato-Butter Sauce (page 214)

½ cup all-purpose flour

Freshly cracked black pepper

2 cups freshly Microplaned Pecorino Romano cheese

1¼ cups breadcrumbs (the finer, the better)

2 large eggs

Extra virgin olive oil

2 cups low-moisture mozzarella cheese, or fresh mozzarella cheese grated on the medium side of a box grater and patted with a kitchen towel

1. Prep the cutlets: In a zip-top bag or snug container, cover the cutlets with the lemon juice, garlic, and 2 teaspoons salt. Let sit sealed in the fridge for 30 minutes.

2. Meanwhile, make a batch of Not Exactly Three-Ingredient Sauce without any pasta or ricotta (just the sauce!).

3. As the sauce simmers, remove the cutlets from the fridge and extract them from the marinade, scraping off any garlic. Set out three plates and a small bowl. On one plate, combine the flour, about ½ teaspoon salt, a pinch of pepper, and ½ cup of the grated Pecorino cheese and fork or whisk gently to distribute evenly. On the second plate, sprinkle the breadcrumbs. Crack the eggs into the small bowl and whisk or fork to combine. Press a cutlet fully into the seasoned flour, then dredge it through the egg to cover, then press hard into the breadcrumbs until fully coated. Place it on the remaining clean plate. Repeat with the rest of the breasts.

4. In your largest Dutch oven, heat enough oil to come about ⅛ inch up the sides of the pan over medium-high heat until a bit of stray breadcrumb dropped into the oil vigorously bubbles. Add the breaded chicken to the pan, making sure not to crowd it. Cook until the bottom is deep golden brown, 3 to 4 minutes, then flip. (If your Dutch oven isn't large enough to hold all the cutlets at once, work in batches, then layer them back in for step 6, overlapping if needed. Or you can use two skillets, side by side.)

5. Heat the broiler.

6. Meanwhile, top each cutlet with the sauce, then a handful of mozzarella cheese and a few tablespoons of the remaining Pecorino cheese. Cover with a lid and cook for another 3 to 5 minutes, until the cheese is melted and when you cut into the center of the thickest cutlet to check, it's fully cooked through. Throw the uncovered Dutch oven under the broiler for a minute or two, until the cheese is bubbling and browned in spots.

7. Serve hot with any leftover sauce on the side.

17

Actually Chewy Fresh PASTA

MISSION

Fresh pasta that is executable by a home cook with no special equipment, and which is chewy enough to satisfy even the most passionate fresh noodle detractor.

WHAT I TESTED

Ratios of flour to moisture • Types of flour
Kneading techniques • Amount of kneading
Techniques for ingredient integration
Amount and temperature of rest
Rolling method
Additions and cooking tweaks

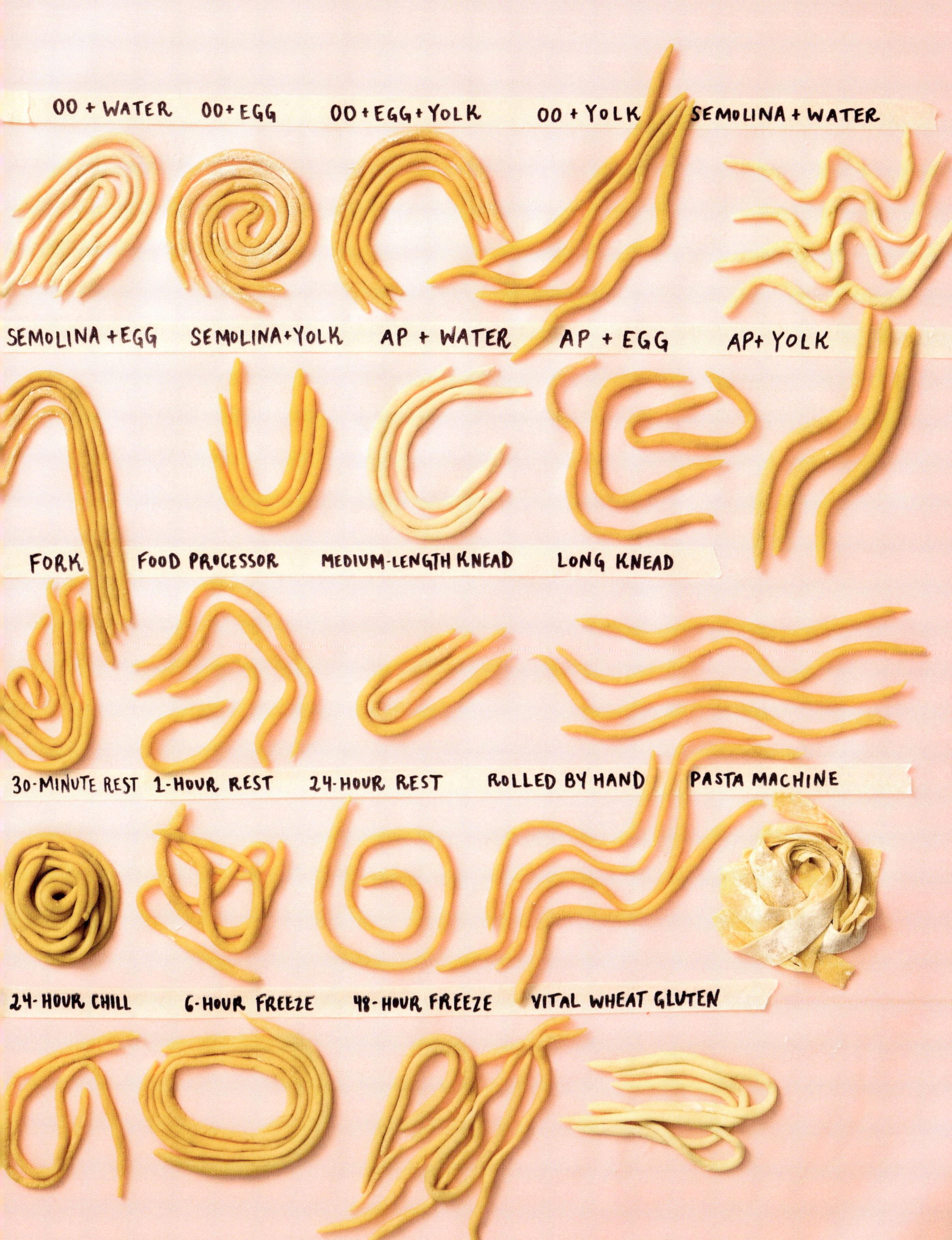

00 + WATER
00 + EGG
00 + EGG + YOLK
00 + YOLK
SEMOLINA + WATER
SEMOLINA + EGG
SEMOLINA + YOLK
AP + WATER
AP + EGG
AP + YOLK
FORK
FOOD PROCESSOR
MEDIUM-LENGTH KNEAD
LONG KNEAD
30-MINUTE REST
1-HOUR REST
24-HOUR REST
ROLLED BY HAND
PASTA MACHINE
24-HOUR CHILL
6-HOUR FREEZE
48-HOUR FREEZE
VITAL WHEAT GLUTEN

I AM A REFORMED HOMEMADE FRESH PASTA HATER.

The key issue, as I saw it for much of my life, was that a lot of fresh Italian-style noodles I encountered outside of restaurants lacked chew. It is not easy to make halfway chewy fresh pasta at home. Anyone who tells you the opposite is trying to sell you something. Fresh pasta the way I like it presents challenges:

- My ideal fresh pasta is bouncy, but still pliable and silky in mouthfeel. But to build the gluten necessary to produce chew, one needs to knead the dough well. And to knead comfortably, a home cook requires enough moisture. Except that too much moisture makes for limp, sodden noodles.
- Egg sizes (and thus the amount of hydration you're introducing to the flour on a per-gram basis) vary wildly.
- Flour (type, protein level, dryness) varies wildly.
- One loses quite a bit of flour and moisture in the initial stages of kneading, and it's impossible to tell how much and of what.
- I'm convinced my cutting board sucks moisture from my dough, since it's not a proper pasta board, and I have no idea how much or how to stop it.

I have spent an entire personal Book of Job amount of time trying to work around these many tribulations. (See: My dad falling into a drainage ditch on page 70.) I traveled around Emilia Romagna, a region known for egg doughs that swaddle pockets of tender meat, pleading with sfogline to show me their ways. (A key one involved using my belly, aka my *pancia*, to hold the dough in place as I rolled it super thin.) I learned about buckwheat dough from a soba expert in Yamagata, Japan, and how to produce elegant chewy udon by kneading with my feet and body weight from a chef in Osaka whose restaurant, UDONZIN Beat, is filled with hip-hop relics.

One can't necessarily "hack" chewy fresh pasta—because, surprise, the people around the world who have dedicated their lives to mastering this traditional art of making pasta or udon or any kind of noodle you can think of have been doing it the best all along (don't talk to me about my attempt to incorporate vital wheat gluten). But as I learned, there are infinite ways to fine-tune your own technique and ingredients.

Ultimately, as I lay awake in bed one night with arms that ached from kneading over a dozen types of dough with differing flour compositions and moisture ratios, I set a goal: I would create a recipe that produced fresh pasta with a professional level of chew, one that even my husband could execute. (My husband had ever only been in our kitchen twice, both times to get seltzer.)

I ended up with two doughs, one for egg-based pasta and one for water-based pasta. Each has a slightly higher ratio of hydration (aka the amount of liquid to the amount of flour) than a fancier book would recommend for an Italian-style pasta dough like this one. Once you've gotten a feel for the process and you're ready to move on, grab something from the experts. I like *Essentials of Classic Italian Cooking* for a no-nonsense traditional approach, *Pasta Grannies* for unique shapes and combinations, and *American Sfoglino* for precision. And once you have the hang of it, experiment with flour swaps, and with different ratios of yolks and whites, or altogether different sources of moisture (like the green water wrung from blanched spinach, or squid ink). Another disclosure: There are a number of the techniques I recommend that would be met with clucking disapproval by several of the nonnas and sfogline who donated their time to my cause. Like the wet fingertips thing, or the thing where I have you reserve some flour up front to make it easier to knead at first.

One of my favorite bits of fine-tuning came from a chef named Robin Frings, who demonstrated his methods at the Michelin-starred L'Erba del Re in Modena, Italy. In between shaping lessons and a lecture on flouring one's rolling board with much discretion, Frings revealed something the restaurant does with any type of fresh pasta to enhance its chew: flash freezing. It sounds like the type of thing that would send Gordon Ramsay into a spiral on a reality show, but my gosh did it make a difference, once I adapted it for my home freezer. It adds a certain mellow toughness and helps larger or more complex shapes retain their structure.

Or so I told my husband, when he complained about the wait time around midnight on a recent Tuesday. I had set out to create a recipe for professionally chewy pasta that even he could execute, but that degree of hubris was put to the test much sooner than I had planned for when, one day on set, a humidity-related snafu meant we spent most of a night remaking all several dozen kinds of dough for photographs the next day. When he was indeed able to follow my instructions to make a perfect coil of pici, it almost felt irrelevant. Because as I said—and as I neglected to tell him—it's not easy to make actually good fresh pasta at home. It's so not easy that at one point, after he left the room for a "cool down shower" and returned to his rolling station with his jaw set the way I've only seen it during a Cleveland Browns game, after he accidentally overturned a cutting board coated in egg and flour from kneading onto our only nice carpet and got a bit in our dog's tail, he threatened to quit. And I might have let him, had I not just cooked the scraps of dough that hadn't become neat farfalle. I tossed them with butter, salt, and a bit of olive oil, and we ate them hot and plain. They were bouncy and chewy, perfectly salted from the cooking water, and tauntingly good, ribboning around a bowl, releasing their steam.

It wasn't just a reminder to both of us that when you make fresh pasta at home and it's excellent, you'll find that all this is worth it—it was enough to keep us going.

THE BEST METHODS

FOR THE BEST EGG PASTA DOUGH: see page 228.

FOR THE BEST WATER PASTA DOUGH: see page 234.

WATER PASTA DOUGH

EGG PASTA DOUGH

MOTHER RECIPE #1

EGG PASTA

LEVEL

A bit of skill required

TIME

1 hour, plus time to freeze (or not!) and cook

MAKES

A little less than 1 pound noodles, roughly 13 ounces (before cooking)

Making fresh pasta by hand is not easy. The opposite belief—that turning out a decent noodle with enough chew is quick for the average home cook—is a dangerous myth perpetuated by those 120-minute vacation cooking classes you and I exchanged a dead-eyed hello at before absconding with our free aprons to drink the provided wine. Fresh pasta presents a few challenges, outlined in more detail on page 224; chief among them is what I'll call the Problem of Chew. Good fresh pasta should be bouncy. Below are my best attempts at outlining a ratio of ingredients I think is ideal for beginners, then explaining the steps with as much transparency as possible. This is a higher hydration ratio than a fancier book would recommend for Italian-style noodles, but no one thought to buy you the fancy book, did they? J.K., even if you own it, start here to get your sea legs. Then grab something from the experts—see page 225 for my recommendations. Another disclosure: There are several steps below that would likely be denounced by the sfogline who dedicated time to my mission when I traveled around Italy, learning to use my pancia. *Which is to say, my final method is entirely inauthentic, and not intended to offend; if anything, it's merely intended to make that myth—the one about good fresh pasta being accessible for home cooks—true.*

260 g "00" flour, plus more as needed

2 whole large eggs

2 large egg yolks

A small dish of room-temperature water

EGG PASTA USING A SCALE *(Recommended for Beginners!)*

1. Set a bowl on a scale and weigh the flour into it. Gently dump the flour into a mound in the center of a large wooden or marble board. Use the bowl you measured the flour into or a mug to press a graciously large, several-egg-size well into the middle of the flour, all the way down to the board. Remove 2 spoonfuls of the flour from the very outside of the flour wall and set them a few inches away on your board to incorporate later.

2. Set the bowl back on the scale and crack the whole eggs into it along with the yolks (reserve the whites for some other purpose, like a virtuous omelet). You want your total liquid weight to be 160 g to begin, so supplement whatever your eggs weigh (probably around 130 to 145 g) with water to get to 160 g. (Note: If it's a humid day, you'll want to add just enough water to get to 150 g. Stop there for now; you can always add more drops later.)

3. Pour the eggs and water into the well you created in the center of the flour. Use a fork to break the yolks and scramble the liquid together without adding air, if you can help it—do that by keeping the tines of the fork as perpendicular as you can to the board, so they're doing the mixing under the liquid's surface. Once it's a homogeneous color, begin slowly, a little at a time, drawing in forkfuls of flour from the inner walls. Incorporate one, then add another, and so on, until your center liquid has become a thick yellow paste ringed by any remaining flour. Grab a pastry cutter or a large chef's knife and use the dull back of the blade to scrape any paste you can from the fork. Then use the cutter or knife to drag any remaining flour into the paste, a bit at a time, and cut it in like you're dividing it up. Drag, cut, drag, cut. And again until there's no flour rim around the shaggy, floury dough.

4. Now, use the fork you thought you were done with (lol) to scrape the paste off the pastry cutter or knife, then the cutter to scrape the fork, and so on until you've gotten as much as possible onto the pile of dough. (It doesn't look like dough, but it will kind of soon!) Use your hands to begin the kneading process: With your nondominant hand, anchor the mass, and with the heel of your dominant hand, press its center away from you, then flip that faraway edge back over itself. Turn it about 45 degrees, then repeat the motion: Hold, press with heel away, fold back, turn. If and when all the flour has become incorporated, gradually knead the ball into the two spoonsful you set aside to incorporate a little at a time. Continue to do this until a very rough, lumpy ball forms, at least 3 minutes but up to 6.

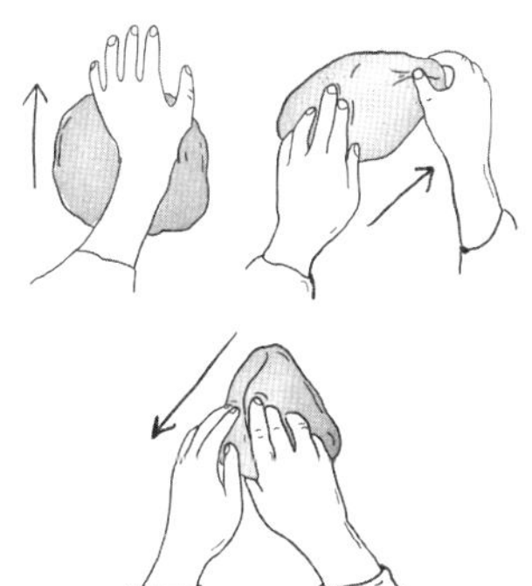

5. ***Is it time to add a few drops of water? you may find yourself wondering at this point, or at any future point in this recipe. Here's how you'll know:***

- You got past the initial kneading phases but now when you fold the dough back onto itself, it won't stick or re-form into a cohesive ball; the seam you've created by pushing and folding is just sitting there looking up at you accusatorily.
- The dough is nearly impossible to knead, but nowhere near as smooth and silky as the seats in a new car, much less plush than a stress ball; in fact, it's lumpy and dimpled and when you press it with your palm, it barely budges.

6. ***Okay, cool, then add a few drops of water from your fingertips, into the crags and seams. Not too much!*** Knead at least three times to incorporate the moisture before determining if you should add a little more. You never want the dough (after you've incorporated the liquid) to feel tacky; if you overdo it, supplement with the lightest feathering of additional flour.

7. After the initial 3- to 6-minute kneading phase, which results in a uniform-ish ball with a lumpy surface (in *American Sfoglino,* Evan Funke and Katie Parla compare it to cellulite), set a timer for 8 minutes. Keep kneading in this same fashion, adding sparing drops of water only as needed: anchor, push, fold. As you knead, the dough will transform, first into something not dissimilar to a tiny beanbag, then into a stress ball, and then the surface will begin to feel incredibly silky and smooth, like it's alive and like it takes much better care of itself than you or I do. I did not truly internalize the meaning of "supple" until I poked a ball of hand-kneaded sfogline dough in Bologna. This could happen a bit sooner than the 8-minute mark, depending on your pressure and rhythm,

continued

or it could take longer; be patient. If you think it's close, poke it; the indent should slowly spring back and fill the hole.

8. Form the ball into an even rounded disc and wrap it extremely tightly in plastic wrap, so it isn't exposed to ***any*** air. Let it sit for at least 1 hour at room temperature or let it chill in the refrigerator wrapped like this for up to a day. I encouraged you (above) to work the dough fairly thoroughly, so if you're met with resistance when you try to roll it out, like it wants to clench back together, rewrap it tightly and let it rest more.

SHAPING PASTA

When you're ready to shape the pasta, I recommend working in portions with the rest of the dough tightly wrapped, so it doesn't dry out. Get a small bowl of water and set it nearby.

Shaping Farfalle (aka Bowties)
An easy shape to start with is farfalle. Very, very sparingly feather your board with a few pinches of "00" flour; the less, the better (but use a bit to avoid sticking). Place the dough piece you're ready to roll on the board, and use the heel of a hand to press it into a roughly even, flattened disc. Hold the bottom in place with the heel of your nondominant hand, and with your dominant hand, use a rolling pin to make a long, firm stroke from the center of the disc away from you (if the dough were a clock, roll toward what would be "12"). Roll it back toward the center with the same pressure. Use your nondominant hand to rotate the dough 90 degrees, and repeat. Continue to roll from the center, rotating as you go for an even thickness. When the dough gets long enough to drape over the side of the board, use your belly (your *pancia*!!!) to hold it in place so you can roll with both hands, applying even pressure. Keep rolling and flipping until it's thin enough to see the grain of the board beneath it, or, when you drape it over the back of one hand, thin enough to see any veins.

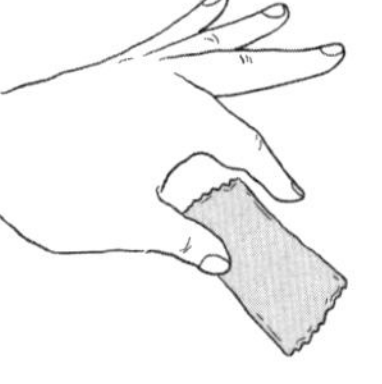

Cut—with a normal sharp knife or else, if you for some reason have it, with a crinkle cut knife—vertical slices about 3 inches apart, and horizontal slices about 2 inches apart, so you end up with little rectangles wider than they are tall. Pinch the top middle and the bottom middle firmly into the middle-middle, to make a bowtie, and set aside.

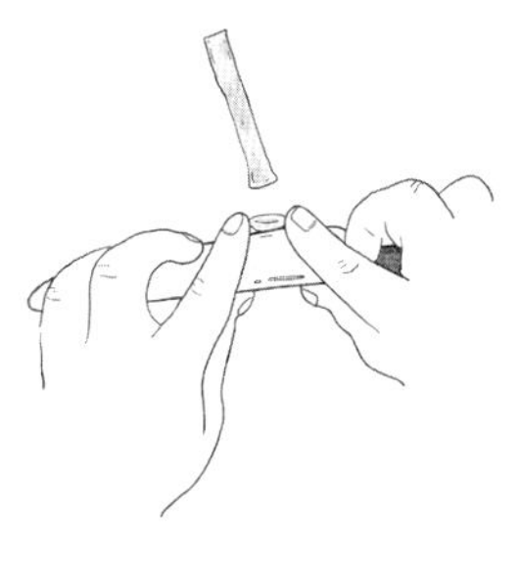

Shaping Orecchiette

Another easy shape to try, which is traditionally much more commonly found with water-only pasta dough, is orecchiette.

Pinch off about one-quarter of the dough and roll with both hands into a roughly ¾-inch-thick rope. Use a knife to cut into roughly ½-inch pieces. Take each piece and place it on a cutting board. Press the knife into one of the cut sides at a 45-degree angle and hold the dough segment with your other hand.

Press the knife as you hold the dough, so it stretches into a sort of demented circle with an indented belly; it will stick to the knife, so use the thumb on your opposite hand to unroll the dough in the opposite direction, pressing in your thumb to make a concave indent.

Set aside on a surface sprinkled with more flour and repeat.

FREEZE YOUR PASTA!

I know, I know. But trust me, if you want extra chew, try this. **For the very chewiest pasta**, freeze it on a sheet tray, then transfer to an airtight bag and freeze for at least 6 hours or up to several weeks before cooking right from frozen. (If you don't want to, you can store shaped uncooked pasta in the refrigerator in an airtight container for several days.)

COOKING PASTA

Bring a pot of heavily salted (2 heaping teaspoons Diamond Crystal kosher salt per quart of water, which I hope you know by now) to a boil. Cook the noodles until they float. If you made farfalle, let them cook for about 1 minute more, then taste for doneness and reserve a cup of water for saucing before draining. If you made orecchiette, let them cook about 2 minutes more once they float, then taste for doneness and reserve a cup of water for saucing before draining.

- Roughly 2¼ cups "00" flour, plus more as needed
- 2 whole large eggs
- 2 large egg yolks
- 1 tablespoon water
- A small dish of room-temperature water

EGG PASTA WITHOUT A SCALE

(What's It Like to Be the Most Confident Person Alive?!)

1. Pour the flour into cup measures (rather than scoop it) for more accuracy. Gently dump the flour into a mound in the center of a large wooden or marble board. Use a bowl or mug to press a graciously large, several-egg-size well into the middle of the flour, all the way down to the board. Remove about 2 spoonsful of the flour from the very outside of the flour wall and set them a few inches away on your board to incorporate later.

2. Crack the eggs into the well you created in the center of the flour. Add the water. Use a fork to break the yolks and scramble the liquid together without adding air, if you can help it—do that by keeping the tines of the fork as perpendicular as you can to the board, so they're doing the mixing under the liquid's surface. Once it's a homogeneous color, begin slowly, a little at a time, drawing in forkfuls of flour from the inner walls. Incorporate one, then add another, and so on, until your center liquid has become a thick paste ringed by any remaining flour. Grab a pastry cutter or a large chef's knife and use the dull back of the blade to scrape any paste you can from the fork. Then use the cutter or knife to drag any remaining flour into the paste, a bit at a time, and cut it in like you're dividing it up. Drag, cut, drag, cut. And again until there's no flour rim around the shaggy, gritty dough.

3. Now, use the fork you thought you were done with (lol) to scrape the paste off the pastry cutter or knife, then the cutter to scrape the fork, and so on until you've gotten as much as possible onto the pile of dough. (It doesn't look like dough, but it will kind of soon!) Use your hands to begin the kneading process: With your nondominant hand, anchor the mass, and with the heel of your dominant hand, press its center away from you, then flip that faraway edge back over itself. Turn it about 45 degrees, then repeat the motion: Hold, press with heel away, fold back, turn. If and when all the flour has become incorporated, gradually knead the ball into the two spoonsful you set aside to incorporate a little at a time. Continue to do this until a very rough, lumpy ball forms, at least 3 minutes but up to 6. If at this point the dough still feels sticky and tacky, add flour by the pinch until it feels more neutral, supple but not wet.

4. Pick up at step 5 in Egg Pasta Using a Scale (page 228).

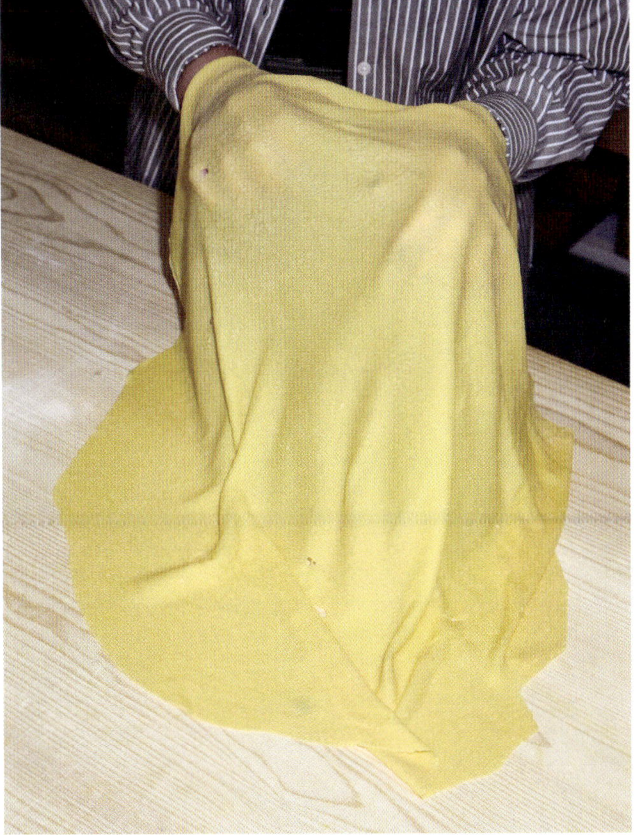

MOTHER RECIPE #2

WATER PASTA

LEVEL

A bit of skill required

TIME

1 hour, plus time to freeze (or not!) and cook

MAKES

A little less than 1 pound noodles, roughly 13 ounces (before cooking)

260 g semolina flour, plus more for keeping the noodles from sticking later

115 g water

A small dish of room-temperature water

WATER PASTA USING A SCALE

(Recommended for Beginners!)

1. Set a bowl on a scale and weigh the flour into it. Gently dump the flour into a mound in the center of a large wooden or marble board. Use the bowl you measured the flour into to press a wide (say 4-inch) well into the middle of the flour, all the way down to the board. Remove about 2 spoonsful of the flour from the very outside of the flour wall and set them a few inches away on your board to incorporate later.

2. Set the bowl back on the scale and use it to weigh out the 115 g water. (Note: If it's a humid day, you'll want to add just enough water to get to 110 g. Stop there for now; you can always add more drops later.)

3. Pour the water into the well you created in the center of the flour. Use a fork to begin slowly, a little at a time, drawing in forkfuls of flour from the inner walls. Incorporate one, then add another, and so on, until your center liquid has become a thick paste ringed by any remaining flour. Grab a pastry cutter or a large chef's knife and use the non-sharp back of the blade to scrape any paste you can from the fork. Then use the cutter or knife to drag any remaining flour into the paste a bit at a time, and cut it in like you're dividing it up. Drag, cut, drag, cut. And again until there's no flour rim around the shaggy, gritty dough.

4. Now, use the fork you thought you were done with (lol) to scrape the gritty paste off the pastry cutter or knife, then the cutter to scrape the fork, and so on until you've gotten as much as possible onto the pile of dough. (It doesn't look like dough, but it will kind of soon!) Use your hands to begin the kneading process: With your nondominant hand, anchor the mass, and with the heel of your dominant hand, press its center away from you, then flip that faraway edge back over itself. Turn it about 45 degrees, then repeat the motion: Hold, press with heel away, fold back, turn. If and when all the flour has become incorporated, gradually knead the ball into the two spoonsful you set aside to incorporate a little at a time. Continue to do this until a very rough, lumpy ball forms, at least 3 minutes but up to 6.

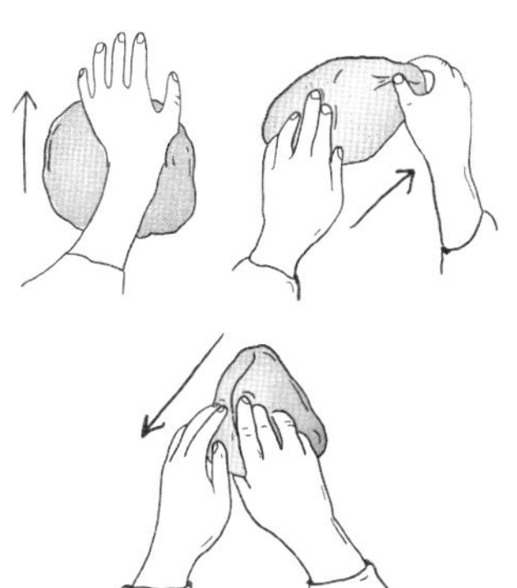

5. ***Is it time to add a few drops of water? you may find yourself wondering at this point, or at any future point in this recipe. Here's how you'll know:***

- The dough is nearly impossible to knead, but nowhere near as smooth and silky as the seats in a new car, much less as plush as a stress ball; in fact, it's lumpy and dimpled and when you press it with your palm, it barely budges.
- You got past the initial kneading phases but now when you fold the dough back onto itself, it won't stick or re-form into a cohesive ball; the seam you've created by pushing and folding is just sitting there looking up at you accusatorily.

6. ***Okay, cool, then add a few drops of water from your fingertips, into the crags and seams. Not too much!*** Knead at least three times to incorporate the moisture before determining if you should add a little more. You never want the dough (after you've incorporated the liquid) to feel tacky; if you overdo it, supplement with the lightest feathering of additional flour.

7. After the initial kneading phase, set a timer for 6 minutes. Keep kneading in this same fashion, adding sparing drops of water only as needed: anchor, push, fold. As you knead, the dough will transform, first into something not dissimilar to a tiny beanbag, then into a stress ball, and then the surface will begin to feel silkier, like the grit has absorbed water and become smooth. This could happen a bit sooner than the 6-minute mark, depending on your pressure and rhythm, or it could take longer; be patient. If you think it's close, poke it; the indent should slowly spring back and fill the hole.

8. Form the ball into an even rounded disc and wrap it extremely tightly in plastic wrap, so it isn't exposed to ***any*** air. Let it sit for at least 1 hour at room temperature or let it chill in the refrigerator wrapped like this for up to a day. I encouraged you (above) to work the dough fairly thoroughly, so if you're met with resistance when you try to roll it out, like it wants to clench back together, rewrap it tightly and let it rest more.

9. When you're ready to shape it, I recommend working in portions with the rest tightly wrapped, so the dough doesn't dry out. Get a small bowl of water and set it nearby.

SHAPING PICI

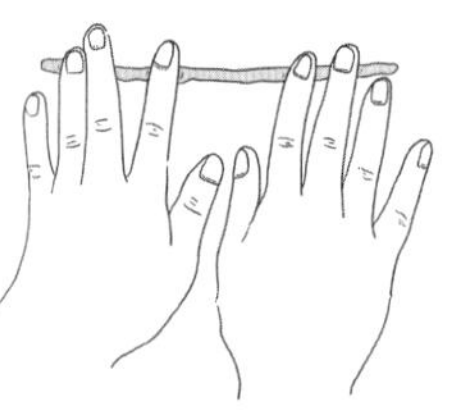

Start by making pici, aka thicker hand-rolled spaghetti. There are a few ways to shape this. One way is to use a rolling pin to flatten the dough disc into a slab about ⅓ inch thick, then cut it into roughly ⅓-inch-thick strips. Use one hand to hold a strip steady and the other to firmly roll and stretch the other end of the strip in the opposite direction until a rounded noodle a bit thicker than a shoelace is formed. Apply pressure with both hands starting in the middle and moving toward the ends, gently rolling, to achieve an even thickness, then, if the noodle is longer than a strand of spaghetti, cut or gently tear it into spaghetti-length pieces and roll the ends to a slight point. Toss each noodle in a bit more semolina flour so it doesn't stick to the others before cooking.

If this method proves too difficult, you can also use my preferred method of pinching off a bit of dough and using both hands to roll it from the middle, working toward the edges, until even and a little thicker than a shoelace, with slightly pointed ends.

If your dough gets too dry at any point, dampen your palms slightly with water.

See page 231 for information on freezing, refrigerating, and cooking pasta, and for instructions on how to shape orecchiette.

WATER PASTA WITHOUT A SCALE

(What's It Like to Be the Most Confident Person Alive?!)

About 1½ cups semolina flour, plus more for keeping the noodles from sticking later

½ cup plus 1 tablespoon water

A small dish of room-temperature water

1. Pour the flour into the cup measures (rather than scoop it) for a more accurate amount. Gently dump the flour into a mound in the center of a large wooden or marble board. Use a bowl or mug to press a wide (say 4-inch) well into the middle of the flour, all the way down to the board. Remove about 2 spoonsful of the flour from the very outside of the flour wall and set them a few inches away on your board to incorporate later.

2. Pour the water into the well you created in the center of the flour. Use a fork to begin slowly, a little at a time, drawing in forkfuls of flour from the inner walls. Incorporate one, then add another, and so on, until your center liquid has become a thick paste ringed by any remaining flour. Grab a pastry cutter, or if you don't have one, grab a large chef's knife and use the non-sharp back of the blade to scrape any paste you can from the fork. Then, use the cutter or knife to drag any remaining flour into the paste a bit at a time, and cut it in like you're dividing it up. Drag, cut, drag, cut. And again until there's no flour rim around the shaggy, gritty dough.

3. Now, use the fork you thought you were done with (lol) to scrape the gritty paste off the pastry cutter or knife, then the cutter to scrape the fork, and so on until you've gotten as much as possible onto the pile of dough. (It doesn't look like dough, but it will kind of soon!) Use your hands to begin the kneading process: With your nondominant hand, anchor the mass, and with the heel of your dominant hand, press its center away from you, then flip that faraway edge back over itself. Turn it about 45 degrees, then repeat the motion: Hold, press with heel away, fold back, turn. If and when all the flour has become incorporated, gradually knead the ball into the two spoonsful you set aside to incorporate a little at a time. Continue to do this until a very rough, lumpy ball forms, at least 3 minutes but up to 6. If at this point the dough still feels sticky and tacky, add flour by the pinch until it feels more neutral, supple but not wet.

4. Pick up at step 5 in the previous recipe, Water Pasta Using a Scale (page 234). See page 231 for information on freezing, refrigerating, and cooking pasta.

GIANT FROZEN BOWTIES
(Trust Me!)

LEVEL

A bit of skill required

TIME

1 hour, plus 6 hours to freeze

MAKES

A jaunty little pasta course for 6 to 12

I still cannot explain, in scientific terms, why, but: off a tip from a chef in Modena, I found that freezing your fresh pasta before you cook it makes for chewier, silkier noodles. It sounds like blasphemy, I know! As I described on page 225, I was introduced to this lesson by the sous chef Robin Frings at Michelin-starred L'Erba del Re. Frings is, fittingly, not from Italy. But my god can the man make a silky, tender noodle that retains enough bite to make even the most fervent fresh pasta hater forget about the boxed Barilla on the shelves of the nearest grocer. The tip works especially well here for these oversize bowtie noodles, since freezing them before you boil helps to keep their shape intact. I like to serve one or two saucy noodles at a time to each guest on a tea-size plate, as a course in a series of pasta dishes, which I recognize reveals how insane I am.

FOR THE NOODLES

1 batch Egg Pasta Dough (page 228); stop before you get to the shaping

Additional "00" flour, for dusting

Diamond Crystal kosher salt

FOR THE PESTO

2 garlic cloves, peeled

¾ teaspoon Diamond Crystal salt, plus more as needed

4 cups fresh basil leaves (look for bunches with small, tender leaves)

¼ cup Italian pine nuts, untoasted (or swap in walnuts)

Heaping ⅔ cup (about 3 ounces) freshly grated or Microplaned Parmesan cheese (swap up to half with Pecorino for more saltiness), plus more for topping

⅓ cup extra virgin olive oil, plus more as needed

1. Make the giant farfalle: Very, very sparingly feather your board with a few pinches of "00" flour; the less, the better (but use a bit to avoid sticking). Place the dough piece you're ready to roll on the board and use the heel of a hand to press it into a roughly even flattened disc. Hold the bottom in place with the heel of your nondominant hand, and with your dominant hand, use a rolling pin to make a long, firm stroke from the center of the disc away from you (if the dough were a clock, roll toward what would be "12"). Roll it back toward the center with the same pressure. Use your nondominant hand to rotate the dough 90 degrees and repeat. Continue to roll from the center, rotating as you go for an even thickness. When the dough gets long enough to drape over the side of the board, use your belly to hold it in place so you can roll with both hands, applying even pressure. Keep rolling and flipping until it's just thin enough to see the grain of the board beneath it, about the thickness of a manila envelope.

2. Cut—with a normal sharp knife or, if you have one (you're fun!), a crinkle cut knife—vertical slices about 6 inches apart and horizontal slices about 4 inches apart, so you end up with rectangles wider than they are tall. Pinch the top middle and the bottom middle firmly into the middle-middle, to make a giant bowtie, and set aside. Knead any scraps into a ball with damp hands if they've become too dry to stick together, roll out, and cut into more bowties. You should get 12 total.

3. Freeze the farfalle on a metal tray or plate, then transfer them to an airtight bag or container and freeze for at least 6 hours or up to 2 weeks.

4. When you're ready to cook the pasta, make the pesto. In a food processor fitted with the S-blade (or in a mortar, or molcajete, or blender), pulse together the garlic and salt until it's in small pieces. Add the basil, nuts, and cheese and pulse until broken down into a rough, chunky paste, stopping to scrape down the sides every few pulses. Run the processor as you drizzle in the oil. Taste and adjust the seasoning with more salt if needed. Cover with another tablespoon of oil and set aside.

5. Bring a very large pot of heavily salted water—about 2 heaping teaspoons per quart of water—to a boil on your scariest burner. When the water comes to a boil, add the noodles and cook until they begin to float. Cook for another 4 minutes or so, then check for doneness; they should be tender with just a bit of bite. Before draining, reserve 1 cup of starchy cooking water.

6. Drain the pasta and return it to the pot. Toss with the pesto and a splash of the cooking water. Keep tossing until the sauce is thick and glossy and clings hard to the noodles (this happens when the cheese in the pesto melts and melds into the pasta water). Add more reserved water, or turn the heat on super low, if needed to get to this point.

7. Serve one or two noodles per plate.

GIANT FROZEN BOWTIES
(TRUST ME!), PAGE 238

10-MINUTE TONNATO PASTA

LEVEL

A bit of skill required (just for the noodles; you can swap in store-bought if you prefer)

TIME

10 minutes, once you have your noodles

MAKES

Dinner for 2 to 4

This may or may not be the second tonnato recipe in the book; mind your business. Tonnato is not used as a sauce for pasta in its motherland, Northern Italy, but I am pretty much always looking for ways to more or less sip tonnato straight up. Here, I toss it with fresh pasta rolled into slightly thicker, irregularly shaped pici noodles, though if you haven't yet stocked your freezer with my noodles, you could use store-bought fresh pasta, or boxed dried, to make this a truly 10-minute dinner.

Diamond Crystal kosher salt

1 batch pici noodles made from Water Pasta (page 234) or 1 batch farfalle noodles made from Egg Pasta (page 228); if you're using store-bought dried or fresh noodles, you want about 13 ounces

Two 5-ounce cans tuna in oil, drained

¼ cup capers in brine, drained, plus 3 tablespoons more for topping

3 garlic cloves, peeled

⅔ cup mayonnaise, preferably Hellmann's

3 oil-packed anchovy fillets, drained

2 tablespoons freshly squeezed lemon juice, plus more as needed

½ teaspoon freshly cracked black pepper

⅓ cup extra virgin olive oil, plus more for frying capers, plus more as needed

1 to 2 ounces Pecorino Romano cheese, freshly Microplaned

1. Bring about 3 quarts of heavily salted water—6 teaspoons of salt for 3 quarts—to a boil. Cook the fresh pasta until it floats, then give it another 2 minutes and check a noodle for doneness; you want it to retain a bit of bite. (For store-bought pasta, cook according to the package instructions, minus 2 minutes.) Reserve 1 cup of cooking water and drain the noodles.

2. Meanwhile, while the water comes to a boil, combine the following ingredients in a food processor fitted with the S-blade: the tuna, the ¼ cup drained capers, the garlic, mayonnaise, anchovy fillets, lemon juice, and black pepper. Pulse until well mixed into a rough paste. Run the food processor as you stream in the oil. You're looking for a smooth sauce with a bit of shreddy texture; you may need to scrape down the sides and continue to blend. (You can also use an immersion blender or a blender here.) The sauce should be the thickness of melted ice cream. Add more oil as it blends to achieve this consistency, if needed. Taste. Add more lemon juice or salt to make sure it's incredibly punchy and briny and addictive.

3. Fry the capers for the topping: Add a few tablespoons oil to a cast-iron skillet until it just coats the bottom. Heat over medium-high heat until it's shimmering and produces tiny aggressive bubbles around the tip of a wooden spoon inserted into the oil. Add the remaining 3 tablespoons drained capers and fry for about 1 minute, until fluffy and crisp. Transfer to a paper towel–lined plate.

4. Transfer the drained noodles to a large bowl. Toss the sauce with the cooked noodles. Add reserved pasta cooking water by the spoonful as needed to thin and warm the sauce to the consistency of tomato bisque; it should tightly coat the noodles.

5. Serve topped with cheese and fried capers.

18

Creamy, Crispy-Topped

MACARONI AND CHEESE

MISSION

Baked macaroni and cheese that is neither dry nor gloppy, with areas of molten cheese and sections of crunch to offset the richness.

WHAT I TESTED

Depth and material of cooking vessel • Noodle shape
Cheese type and mixture and integration method
Dairy type • Toppings and mix-ins
Bake temperature

EVERYTHING THAT IS TAILOR-MADE TO LOOK EASY IS ACTUALLY HARD,

which applies to making a cookbook and pulling off perfectly creamy baked macaroni and cheese. The latter is a challenge because too little cheese and sauce (roux-based or otherwise) makes for an arid dish closer in texture to an uncharitable interpretation of kugel, and too much sauce can induce a stomachache. The former, the cookbook, was a bit like an anesthetized root canal; there were over one hundred carrots and a constantly ringing buzzer and melting buttercreams and lunch orders that arrived without one person's salad and me issuing lamentations that "I thought we were going to do Dalí on that last shot" and everyone else politely, gently reminding me that Dalí had never been on the table. There was a lot to get done and not so much time, a lot of personality and vision, very little sleep. As tensions mounted and people had to leave rooms when their least favorite foods entered in multiples of twelve and stylists' expressions twitched and bacon lay sweating, I was often tempted to call out, "The patient is coding!" Every so often, the "heat gun" was evoked to melt chocolate discs at my behest, and it felt like a hunting rifle would have caused less distress.

One day on set, as communal stress levels reached a fever pitch, we set out to shoot a recipe I was calling "never dry, never soggy" mac and cheese. It emerged, looking both dry and soggy, but an overhead shot was already set up, and we had a half dozen more recipes to get through before everyone could go sit in a dark, quiet room. I'll skip to the good part since we're both already worked up: Our very talented, very graceful food stylist, whom I had never seen so much as shiver, somehow fully tripped while setting down the hot saucepan of kale-sauce baked mac. She fell forward and the whole thing sprayed across the setup and another finished dish, splattering the tripod with a pattern that looked like a crime scene at Shrek's place. And it was the best thing that could have happened: an instant reminder

EVAPORATED MILK ROUX
PYREX
CHEDDAR + AMERICAN
EXTRA CHEESE
PANKO
RITZ
400°F
KALE
GOUDA + PARM + GRUYÈRE
325°F
SHEET PAN

ROUX
ELBOWS
DUTCH OVEN
SHELLS
CHEDDAR + MOZZ
VEGETABLE SAUCE
METAL
CAVATAPPI
CREAM CHEESE + CHEDDAR + AMERICAN
MILK

not just that we weren't performing open-heart surgery, but that food was most beautiful when it was spontaneous. And a little bit surreal, like Dalí, dammit. And that even though everything that is tailor-made to look easy is hard, it can be fun and surprising and delightful, too.

I set out to create a baked macaroni and cheese with a roux-based sauce (or roux-*like* sauce) coating the noodles. (For one bound primarily by cheese, Jessica B. Harris has a recipe from Rufus Estes's *Good Things to Eat* in *High on the Hog*[1] that I love, in which you layer cooked noodles with grated cheese, pepper, salt, and melted butter, then moisten the baking dish with milk before baking. I also often turn to Lesley Enston's recipe for Trinidadian Macaroni Pie on the *New York Times Cooking* site.[2])

As far as a creamy sauce–based mac, I have long faced an enduring problem: One pound of cooked pasta requires a huge amount of cheesy binding to keep it from turning into cemented, dried-out noodles in the oven. I love a saucy mac, but I also want to be able to eat a large bowl of it. So I set out to find a sauce formula that wasn't too cloying, with noodles that retained a bit of bite despite two rounds of cooking.

For the creamiest texture with the least potential for dryness, a roux (roughly equal parts flour and butter) cooked with whole milk or evaporated milk worked best; the evaporated milk made for a sweeter sauce and the whole milk was more neutral. The vegetable sauce trial also made a sauce with quite a bit of flavor and body without richness, which lightened the final dish without thinning it out. I eventually settled on adding a decent amount of pasta water to my sauce, along with some amount of roasted or sautéed vegetables, to reduce the richness. As in cacio e pepe, the starchy water lightened my final pasta while keeping it cohesive. A temperature of 400°F did not cause the cheesy sauce to break in the oven, so I preferred it since the noodles and sauce were already essentially cooked and needed just a short foray into the oven to meld and fully heat. A broiler blast at the end was integral.

American cheese melted into the silkiest texture, because it's made with a stabilizing emulsifier, sodium phosphate. Cheese preferences are, of course, one of the more intimate pursuits known to man, so I won't comment other than to say that the fancy mix had superior stretch and pull.

A metal pan produced the crispiest edges and corners, but a Dutch oven was my favorite vessel because it didn't require the transfer from a pot to a second pan, and still produced a crusty ridge where mac met side. Shape of noodle was a matter of personal preference, one less personal than cheese, so I'll share: Mine was cavatappi, for its crazy straw energy. Tiny shells (sauce boats) were also lovely. Finally, to grate cheese super quickly, use the shredder attachment in your food processor. You'll be so thrilled that you did.

THE BEST METHODS

FOR A CREAMY, ROUX-BASED MAC: Cut through the richness with black pepper and (!!) kale, as on page 249. Lighten your sauce by adding pasta water. Add a texturally contrasting topping.

FOR A LOW-MAINTENANCE MAC: Let a sheet pan do much of the work for you, as on page 251.

MOTHER RECIPE

GREEN MAC AND CHEESE

LEVEL

Anyone can execute

TIME

1 hour

MAKES

Dinner for 8

Kale pairs extremely well with creaminess; Joshua McFadden can take some credit for that one, with his moss-colored kale pasta. Collard greens can take the lion's share, setting a ubiquitous example of the power of a hearty green to cut through smothered pork chops. I ran with the greens-and-cream pairing after observing that the addition of thinly sliced kale, sautéed with lots of browned onion (or shallot, or garlic, or all three) made for a baked mac with enough lift to entice me to finish a whole bowl. Another way I get around a dense final product: Rather than drowning the noodles in an outsize amount of dairy, I drown them in a moderate amount of dairy, and then a lot of pasta water. As in cacio e pepe, this lightens the sauce while keeping it cohesive. (I throw in a substantial amount of cracked black pepper here, too.) The super-starchy water—because I only let you use a few quarts to boil the whole pound—makes for a silky, glossy sauce that grips the noodles. The kale cooks in an onion fond to add more flavor to the roux later, without calling in a third or fourth cheese. I top this with Ritz shards to play off the butteriness of the sauce, and to ensure crunch on top of the noodles (which I way-undercook before they go into the oven, so they don't turn soggy). You can and should tweak this with spices to your palate; red chile flakes or chile crisp or minced Calabrian chiles all add heat; lemon zest or a bit of champagne vinegar brings acid. Last, I really think you should try this with cavatappi, which end up as tiny silly straws for the cheese. (If you can't find cavatappi, shells work, too.) I call for fresh bunches of lacinato kale, but the recipe actually works even better with leftover greens that you cooked with plenty of alliums. Just chop them up and skip the onion-kale steps. Save yourself 15 minutes of prep work by grating the cheese with the grater attachment in the food processor. If you don't have a Dutch oven, or if you like your mac and cheese even crispier than I do, make this in a large saucepan, or transfer it to a sheet pan for the oven portion.

continued

2 heaping tablespoons plus 2 teaspoons Diamond Crystal kosher salt, plus more as needed

1 pound dried cavatappi noodles

3 tablespoons extra virgin olive oil

1 yellow onion (or a mixture of garlic, yellow onion, and shallot), diced

2 large bunches lacinato kale, roughly chopped, bottom 2 inches of stem removed and discarded

6 tablespoons unsalted butter

2 teaspoons freshly cracked black pepper, plus more as needed

Heaping ⅓ cup all-purpose flour

3½ cups whole milk

12 ounces sharp cheddar cheese, grated (about 4 cups tightly packed), plus 1 handful grated for topping

8 ounces Gouda, grated (about 2 cups loosely packed; substitute Gruyère or American if you prefer)

32 Ritz crackers (1 sleeve), roughly crushed

6 ounces Parmesan, grated (about a scant 2 cups)

1. Fill a large Dutch oven with 3 quarts (12 cups) of water and 2 heaping tablespoons salt. (You'll use this cooking vessel for the whole recipe; pick one that's wider than it is tall, so the mac and cheese will have room later to spread out, for the most possible crispy topping.) When the water comes to a boil, add the noodles and cook for 3 minutes less than the package says. When you bite into one, it should seem 75 percent cooked. Reserve 1½ cups of the water, then drain.

2. Set the large Dutch oven over medium-high heat. Add the oil and onion and sauté for 7 to 10 minutes, until they have begun to brown around the edges. Deglaze with a big splash of water. Add the kale and 1 teaspoon of the remaining salt, cover, and let steam. Lift the cover after 1 minute and cook for another 5 minutes, stirring occasionally, or until the kale is wilted and tender. Cut the heat and transfer the kale and onion to a high-powered blender. Wipe out any straggler bits.

3. Heat the oven to 375°F.

4. Set the same Dutch oven (I'm sick of her!) over medium-low heat. Add the butter and bring to a simmer. Cook for 2 to 3 minutes. Add the pepper and flour and cook, whisking, until the roux becomes smooth like gravy, about 1 minute. Cook for another 3 to 4 minutes, whisking, until it has turned the color of light khaki pants. Increase the heat to medium. A little at a time at first, then more steadily as it gets absorbed and smooth, whisk in the milk. Raise the heat to high and bring to a rolling simmer, whisking constantly, then immediately reduce the heat to low and continue simmering and whisking until the sauce is about as thick as cold ranch dressing, about 3 minutes. Add half of the cheddar and Gouda, whisk to combine, then add the rest (excluding the handful of cheddar you're reserving for topping). Whisk. Cut the heat.

5. To the blender, add 1 cup of the cheesy white sauce, and ¾ cup of the reserved starchy pasta cooking water. Blend until very smooth and bright green. If the sauce is already super thick, like finished mac and cheese coming out of the oven, add more reserved starchy water in 2-tablespoon increments until the sauce is closer to the thickness of movie theater nacho cheese. Taste and adjust the seasoning if needed with more salt or pepper.

6. Add the green sauce to the cheesy sauce in the Dutch oven and thoroughly combine. Add the drained noodles, and toss to coat.

7. Gently flatten the cheesy, sauced noodles in the Dutch oven and top evenly with the crushed crackers, the remaining handful of cheddar, and the Parmesan. Bake for about 15 to 20 minutes, uncovered, until the kitchen smells like butter and the crackers have become a golden topping, with happy bubbling around the sides. Broil until you see spots of brown across the top, and then serve warm.

MINIMALIST MAC WITH BURNT MISO AND BUTTERNUT SQUASH

LEVEL

Anyone can execute

TIME

1 hour 15 minutes

MAKES

Dinner or a side for 8

This is a baked macaroni and cheese for fans of crispy edges, who feel that my celebration of creamy kale mac on page 249 is all wrong. I call it "minimalist" not because it has two ingredients (it doesn't), but because you don't need to make a roux. In fact, the sauce is made right in a blender or food processor. You can swap in two honeynut squashes for the butternut, prepared in the same way, if preferred.

2½ teaspoons Diamond Crystal kosher salt, plus more for the pasta water and as needed to taste

One roughly 3-pound butternut squash, peeled, seeds removed, and diced into roughly ½-inch(ish) cubes

2 medium yellow onions, each roughly sliced into about 8 half-moons

¼ cup olive oil

½ teaspoon freshly cracked black pepper

5 tablespoons shiro miso

12 ounces Gouda cheese, freshly grated (2½ cups packed)

8 ounces cheddar cheese, freshly grated (1½ cups packed)

One 12-ounce can evaporated milk

4 tablespoons unsalted butter, plus more for the sheet pan

1 pound dried cavatappi

1. Heat the oven to 450°F. Set a covered pot of heavily salted water (2 heaping teaspoons of salt per quart of water) to boil over high heat.

2. In a large bowl, toss the squash cubes and onion pieces with the oil, 2½ teaspoons salt, and the pepper.

3. Line a sheet pan with parchment. Spread the miso over the parchment as thin as you can without letting it go past the edges. Spread the oiled, seasoned butternut squash cubes and onion over the miso. Roast until the squash is tender and browned all over and the exposed miso is nearly burnt, about 35 minutes. (Leave the oven on; you'll use it to finish the pasta soon.)

4. Add the miso, squash, and onions to a high-powered blender and let cool for 5 minutes. Remove the parchment paper from the sheet pan and discard. Butter the pan once it's cool enough to touch.

5. To the blender with the squash, onions, and miso, add about two-thirds of both types of cheese (reserve the rest for topping), the evaporated milk, and the 4 tablespoons butter. Run on low until you have a dip-textured sauce, then run on high until the sauce becomes smooth, like a thick soup.

6. When the water comes to a boil, add the pasta and cook for 5 minutes. Reserve 1 cup of the starchy, salty cooking water, then drain the pasta. Combine the drained pasta and sauce over low heat, using about ½ cup (but up to 1 cup) of reserved pasta water to thin the sauce and help it coat the noodles; the sauce should be roughly the thickness of queso. Taste and add more salt if needed.

7. Transfer the sauced noodles to the buttered sheet pan. Top with the remaining cheeses in an even layer. Bake for 15 to 20 minutes, until browned, bubbling around the edges, and crisp on top.

MINIMALIST MAC

NEVER DRY, NEVER SOGGY BAKED MAC & CHEESE

THE BACON BOYS

About a year before I sat down to draft this essay, someone at HarperCollins made a huge mistake and offered me money to write a book. I had never made a book in the traditional sense, though when I was a child, my older sister Zoe and I had sketched many disparaging comic strips about members of our family. (At least one, about our grandmother's order at a local Jewish delicatessen, used the term "knish" as a double entendre.) But like hanging a floating shelf from IKEA on the wall of a rental apartment or keeping a Shih Tzu alive, writing a book was just something I assumed I could do if I were reasonably sober. It would afford many opportunities to look smart and make people like me, which were two of my three key interests. The third was having a floating shelf that didn't tip to one side or the other, but I reasoned that even a modern woman couldn't have it all. The book was commissioned on the strict-seeming condition that it be turned in, so about a year minus two days before I sat down to write this, I went to Iowa because I wanted to tell a story about the American obsession with the best.

At first I thought that the story I wanted to tell was about clout. About how in the age of internet antics and late-stage capitalism and the new, new American dream (going viral), there was a group of women all competing to become the Queen of Bacon. I wanted to tell a story about how after the pandemic, it seemed harder and more expensive to access the flight paths I'd need to take to arrive in Des Moines in time for the fifteenth-annual Blue Ribbon Bacon Festival than it would have been to get to the Black Forest. In spite of that, I arrived, and I sat in the front row and watched as five women took part in a pageant for the obscure title of Bacon Queen and a $500 cash prize. Just before the talent show portion of the competition, a man named Mike sat next to me and asked what I was doing later. "Are you asking me out, Mike?" I said with a blush. "No," he said. One woman performed a mournful rendition of "I Like Big Butts" by Sir Mix-a-lot with the word "bacon" occasionally substituted in for the word "butt." A former pro wrestler named Hacksaw served as one of the pageant judges. With very little effort he frothed the crowd into a "USA" chant and then said quietly into his mic, "If that don't make you feel free, I don't know what would; God bless America." ("Amen," said Mike.) The contestant who took the crown demonstrated a talent for chanting the names of former presidents in order. Then the Bacon Queen hopefuls were shooed away so a Tom Petty cover band could set up for a concert. And I wanted to tell you about how it made me think about all the ways a woman could perform for a prize, and how we're all just looking for meaning—how some people have religion, others have astrology, and some have the Bacon Queen pageant.

Then, abruptly, the story I wanted to tell changed. I thought then that I wanted to tell you about a place and a moment in time where and when cured pork and freedom converged and then twisted, like a floating shelf hung on nails that couldn't bear its weight. Just as I arrived in Des Moines, a watershed Supreme Court decision about hog farming standards had passed, apparently devastating Iowa's producers, who were already in crisis as corporations pushed out family farms and overproduction drove down prices. Still, the good people of Des Moines gathered on a boundless fairground to eat as much bacon as they could stomach, to vibe together in a silent bacon disco, to smash a mallet onto a carnival sensor in an effort to earn a score of 999 and thusly win a free National Guard hoodie. And I wanted to tell you about how two nearby rivaling Donald Trump and Ron DeSantis rallies planned for the same day, the second day of the Blue Ribbon Bacon Festival (when attendance hovered in the thousands), sent a rumor through the fairground that Trump might show up for a slice of bacon-and-banana pizza, or a bacon and American cheese–stuffed meatball on a stick. Or so I overheard while eating my second bacon and American cheese–stuffed meatball of the morning. How for a moment it seemed like a race to be "the best" meant being the most tangible and how, as if to underscore this, after Trump canceled his rally due to an unfulfilled tornado warning, DeSantis posted up at the BBQ spot Jethro's to thumb his nose at his challenger. How before any of that had unfolded, I loitered by the National Guard hoodie carnival game, eating free slices of bacon and showing off my strength. I scored in the 300s. One guy got an 892. "Don't be a pussy, Josh," his friend screamed as he hit the sensor again as hard as he could and got a 604. The hoodie rippled tauntingly in a breeze that only it could feel, and the lost Supreme Court debate about twenty-four square feet of pen space per hog and whatever would befall us in the next eighteen-month election cycle both seemed impossibly complex and laughably simple, faraway and too close.

But then I met Brooks Reynolds, a founder and the face guy of the Blue Ribbon Bacon Festival, and immediately I knew that *his* was the story I wanted to tell. Brooks has curly hair down to his shoulders, and the first time I caught sight of it he was nearly mowing me over in a utility vehicle, which was thrilling to me, as the most danger I typically encounter is when I lose track of what I'm doing with the sharp little scissors I use to trim the hairs from my face twice monthly, in case someone looks at me closely for the first time ever. Nearly being run over by Brooks was a fitting way to meet him, since he is almost always in motion. I never actually saw him pause to eat a strip of the bacon he deals on the Iowa State Fairgrounds in increments of hundreds of pounds. As soon as he became aware of my presence at the festival, he came to find me and ordered me onto his cart. We whizzed around as he shouted status reports at his designated "beer meisters," two gentlemen named Pumpkin and The Hopper, who manned their own utility vehicle and who each had beards that were nearly one foot long, one beard sand-colored and the other brunette. He fielded inquiries from the Bacon Buddies—a fleet of teens who worked the grounds in neon orange shirts moving cured pork from one point to another. We buzzed between the guys who were there to worship him (one, Walt Jr., used to play the festival with his folk rap band, known locally for irreverant lyrics), and Hacksaw, and Miss Iowa 2022, and the onetime 2018 "Bacon King." And I became so compelled by this person who was a few things at once—a character who posted online under the moniker "ohhhhbacon," and also infectiously joyful, and proud of where he was from, and kind, and a beacon of his community who donated his time to make something beautiful for everyone else—that I nearly forgot I was there because I wanted to tell you a story that would make you think I was smart. A story that would make up for the fact that I had aimlessly left a career on Wall Street to become a writer and then had, perhaps even more aimlessly, sold this nebulous book about "the best" with very little idea of who or what would fill it. That HarperCollins had not made a grave mistake. Brooks ripped me away from that. I couldn't stop watching him rove around the fairground in his bacon-printed leisure shorts, heckling friends, comforting strangers.

Brooks's sister put it best beside a table where Hacksaw signed photos of himself for attendees: "He's up to no good, but he's very philanthropic; he has a heart full of gold, and he's naughty." In its years of operation, the festival has helped raise over $1,000,000 for local causes, and if that sounds out of character for an event themed "bacon and beer," it might help to know that Brooks's mother was a Red Cross nurse during the Vietnam War who spent decades working for an Iowan children's charity. I followed him around all weekend, and when Monday came, I was so smitten with his whole shtick that I realized I'd never asked if anyone won the hoodie.

I'd wager that he has that effect broadly. Brooks is one of those people who commands a mythology, like my uncle Dan. For many decades, Uncle Dan (my mother's youngest brother) was perhaps the only uncomplicated and charismatic person anyone in my Philip Roth-ian family had ever met in real life. (Dan briefly played organized sports and was blond as a child; later, after he became an anesthesiologist, he purchased a red car.) And so by default anyone that any of us met and found charming was instantly compared to him. Our favorite family dog was "a lot like a chocolate Lab version of Uncle Dan." One of my sister's first boyfriends was "like Uncle Dan but shorter and more surly and with a possible drinking problem." When Barack Obama first ran for office in 2008, I swear to god that my dad said Barack was "like a taller, more serious, more presidential-seeming Uncle Dan, who smokes."

Brooks was Uncle Dan but in Iowa, spreading the values of one of his home state's biggest exports, bringing people together, and making them feel good.

It's how I found myself not far from Brooks's side again six months later, that time in Kofu, Japan, twenty minutes before the scheduled start of the Shingen-kō processional. Shingen-kō is an annual festival in which many attendees dress in Sengoku-period garb to honor an ancient samurai conqueror, Takeda Shingen, who I imagine was a bit like the Uncle Dan of the Yamanashi prefecture in 1542. Right before the parade began, Brooks and his roving, faithful gang of bacon-slinging Iowans took their places in line. Their outfits, selected by the festival organizers, consisted of gold and black jackets and pointy black hats poking upward toward the blue sky. Beneath one that stuck out above the crowd, Brooks's curls flowed to his shoulders.

He and his comrades had arrived after a day and a half of flying, with one mission in mind: to promote the fine bacon of Iowa, far and wide, just as they did on their home turf. To explain that it was the best. I guess I was there because I still wanted to tell a story, although I wasn't totally sure what it was about anymore. There was this guy who evangelized Iowa bacon on his own dime all around the world—he was heading to the Philippines the next day for the same reason—whom I privately had dubbed "Bacon Jesus." A sixth-generation Iowan who had lovingly erected a sub-festival within the Shingen-kō festival called "Porktoberfest," at which two-inch-thick bacon was grilled over an open flame and local boys competed in teams of three to down as much crisped pork as they could, pausing to chug water as they began to glisten like the bacon. And I was there, I suppose, because I still wanted to understand why Brooks was doing it. I got some surface answers—Kofu was Des Moines, Iowa's sister city, and a sibling of Kumi, one of the co-organizers from Kofu, had gone abroad to Brooks's turf in high school. Perhaps relatedly, a Costco would be opening near Kofu later that year. But still it wasn't obvious to me why Brooks, a retired insurance salesman, had spent his own money and time to be there, to bring so many others with him to spread the lore of Iowa's spoils. A more cynical observer than me (I'd hate to meet her) might have thought of colonization, or of overseas missions, but Brooks wasn't forcing anything on anyone.

Most obvious, then, was pride. Americans have been proud of our agricultural output for at least as long as we've been putting on state fairs with municipally funded scenes sculpted out of locally produced butter. More than that, though, in between bites of "American Breakfast" (two defrosted pancakes soaked in bacon juices swaddling a sausage patty), I was struck by the idea of ego. Not Brooks's, but my own. Where Brooks was from had everything to do with where he was going, with what stories he was telling. I couldn't help but see my own attempts at cultural commentary in relief: I had grown up the daughter of two lovely and extremely particular writers in a home that prioritized observation and storytelling, and in lieu of actually generating a story, I had sold the idea that I might come up with a bunch of them. I was crafting a mythology in real time to avoid the fact that I was not in touch with my own.

My own was something like this: The first time I thought I might not know what I wanted to be in life, I was seven-ish. I'd just locked myself inside a bathroom in our home on Long Island. I was wearing a tangerine-colored bathing suit, textured with the dots you'd see on no-slip-grip hospital socks. My babysitter was knocking on the door and jiggling its knob in bursts, like it might just magically open itself. (I'd told her it was jammed and I couldn't figure out how to twist free the lock.) We were twenty-five minutes late for swim, so I could understand her urgency, in theory. But I wasn't sure I wanted to go. I was only sure I did not know. I started to feel bad for the fuss when I realized (gruff low voices, the corner of a neon stripe through the keyhole) that she'd called a bunch of firefighters to help. They debated the best course: Either try to pry open the door with a crowbar or lift me out through a window, since we were on the ground floor. Later, when I mentioned this to my mother, a journalist, she disputed my recollection, gently—was it a neighbor who came by to help? If it really was firemen, were they already on our block for something else? ("Well, who does it help to fact-check your own life, anyway?" I said, before changing the subject to her friend's recent gum surgery.)

Back then I used to eat Top Ramen every day for breakfast. Gargantuan mugs of hot, salty soup, Brillo-tangles of undercooked noodles still clinging to one another, the odd rehydrated scallion floating by as if I was dreaming it. Then we moved across the country and I was a new person. I never thought about ramen, my front teeth sinking over and over again through the plasticine flesh of a California avocado, squeezed out from its peel onto a slice of toast. When I got to college, back in New York, "I used to live here," I said a lot, pausing wistfully (I'd recently begun to smoke). I ended up in finance. Each person was like a character in a show I could not stop watching. Busy. Important. Impenetrable. I fell in love with every single one of them. I had a cubicle full of papers and staplers and I kept six pairs of high heels in one of my drawers. Sometimes, late at night, the motion-sensor light system would sputter into darkness and I would have to stand on my chair, waving my arms around wildly—a shipwreck victim—until the room became illuminated once again. We got off planes in Dallas. In the middle of nowhere. In Los Angeles. I would eat almonds from a minibar for breakfast and I started to say things like "we're not trying to reinvent the wheel here." I made a list:

- Buy tights
- Read *WSJ* 1x weekly
- Dentist?

One year, the head of our group invited us all to a farm he owned upstate. We chased each other around a field with paintball guns. We ducked behind wooden barrels and down into dirt dugouts as his kids pelted us and we compared welts (they had perfect aim). Later in the day, a Led Zeppelin cover band appeared in a barn and one of my bosses closed his eyes and sang along ruefully to "Stairway to Heaven." On Fridays, I curled into a hideous ball on a hideous couch at my boyfriend's apartment. "What do you want to do?" he asked. Usually, the answer was "order Indian food." Or "pick all of the polish off of my toenails and arrange it in a small pile of cherry-colored flakes on the edge of a suede cushion" or "sit there forever" or "perch on the bathroom sink like a gargoyle and take all the lightbulbs out of their fixture so I can buff away the dust that's built up between each one" or "threaten to think of an idea for a screenplay."

By the time I got a new job as a writer—a new life, again—my new life seemed, as it always did, like it had been my life forever. Like I had always been the sort of person who writes back "o.k." when a friend asks to have dinner too late (9 p.m.), too last-minute, on a Friday, too far away. Like I didn't mind taking the subway for ninety minutes to get to an Italian restaurant, and like I didn't mind when she was thirty minutes late and I was left to make small talk with a server who introduced himself as Stefano, but whom I had heard another server call Brian, and who suspected I was being stood up.

Everything was so amusing, everyone was so charming. People were *stressed*, they reported. Very worn out. Very serious. We worked at a food blog. I told them I used to eat Top Ramen every day for breakfast, and they smiled, encouragingly. "Sometimes," I added hopefully, "I'd crack an egg into it." "Maybe there's a story in that," they'd say.

I was a mole person who had just stepped aboveground for the first time in a century. The stylists from the test kitchen ran over to my desk and spoke as if they were E.R. doctors, working to stabilize my daughter after a terrible car accident in the rain: "Your pear cake's out," they said, touching my shoulder. "We've inverted it successfully. There was a second where"—they paused, sucked in a breath—"one of the pear slices fell off. But we were able to reattach it for the photo. You'd never know the difference." I went to a wedding and drank a thimbleful of espresso on a balcony overlooking green hills and it was so pretty I wanted to bawl and then I did and what was left of my coffee tasted a little bit like an ocean and I thought to myself, *Maybe there's a story in that.*

I would text my mother to confirm bits of our family history that I'd always believed to be true, which all turned out to be misremembered—that my grandfather, a pharmacist, had gone bankrupt in the wake of big-box chain drugstores and retaliated by maybe becoming the Tylenol killer. "El: No. He loved working for someone else," my mother would write. She gently corrected my memories again and again. Her father hadn't gone with the family from Chicago to Kentucky for the holidays each year like I'd thought; in the 1970s he'd once spotted a long snake in the road from inside a car and never returned. She texted black-and-white photos and I learned I had once had a hot great-uncle who was killed in a freak car accident in the 1950s that "people thought" was "the mob getting back at Jack for refusing to do their books in Florida." At one point she texted the following sentence and I wrote it down in pencil in a notebook, in case I ever needed to plagiarize her: "I don't understand why people claim childhood is a happy time; it's just a time when people who are dumber than you make you do stuff you don't want to do." At another point, she texted the following sentence and I wrote it down in pen: "It's actually marvelous that in each of our lives, we have the capacity to capriciously change in ways that are illogical, surprising, and mysterious even to ourselves. Keeps it fresh."

I was smug and serene. I bought a bunch of scarves from a thrift store. For the first time in six years, I started to talk to my best friend. I started to talk to my boyfriend. I called my sisters. I was finally a writer. It turned out fairly quickly that such a distinction was meaningless without much to say.

And so I went to Iowa, because I wanted to tell a story.

I wanted to at least *see* if I might have something to say. Then I flew to Japan in the back row of a very full airplane with very few free snacks. And the story I had set out to tell began to take shape. I was all geared up to tell you how the pursuit of the best is born from longing. How our obsessions stem from this creatural yearning for identity. How it's hard to be a person with an ego and emotions and how "the best" is just something we all do to keep ourselves going. I was born of two writers and I grew up craving praise and that praise came when I said something astute or made adults laugh and so in lieu of anything else more pressing to do, I had flown around the world constructing this story about a guy and his pleasures, his dead-set quest to tell people that Iowa bacon was the best. His pride in a place that was known for producing the best possible version of a very good thing. Instead of saying that I was afraid I might be faking it, I had come up with a play in several acts about a guy I called Bacon Jesus who represented America, who might have won the National Guard hoodie if he had wanted to, because he cared enough. About his people, his family, the place he was from, the bacon he had grown up with.

He had proven something I hadn't realized I'd been wondering about for the better part of the year, or maybe since I locked myself in that bathroom: that people are infinitely capable of reinvention as the opportunity arises. And that doing so is not something to be ashamed of—life is not some one-dimensional novel in which we each have an arc that makes sense at the right points. That "it's actually marvelous that in each of our lives, we have the capacity to capriciously change in ways that are illogical, surprising, and mysterious even to ourselves. Keeps it fresh." The idea of a "best" is actually just a tool for reinvention, a moving goalpost that allows us to keep defining ourselves in new and different ways.

And I had Brooks just where I wanted him. He was trawling the globe, peddling the thing that mattered to him most, convincing us it was the best because doing so was literally in his DNA. His pride was his identity. Where he came from was where he was going. He had, in a certain sense, lots of clout. He was freedom and pork personified. I had put the cart before the horse, but just this once, it seemed to be working out.

Then, just to make sure, I sent him a text.

"By the way," I wrote, "it occurred to me, in all the time we chatted in Iowa and Japan, I never asked: Why did you choose bacon specifically? Is there a personal significance?" He sent a vague response. "Did you grow up eating a lot of bacon?" I prodded.

A few dots appeared as he typed. Then they disappeared. A minute later, they began to flicker again. I held my phone with both hands, staring at the screen, waiting for the final piece of the myth of Bacon Jesus to materialize.

And then two words came into focus: "Not really."

DESSERTS *TO* EAT *in* BED

OR STANDING OVER THE SINK *OR* SEATED LIKE A LADY

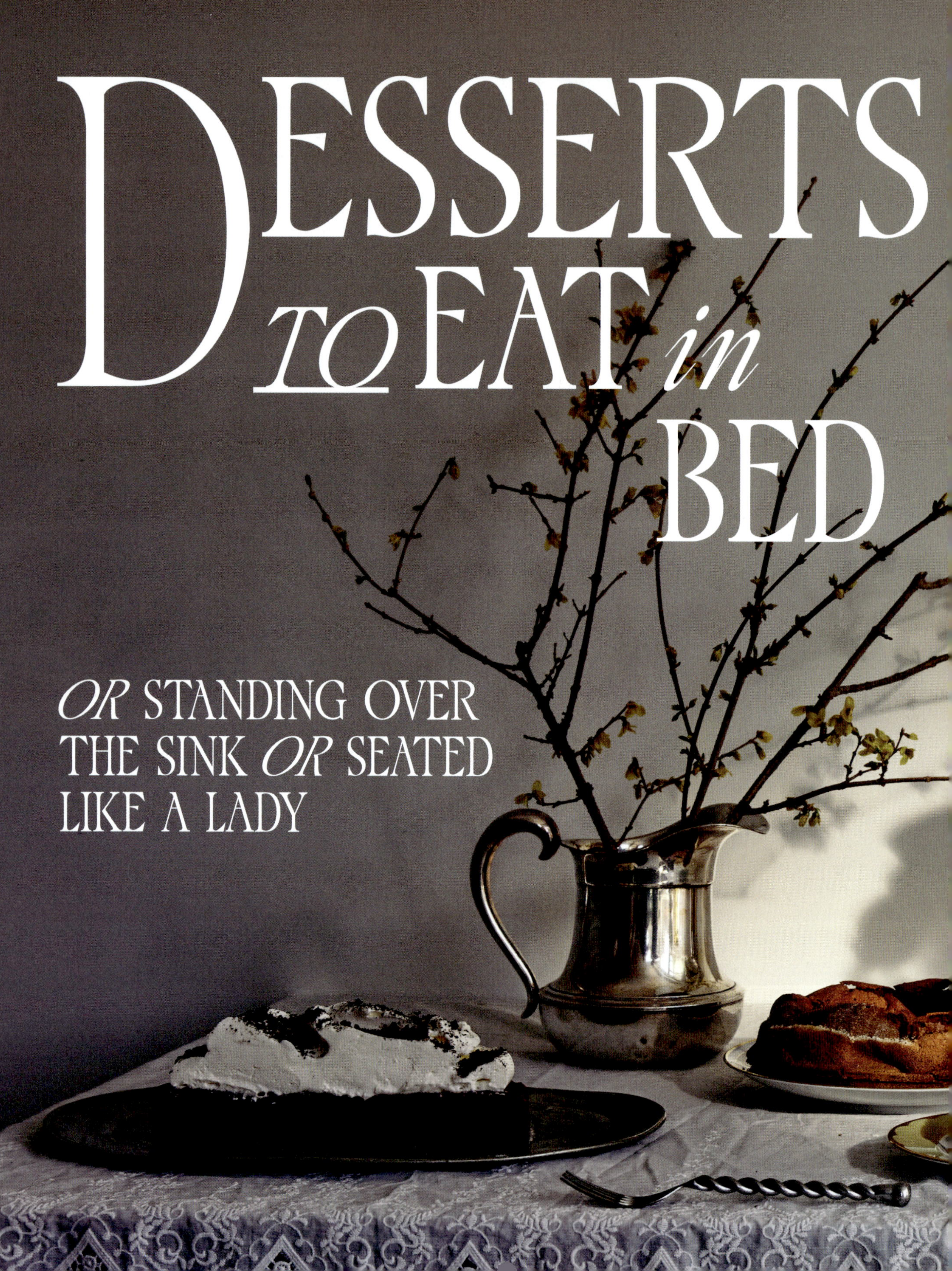

19

Cloudlike Whipped CREAM

MISSION

Whipped cream good enough to eat on its own.

WHAT I TESTED

Whipping method • Stabilizers and flavor enhancers
Temperature of equipment • Temperature of cream
Sweeteners

MAPLE SYRUP
AGAVE
CREAM HEESE ADDED LATER
MELTED MARSHMALL
CONFECTIONERS' SUGAR
COCKTAIL SH
BUTTERMILK
HIGH-SPEED BLENDER
HAND MIXER
MILK POWDER
HONEY
CRÈME FRAÎCHE
ROOM-TEMPERATURE CREAM
CHILLED CREA
GREEK YOGURT
MERSION BLENDER
CREAM CHEESE ADDED FIRST
FOOD PROCESSOR
STAND MIXER–PADDLE
BOWL + WHISK CHILLED
GELATIN
ROOM-TEMPERATU CREAM
HAND WHISK
STAND MIXER–BALLOON
JAR SHAKE

THERE ARE EXACTLY TWO THINGS THAT,

when executed properly, have infinite transformative power: haircuts and whipped cream. I cannot help you with the former—I recently forgot about my face shape and got a "blunt bob"—but as for the latter, I can offer a few suggestions. The first is that whipped cream can and should be the whole dessert. If you want to experience its transformative powers without any insulation, see page 269 for ideas about how ethereal, velvety whipped cream can replace fussy puddings as a last-minute sweet course. Another piece of evidence: Whipped cream can transform an average baked good. My former colleague (and the brilliant food writer) Emma Laperruque turned me onto this when she wrote[1] about a passage in *BakeWise* by Shirley O. Corriher, in which Corriher discovered that whipped cream vastly improved her pound cake. As Laperruque pointed out, Rose Levy Beranbaum has a recipe in *Rose's Heavenly Cakes*[2] that calls for whipped cream rather than butter in its typical form. (The eggs and sugar get beaten right into it.) To try it for yourself, see my Strawberries-Three-Ways Cake recipe on page 280, in which whipped cream not only forms a gently tangy frosting layer with mascarpone and vanilla bean but also helps to keep the sheet cake from drying out or having the mouthfeel of a couch cushion. Another example is my Whipped Corn Muffins on page 272, in which whipped cream helps to provide a bakery-style rise and crumb. Whipped cream can also lighten a denser frosting—as in my American Buttercream on page 323, which has you whip unsweetened heavy cream into the bowl—or even a traditional mousse or pudding. I use it as a second form of aeration in my milk chocolate mousse on page 276, for extra richness and more firmness than whipped eggs would provide alone. Whipped cream can, incidentally, also positively transform a day spent being bummed that you got a blunt bob—if you eat enough of it while supine.

THE BEST METHODS

BEST SPECIAL EQUIPMENT METHOD: A stand mixer fitted with the balloon whisk consistently produced the fluffiest whipped cream across all my trials, measured in volume and mouthfeel.

Chill your bowl and beaters in the freezer before you begin, and use cold cream. Start on a medium speed until splattering ceases, then whip on medium-high.

BEST NO-EQUIPMENT METHOD: A whisk and a bowl, or even a jar with a sealable lid, will produce aerated cream, and the slightly denser texture would hardly be perceptible if you weren't performing side-by-side taste tests. You'll get fluffier hand-whipped cream with a whisk than you will from a sealed jar.

BEST EASY UPGRADES: As far as sweeteners: Granulated sugar works perfectly well (I reach for this when it's used elsewhere in the recipe), and confectioners' sugar is even better since it comes with a bit of cornstarch, which will contribute to stability. (Though I found that cream whipped with granulated sugar still held up at least 3 days without weeping when stored tightly covered in the refrigerator.) You could also turn to honey, or maple syrup, or agave syrup for more flavor, depending on the other flavors in your recipe. Salt is nonnegotiable; if this freaks you out, start with a little pinch. You'll immediately notice a lift in the richness of the lightly sweetened cream.

WHAT TO DO IF YOU OVER-WHIP: Don't panic! At least you didn't get a blunt bob. Just let the mixer (or your whisk-holding hand) run on low and drizzle in more cold cream by the tablespoon, until it reverts to a fluffy texture.

TO MAKE THE WHIPPED CREAM TANGY AND LOOSE AND SWOOPY: Drizzle in ⅓ cup buttermilk as you reach soft peaks and keep whipping, to regain the thickness you lost by adding liquid.

TO MAKE THE WHIPPED CREAM TANGY: Add ⅓ cup Greek yogurt or sour cream or labneh, at room temperature, as you reach soft peak. Make sure the Greek yogurt or sour cream or labneh is really at room temperature first; otherwise, lumps will form in the cream. If you're wondering about crème fraîche, seek out the Cream Cheese Whipped Cream on page 270 and use the same (reversed) method, to avoid clumpiness.

TO STABILIZE THE WHIPPED CREAM BUT LEAVE IT SWOOPY: Sprinkle ½ to 1½ teaspoons powdered unflavored gelatin (the more you use, the more stable the cream will be, but you'll sacrifice a bit of soft, melty mouthfeel with the full 1½ teaspoons) over 1 to 2 tablespoons water, let sit until soggy and wrinkled, then microwave for 5 to 10 seconds, until the gelatin dissolves. Stir, let cool a few minutes, and add.

TO STABILIZE AND STIFFEN THE WHIPPED CREAM, I.E. FOR DETAILED PIPING: Add 2 tablespoons milk powder, and mix on low just to combine. (The whipped cream will firm up right away; if you need to loosen it for any reason, add a bit more unwhipped cream and mix on low.)

MOTHER RECIPE

SALTED WHIPPED CREAM

LEVEL

Anyone can execute

TIME

15 minutes

MAKES

Whipped cream to cover a 9- or 10-inch cake, or enough whipped cream to top 6 to 8 desserts

Good whipped cream evokes nature. The clichés aren't baseless; a mound of it does imitate the soft bulge of clouds, or the weightlessness of snowbanks that appear overnight and threaten to bury sedans. In fact, an early name for whipped cream, from the Renaissance chef Bartolomeo Scappi, translated to "milk snow." And good whipped cream disappears as quickly as a tuft of fresh snow melts. For that level of ethereality, a stand mixer fitted with the balloon whisk will serve you. That setup consistently produced the fluffiest whipped cream, measured in volume and mouthfeel. With that said, you don't need any special equipment to make worthwhile whipped cream. You can use a whisk and bowl, a hand mixer, or even a sealed jar—any of these will aerate cream, and the slightly thicker texture will hardly be noticeable. See page 269, where I make the case that whipped cream should be the whole dessert, not just the finishing touch—you can find a number of formulas to flavor the cream with everything from cocoa powder to milk powder to raspberry jam.

2 cups cold heavy cream

1 tablespoon vanilla bean paste or extract

2 tablespoons confectioners' sugar or granulated sugar (use confectioners' sugar if you are making it in advance)

Scant ¼ teaspoon Diamond Crystal kosher salt

1. Place the bowl and balloon whisk attachment of your stand mixer—or a regular bowl and a metal whisk, or a regular bowl and the beaters for a hand mixer—in the freezer 15 minutes before you're ready to whip. (Note: If you're pinched for time, don't worry about this; the amount of incremental fluff you'll get from a frozen setup is noticeable, yes, but you'll still get very good whipped cream in a room-temperature bowl.)

2. Add the cream to the bowl. Beat on medium speed for 1½ to 2 minutes, until the cream stops splattering. Add the vanilla, sugar, and salt. Continue to whip on medium-high until soft peaks form (i.e. when you pull out the beater or whisk and flip it, a floppy tail stays affixed even though it doesn't stand up stiff), 30 seconds to 1 minute more. If not using immediately, store tightly covered in the refrigerator for up to a few days, though it might lose some volume and eventually begin to weep after the first day.

NOTE: *See page 265 for variations.*

Whipped Cream Should Be the Whole Dessert

EMERGENCY "CHOCOLATE SANDWICH COOKIE" FRIDGE PUDDING

aka Depression Pudding

I make this on days when my SSRIs feel less effective than PEZ. The barely aerated cream and the salty-biscuit flavor of Dutch-process cocoa become accomplices in a sensory heist that will convince you that this recipe produces two bowls of Oreo milkshake in mousse form. It also tastes like Swiss Miss hot chocolate powder, straight from the packet. Which is at least a bit remedial. While you could use a stand mixer, I do it with a whisk, because, Depression Pudding.

3 tablespoons pure maple syrup

3 tablespoons Dutch-process cocoa powder

¼ teaspoon Diamond Crystal kosher salt, plus more to taste

1 cup cold heavy whipping cream

1. In a large bowl, whisk together the maple syrup, cocoa powder, and salt until fully combined into a thick syrup. (Whisk out all the dry pockets and lumps here.) Add the cream and whisk until the mixture has thickened to the consistency of shaving cream and holds the whisk tracks. Spoon into 2 shallow cups or ramekins. Consume immediately.

TWO-INGREDIENT RASPBERRY MOUSSE-ISH

This is a markedly cheerier variation in Yoplait pink. Unlike its Oreo-flavored cousin, this pert cheaters' mousse (or more accurately, cheaters' raspberry fool) works best in a stand mixer fitted with the balloon whisk attachment, for lighter, fluffier spoonfuls. (You could do it by hand with a whisk, though.) For a marbled top, after you've doled out the pink mousse into individual portions, add an extra tablespoon or so of jam to the top, and use a butter knife to twirl it into a ribbon pattern. If that doesn't have you grinning like a lady eating yogurt in a stock photo, I don't know what will.

1 cup cold heavy whipping cream

Pinch of Diamond Crystal kosher salt

5 tablespoons seeded or seedless raspberry jam

OPTIONAL

Sweetened whipped cream

Fresh raspberries

1. In the bowl of a stand mixer fitted with the balloon whisk attachment, whip the cream on medium speed and then medium-high to soft peaks. With the mixer turned down to low but still running, whip in the salt and then 4 tablespoons of the jam, 1 tablespoon at a time, until combined and light pink.

2. Transfer to 2 short cups or martini glasses or ramekins and use a knife or offset spatula to dollop the remaining jam in a few places over the top of each. Gently swirl it in while keeping it as a defined ripple, then smooth the top, cover with plastic wrap, and refrigerate for at least 30 minutes or up to 2 days. Serve as is or topped with sweetened whipped cream or fresh raspberries.

MILK AND HONEY WHIPPED CREAM

I would give up ice cream forever for this combination. I find milk powder to be incredibly savory and rich, so adding it to cream—which has so much natural milky sweetness—is game-changing. With salty honey, this becomes game-ending. I use my stand mixer method to make sure the milk powder is evenly distributed, but if you prefer to whisk by hand, just add the milk powder earlier in the process.

1 cup cold heavy whipping cream

1 heaping tablespoon whole milk powder

2 tablespoons honey

1 tablespoon vanilla bean paste or extract

¼ teaspoon Diamond Crystal kosher salt

TO TOP

2 tablespoons more honey

Flaky salt

1. In the bowl of a stand mixer fitted with the balloon whisk attachment, whip the cream on medium speed and then medium-high to soft peaks. With the mixer turned down to low but still running, whip in the milk powder, honey, vanilla, and salt. Taste and if you're not tempted to immediately eat the whole thing, add another pinch of salt and taste again; you'll know when it's ready. Spoon into 2 short cups or martini glasses or ramekins. Use a spoon or offset spatula to create a shallow well, about ½ inch in the center of each mound. Pour in the honey and garnish with flaky salt.

CREAM CHEESE WHIPPED CREAM WITH JAM

Not quite a cream cheese frosting, but also not not that. Just trust me.

5 tablespoons cream cheese

1 cup cold heavy cream

2 teaspoons vanilla bean paste or extract

2 tablespoons confectioners' sugar or granulated sugar

Pinch of Diamond Crystal kosher salt

¼ cup jam, to serve

1. Put the cream cheese in the bowl of a stand mixer fitted with the balloon whisk attachment. Beat for 1 to 2 minutes on medium-high speed until fluffy and room temperature, stopping to scrape down the sides of the bowl with a spatula every 20 seconds or so.

2. Add the cream to the bowl. Beat on medium speed for 1½ to 2 minutes, until the cream stops splattering. Add the vanilla, sugar, and salt. Continue to whip on medium-high until soft peaks form (i.e. when you pull out the beater or whisk and flip it, a floppy tail stays affixed even though it doesn't stand up stiff), 30 seconds to 1 minute more.

3. Transfer to 2 serving dishes and use a spoon or offset spatula to dig a 2-inch-deep hole in the center of the top of each mound. Split the jam between each.

BUTTERMILK CHOCOLATE WHIPPED CREAM WITH CHOCOLATE GANACHE

This will become your new go-to dessert for low-effort dinner parties. It's visually stunning—any light, even our horrible, flickering track lighting left over from past residents, glints off the ganache like it's covered in gold leaf. And it tastes like it took all day to make.

FOR THE GANACHE

5 tablespoons unsalted butter, cubed, at room temperature

2 heaping tablespoons whole milk powder

1 cup semisweet chocolate chips (or chopped chocolate)

¼ to ½ teaspoon Diamond Crystal kosher salt

FOR THE WHIPPED CREAM

2 cups cold heavy whipping cream

6 tablespoons Dutch-process cocoa powder

2 tablespoons sugar (any kind)

1 tablespoon vanilla bean paste or extract

¼ to ½ teaspoon Diamond Crystal kosher salt

⅓ cup buttermilk, shaken, at room temperature

Flaky salt

Cherries, fresh or maraschino, for topping (optional)

1. About 10 minutes before you're ready to serve dessert, make the brown butter chocolate ganache: Cook the butter in a small saucepan over medium heat, stirring frequently, until it starts to foam. Add the milk powder and whisk until the milk solids at the bottom of the pan are deeply golden brown and similar to the color of toast, 4 to 5 minutes. Remove from the heat.

2. Stir in the chocolate chips and kosher salt. Cover with a tight-fitting lid; let stand for about 3 minutes. Uncover and whisk the melted chocolate, scraping up the toasty bits from the bottom of the pan. Let the ganache stand, covered, until it is barely warm to the touch. Set aside.

3. While the ganache cools, make the whipped cream: Pour the cream into the bowl of a stand mixer fitted with a balloon whisk attachment. Whip the cream on medium speed until soft peaks form (peaks should barely hold their shape and briefly hold on the whisk before they fall back into the bowl), 4 to 5 minutes. Turn off the mixer and sift in the cocoa powder. Return the mixer to low and add the sugar, vanilla, and ¼ to ½ teaspoon salt; scrape down the sides, as needed. Add the buttermilk and beat the mixture until just combined and medium-soft peaks form, about 1 minute.

4. Spoon about ¾ cup of the whipped cream, mounding it high, into 4 serving cups. Use a spoon or offset spatula to create a deep well, about 2 inches in the center of each mound. Pour in the barely warm ganache (2 to 3 tablespoons per well, or enough to fill the wells to the edge). Garnish with flaky salt and cherries (if using).

WHIPPED CORN MUFFINS

LEVEL

A bit of skill required

TIME

50 minutes

MAKES

12 muffins

In another life (I love to say that, as though I have several thinly veiled romans à clef up my sleeve), I worked at an investment bank. The best part of my very long days was breakfast, even though the on-site offerings were flagrantly mediocre. Some days I'd get a softball-size corn muffin from the grab-and-go cafe in the lobby. I admired the muffin's pillowy, tight crumb, its nearly damp interior (when you pinched some together hard it would stick), and most of all, the slight grit of finely milled cornmeal. I've made a few tweaks in my own rendition, based in part on my father's preferences and in part because I refuse to buy a bakery-size muffin tin. Here, whipped cream provides lift and insurance against a dry crumb. It produces fluffy bakery-style muffins without sacrificing the tender richness of homestyle ones. You can serve these muffins as written, split in two while warm and topped with more butter and maple syrup, or you can griddle them and serve them with eggs, or you can frost them with the Brown Butter French-ish Buttercream on page 321.

3 tablespoons (42 g) plus 1 cup (2 sticks/225 g) unsalted butter, at room temperature

¼ cup (78 g) plus ⅓ cup (104 g) pure maple syrup, plus more for drizzling

2 cups (276 g) fine- or medium-ground cornmeal, plus more for the muffin tin

1 cup (230 g) cold heavy cream

⅔ cup (133 g) granulated sugar

2 large eggs, at room temperature

1¼ cups (286 g) buttermilk, at room temperature

1¾ teaspoons baking soda

1¼ teaspoons Diamond Crystal kosher salt

2½ cups (355 g) all-purpose flour

1. Heat the oven to 400°F.

2. Melt the 3 tablespoons (42 g) butter, and, using a pastry brush, grease a 12-cup muffin tin, including the space between the muffin molds. Set the remaining melted butter aside to use when the muffins come out of the oven.

3. Drizzle each buttered mold evenly with the ¼ cup (78 g) maple syrup, about 1 teaspoon per tin (wipe any that lands on the top of the tin, or it'll burn). Then, pinch about a teaspoon of cornmeal into each, to start melding with the maple.

4. In the bowl of a stand mixer fitted with the balloon whisk attachment (or using a whisk), whip the cream on medium speed, then medium-high, to medium-stiff peaks. Transfer to another bowl and set in the refrigerator to chill; don't bother wiping out the bowl you used to whip it.

5. Fit the stand mixer with the paddle attachment. In the dirtied bowl, beat the remaining 1 cup room-temperature butter and granulated sugar on medium speed until pale yellow and super fluffy, about 6 minutes, scraping the sides throughout. Add the eggs, one at a time, beating until each one is completely incorporated. Add the remaining ⅓ cup maple syrup and the buttermilk and mix just to combine. Add the baking soda, salt, flour, and remaining cornmeal and mix just to combine. Let the batter sit for about 5 minutes to allow the cornmeal to absorb moisture.

6. Use a spatula to gently fold in about one-third of the chilled whipped cream; this will be tough, since the batter is extremely thick and sticky at

this stage, but do your best to fold it in from the bottom and sides, with long strokes. Once it's mostly incorporated with some white streaks and the batter is a tiny bit looser, add the next third and quickly fold it in to the point of seeing streaks, then add the last third and fully incorporate. The batter should look more like what you'd use for drop biscuits at this point, still thick and sticky but fluffier and looser.

7. Ladle the batter among the 12 prepared muffin molds, mounding any excess batter on top (each muffin should have a little batter mountain on top of it, above the rim). Bake for 8 minutes, then lower the oven temperature to 350°F. Continue to bake until the muffins are puffed and golden around the edges and firm in the centers, 20 to 25 minutes more.

8. Slice in half and brush with the remaining melted butter and more maple syrup drizzled over them. Eat warm. Store any leftovers tightly wrapped in the freezer for up to 2 weeks, and toast to serve.

WHIPPED CORN MUFFINS

MILK CHOCOLATE MOUSSE

MILK CHOCOLATE MOUSSE WITH BROWN BUTTER GRAHAM STREUSEL

LEVEL

A bit of skill required

TIME

45 minutes, plus 3+ hours to chill

MAKES

Mousse for 8 to 10

You can streusel any sweet or salty crunchy thing, and you should feel free to experiment with swapping out my graham version for whatever you love here; sesame and chocolate are really nice together, and I would never say no to Ritz or saltines. I serve this in 8 to 10 ramekins or cocktail glasses, but you could also make one large mousse in a bowl and pretend to be in Paris, serving it in big scoops onto guests' plates.

FOR THE GRAHAM CRUMBS

¼ cup (½ stick/56 g) plus 1 tablespoon (14 g) unsalted butter

⅓ cup (47 g) almonds, ideally blanched, but it's not critical

8 sheets (115 g) graham crackers

3 tablespoons (38 g) granulated sugar

¼ teaspoon Diamond Crystal kosher salt

FOR THE MOUSSE

1½ cups (345 g) plus ½ cup (115 g) heavy whipping cream

8 ounces (227 g) milk chocolate, finely chopped

3 large eggs (165 g), separated

2 tablespoons (12 g) Dutch-process cocoa powder

½ teaspoon Diamond Crystal kosher salt

3 tablespoons (38 g) granulated sugar

1. Heat the oven to 400°F. Line a sheet pan with parchment paper.

2. Brown the butter: Melt ¼ cup of the butter in a small saucepan over medium to medium-high heat. Cook, watching like a hawk and stirring occasionally, until the butter foams and smells super nutty and the solids at the bottom begin to turn the color of toasted bread. Remove from the heat (it'll brown a bit more as it sits). Add the remaining 1 tablespoon butter and let it melt into the browned butter.

3. In a food processor, pulse the almonds until they're pebble-size. Add the graham crackers and pulse until everything is fine, like sand. Add the sugar and salt and pulse to combine. As you run the processor, drizzle in the browned butter until the mixture become wet and sticks together in clumps when you press it between your fingers. (Use a silicone spatula to be sure you transfer all the browned butter bits to the crumbs.)

4. Transfer the graham mixture to the parchment-lined sheet pan and use your fingers to make clumps of different sizes, like streusel.

5. Bake for about 6 minutes, until the largest clumps are beginning to turn golden on their highest points and the streusel is fragrant. (It'll keep cooking on the pan, so you don't need to take it further than this in the oven.)

6. Set aside at room temp until assembly; the streusel will continue to clump up as it sits. Store covered loosely at room temperature for up to a day, or cover tightly and store at room temperature for up to 3 weeks; if it goes limp, re-crisp on a sheet pan at 300°F.

7. To make the mousse: In the bowl of a stand mixer fitted with the balloon whisk, whip 1½ cups cream on medium speed, then medium-high, until stiff peaks form. Transfer roughly one-third of the whipped cream to a bowl and chill to reserve for serving. Transfer the remaining two-thirds of the whipped cream to a bowl that sits out at room temperature. Clean and dry the mixer bowl and whisk.

8. Using a double boiler (or short bursts in a microwave if you're responsible, or in a large saucepan directly over low heat if you crave danger), carefully melt all the chocolate in the remaining ½ cup (unwhipped) cream, stirring often from the bottom with a silicone spatula to avoid burnt spots. Once most of the chocolate has melted, mix rapidly until the mixture is fully melted.

9. Dip a finger into the chocolate mixture. When it's cooled to the point that you no longer want to remove your finger, add the egg yolks one at a time, whisking to combine after each. Add the cocoa and whisk to get rid of lumps.

10. In the bowl of a stand mixer fitted with the balloon whisk, beat the egg whites and salt on medium speed until foamy bubbles cover the surface. As the mixer runs, add the sugar a tablespoon at a time. Continue to beat until the meringue has shiny, stiff peaks, meaning if you remove the whisk (or beater), the peak will not droop or fall off when you tip it upside down.

11. Add a third of the meringue, plus all the room-temperature whipped cream, to the melted chocolate mixture and gently fold to combine until only a few streaks remain. Add the next third of meringue and fold to combine until only a few streaks remain. Add the remaining meringue, and repeat, this time fully folding until no white lumps or streaks remain.

12. Fill 8 to 10 ramekins or martini glasses or bodega cups with the mousse. Cover and chill until set, at least 3 hours or overnight.

13. Before serving, top the mousse with the reserved chilled whipped cream and a few tablespoons of graham streusel.

STRAWBERRIES-
THREE-WAYS CAKE,
PAGE 280

STRAWBERRIES-THREE-WAYS CAKE

LEVEL

Slightly challenging, but impressive

TIME

2½ hours start to finish, though you can easily do the jam and macerated berries the day before to streamline

MAKES

Cake for 10

The secret to the best strawberry cake is, I'm worried to say, a pint of raspberries. At least, that's the secret to the flavor of peak-season strawberries when you're still in shoulder season. This cake takes inspiration from strawberry shortcake, Korean cream cake, and, unexpectedly, tiramisu, with its whipped mascarpone layer complementing a soft cakey one. In it, I not only instruct you to use strawberries three ways (as jam, as a macerated topping, and as a juicy soak for the sponge layers), but I also instruct you to use whipped cream two ways (as a tenderizer and leavener, and as a creamy frosting). That's a lot of multitasking! So you'll want to read through the steps before diving in. Like any great literary heroine, this cake's greatest strength is also its Achilles heel, which is tenderness; handle the cake layers with care, and make use of gentle spatula transfers. And feel free to swap in ripe peaches by weight for the strawberries. If you do, you can keep the basil as is, or substitute mint and citrus zest. If you reallllllly want to make a day of it, this cake is so incredible with the Brown Butter French-ish Buttercream on page 321; use the mascarpone whip between layers, then frost the outside in the buttercream and decorate with macerated fruit.

DON'T TOSS YOUR STRAWBERRY TOPS!
Dry them in the oven at 100°F until brittle, and brew them as tea along with fresh mint, or add them when you boil simple syrup.

FOR THE MACERATED BERRIES, JAM, AND WHIPPED CREAM

3 pints ripe strawberries (roughly 2½ pounds or 1130 g), hulled (or greens trimmed) and halved

1 pint raspberries (roughly 8 ounces or 230 g)

½ cup (100 g) plus ⅓ cup (66 g) granulated sugar, plus more as needed

¼ cup (60 g) plus 1 tablespoon (15 g) freshly squeezed lemon juice, plus more as needed

2½ teaspoons Diamond Crystal kosher salt, plus more as needed

1. In a medium bowl, use a wooden spoon to gently mash the strawberries and raspberries into the ½ cup sugar and ¼ cup lemon juice and 1 teaspoon of the salt. Mash and mix until about two-thirds of the berries are at least partially crushed, within a thick juicy stew. Let sit at room temperature, stirring every 20 minutes or so, until the juice covers the berries by roughly ¼ inch—about 1 hour.

2. Meanwhile, in a stand mixer fitted with a balloon whisk, whip the cream on medium speed, then medium-high, to stiff peaks. Set aside 2 cups of the whipped cream, at room temperature, to add later to the cake batter in step 6. To the remaining whipped cream, add the confectioners' sugar, ½ teaspoon of the remaining salt, and the mascarpone in about 10 small spoonfuls (to keep it from clumping). Whip just to combine. Set in the fridge to keep cold.

3. When the juice covers the macerating berries by about ¼ inch, remove ½ cup of the liquid and set it aside to use as cake soak. Add about half of the berries and the remaining liquid to a saucepan with the ⅓ cup sugar and set it over medium-high heat. (Set aside the rest of the macerated berries and liquid until you're ready to construct the cake; cover in the refrigerator if you're doing this step the day before.)

3 cups (690 g) cold heavy cream

¼ cup (30 g) confectioners' sugar

¾ cup mascarpone (about 173 g), at room temperature (important); you can swap in Greek yogurt or sour cream for a similar flavor with slightly less stability

Zest of 2 lemons

1 tablespoon unsalted butter

⅔ cup fresh basil leaves, rinsed and dried and cut in a chiffonade

FOR THE CAKE

Butter, for the pan

2¾ cups (391 g) all-purpose flour

1¾ cups (350 g) granulated sugar

1 tablespoon plus 1 teaspoon baking powder

1½ teaspoons Diamond Crystal kosher salt

⅔ cup (214 g) olive oil, plus more to drizzle on top

1 cup (230 g) buttermilk

4 large eggs, at room temperature

2 tablespoons vanilla bean paste or extract

2 tablespoons freshly squeezed lemon juice

4. Bring the berries and liquid to a boil, stirring and smashing the berries with a wooden spoon. Continue to cook, scraping the bottom and smashing the berries, for 12 to 15 minutes, until the mixture is thick and sticky and any chunks of berry are the size of a large pebble. Turn the heat to medium-low and simmer for another 5 minutes, or until when you dip a frozen spoon into the mixture, let the jam cool on the spoon, then run your finger through the cooled jam, it leaves a clear trail. Turn off the heat, add the remaining 1 tablespoon lemon juice, all the zest, the butter, and basil, and stir. Taste and adjust with more lemon juice, salt, and/or sugar until it's pert and perfect. Let cool in the fridge. (If you're not constructing the cake immediately, transfer to a jar and refrigerate for up to 1 month.)

5. To make the cake: Heat the oven to 350°F. Grease an 18 × 13-inch sheet pan (a standard half sheet pan) with butter. Line the bottom with parchment and butter that as well.

6. In a large bowl, whisk together the flour, sugar, baking powder, and salt. In a second bowl, whisk together the oil, buttermilk, eggs, and vanilla. In two additions, add the wet to the dry and whisk to combine. Add the lemon juice and whisk once more. In two additions, use a spatula to fold the 2 cups reserved plain whipped cream into the batter until no streaks remain.

7. Pour the batter into the prepared pan and gently level it with an offset spatula or knife, taking care not to smash the batter and deflate it. Bake for about 30 minutes, until set (to touch) in the center, with golden brown beauty marks all over its surface (do a toothpick test if you're not sure).

8. Let cool for at least 20 minutes. (This is important; it's a *very* tender cake, so inverting too soon will cause it to quiver and crumble, like me when I didn't get a callback for the role of Éponine.)

9. Carefully invert the cake onto a cooling rack and, using a pastry brush or small spoon, saturate it with the reserved fruit macerating liquid until the cake feels damp to the touch but not soggy (you never want to see excess soak dripping from the bottom of the rack; use only as much as the cake can absorb). When the soaked cake has cooled to room temperature, slice it crosswise into two even rectangles—these are the two layers.

10. Using your widest spatula(s) and your hands, carefully transfer one of the two rectangles of soaked cake onto a serving platter. Top with the strawberry jam, spreading it almost to the edges and leaving about ¼ inch of border space. Spread half of the mascarpone whipped cream on top of the jam, then stack the second cake layer on top of that. Top the cake with the remaining mascarpone whipped cream and the reserved macerated strawberries, plus spoonfuls of their juices. Finish with a drizzle of oil to serve. (Store any leftovers tightly covered in the refrigerator for up to a week; they'll get even more insanely delicious as they sit.)

BROWN SUGAR PANNA COTTA WITH BUTTERMILK WHIPPED CREAM AND FIGS

LEVEL

Anyone can execute

TIME

15 minutes, plus 3+ hours to chill

MAKES

Dessert for 4

This is one of my fifty-nine favorite ways to use fresh in-season figs; it totally makes you look like you have your life together. (The other fifty-eight ways, which include mashing one into a dirty gin martini—try it!—and crushing them onto toast with warm almond butter and salt, unfortunately do not have the same effect.) You can use this panna cotta recipe for nearly any ripe fruit; skip the cardamom or swap in a complementary spice. If you'd like to add vanilla extract, or rum, or almond extract, do so off heat, after you've brought the milk and gelatin to a simmer, to avoid burning off the flavor.

1 cup (227 g) whole milk

½ cup (99 g) brown sugar

½ teaspoon ground cardamom or 1 teaspoon whole cardamom pods, lightly crushed

Scant ½ teaspoon Diamond Crystal kosher salt

One .25-ounce packet unflavored gelatin

2 cups (460 g) heavy whipping cream

Salted Whipped Cream (page 266, using the buttermilk variation described on page 265)

8 to 12 fresh figs, ripped or sliced lengthwise into quarters or halves (whatever you prefer)

⅓ cup port or Sauternes (I prefer Sauternes, but port is a more classic combination)

Olive oil, for drizzling

1. Set 4 deep coupes or drinking glasses or bowls, plus a fine-mesh sieve, beside your stovetop.

2. Combine the milk, brown sugar, cardamom, and salt in a small saucepan. Sprinkle the gelatin over the top. Let sit for about 5 minutes, until the gelatin swells and wrinkles. Set the saucepan over medium heat and whisk until you can see small bubbles sputtering around the edges of the milk and steam rising from the top. Add the cream and heat for another 2 minutes, stirring, until the mixture is warm to the touch but not boiling.

3. Pour the mixture through the fine-mesh sieve, dividing it equally into the prepared glasses. Cover each glass with plastic wrap and set in the refrigerator for about 3 hours (or, wrapped tightly, up to 4 days).

4. When you're ready to serve, make a batch of the whipped cream. In a small bowl, macerate the sliced figs in the port; toss roughly with a spoon or fork a few times after covering the figs, to encourage them to soak up the liquid.

5. Top each panna cotta with whipped cream, juicy figs, and a drizzle of oil.

ANGEL PIE

LEVEL

Some skill required

TIME

3 hours

MAKES

Pie for 6 to 8 (but, like, 1 or 2?)

This rambunctious, overflowing pie turns my siblings and me into feudal warlords, battling one another with fork tines in the days after any family holiday. My mother prepares it ostentatiously over a period of two days, the puffy crust on day one, and then—as the meringue sits on a sideboard in full view, taunting us—the curd and cream on day two. I've adapted it a bit to add more salt to both the curd and cream, but otherwise, it's pretty much her recipe, which was my great-grandmother's formula, so there's no mushroom powder bullshit here. Enjoy.

1 tablespoon butter, plus more for the pan

4 large eggs, separated, cold

½ teaspoon baking powder

Diamond Crystal kosher salt

2 tablespoons vanilla bean paste or extract (use the latter to keep it super white, or the former for more flavor)

½ teaspoon white vinegar

½ teaspoon plus ½ cup room-temperature water

1½ cups (300 g) plus 2 tablespoons granulated sugar

1 tablespoon all-purpose flour

Juice and zest of 2 lemons

2 cups (460 g) cold heavy cream

Grated bittersweet chocolate, for topping (optional)

1. Heat the oven to 275°F. Butter the sides and bottom of a 10-inch pie pan.

2. In a stand mixer fitted with the balloon whisk attachment, whip the egg whites on medium-high until soft peaks form (they'll turn into an opaque, soft cloud). Add the baking powder, ½ teaspoon of the salt, 1 tablespoon of the vanilla, the vinegar, and the ½ teaspoon room-temperature water and whip on high speed for about 2 minutes, until the mixture stiffens further. As the mixer runs, add 1 cup of the sugar, 1 tablespoon at a time, until the mixture is super glossy with firm peaks (meaning that if you remove the beater and flip it upside down, the evil meringue peak at the end doesn't slump over).

3. Transfer the meringue to the buttered pie pan and use an offset spatula or a silicone spatula to gently smooth the meringue into an even layer on the bottom and a slightly thicker layer on the sides and rim of the pie pan. (When it bakes and puffs, you want to leave room in the middle for the curd and whipped cream filling; it should bake into a pie shell, not fill the entire pan.) Bake for 2 hours, then turn off the oven and open the oven door. Let it completely cool, another hour (or up to 24 hours; you can transfer to a countertop to continue cooling, uncovered).

4. Prepare the lemon curd: In a small saucepan, whisk together the egg yolks, ½ cup of the sugar, the flour, the ½ cup water, ½ teaspoon of the salt, and the lemon juice and zest. Set the pan over medium-low heat and whisk constantly until the mixture comes to a simmer. (You can increase the temperature as needed.) Keep whisking, especially scraping the bottom and sides, until it thickens to the texture of a seedless jam and coats the back of a spoon without running off. Cut the heat.

5. Run the curd through a fine-mesh sieve into a medium bowl and fold in the butter. (Save the sweet pulpy stuff that gets caught in the sieve for toast or buttercream.) To avoid a skin on the surface of the curd, cover with a piece of plastic wrap touching the curd as it cools on the counter or in the refrigerator.

6. Make the whipped cream: Place the bowl and balloon whisk attachment of your stand mixer—or a regular bowl and a metal whisk, or beaters—in the freezer for 15 minutes. (Note: If you're pinched for time, don't worry about this.)

7. Add the cream to the bowl. Beat on medium speed for 1½ to 2 minutes, until the cream stops splattering. Add 1 tablespoon of the vanilla, 1 tablespoon of the sugar, and a pinch of salt. Continue to whip on medium-high until soft peaks form (when you pull out the beater or whisk and flip it, a floppy tail stays affixed even though it doesn't stand up stiff), 30 seconds to 1 minute.

8. When the pie shell is totally cool, add the cooled lemon curd and gently, with an offset spatula or silicone spatula or the back of a large spoon, smooth the curd across the bottom. Add a thick (up to the rim of the pie) layer of whipped cream and smooth it in the same way.

9. Decorate with the grated bittersweet chocolate (if using). Chill until you're ready to serve. Serve with any remaining whipped cream on the side.

20

Superlative Chocolate Chunk COOKIES

MISSION

The best chocolate chunk cookie that you've ever had the pleasure of baking, with a chewy, dense center and all of the classic flavor notes—toffee, nuttiness, vanilla—dialed up to an extreme.

WHAT I TESTED

Flavor and texture enhancements
Alternate flours • Chill level of dough
Baking temperature • Length of dough resting time

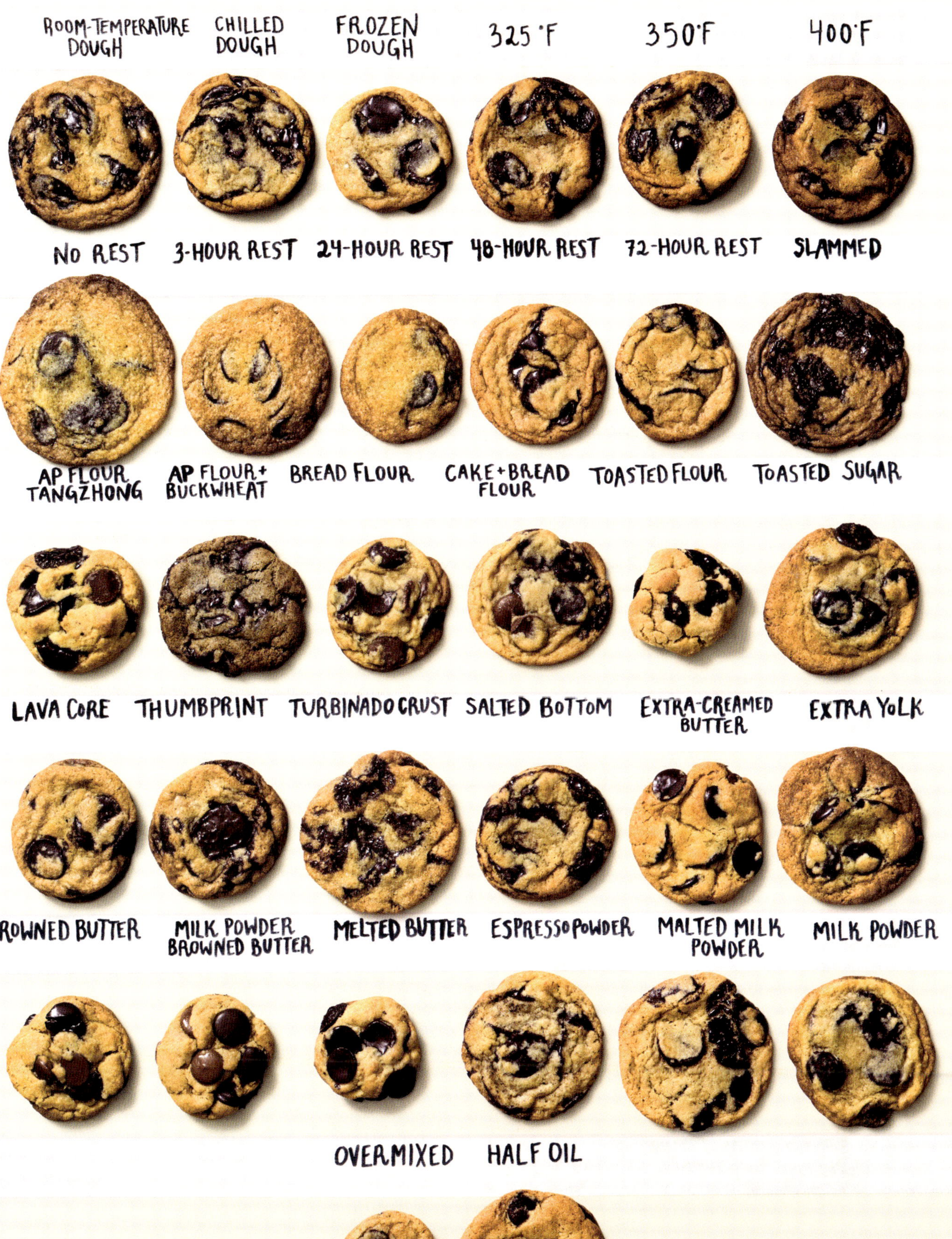

ROOM-TEMPERATURE DOUGH
CHILLED DOUGH
FROZEN DOUGH
325°F
350°F
400°F
NO REST
3-HOUR REST
24-HOUR REST
48-HOUR REST
72-HOUR REST
SLAMMED
AP FLOUR TANGZHONG
AP FLOUR + BUCKWHEAT
BREAD FLOUR
CAKE + BREAD FLOUR
TOASTED FLOUR
TOASTED SUGAR
LAVA CORE
THUMBPRINT
TURBINADO CRUST
SALTED BOTTOM
EXTRA-CREAMED BUTTER
EXTRA YOLK
BROWNED BUTTER
MILK POWDER BROWNED BUTTER
MELTED BUTTER
ESPRESSO POWDER
MALTED MILK POWDER
MILK POWDER
OVERMIXED
HALF OIL

THE CHOCOLATE CHIP COOKIE IS CHARTED TERRITORY.

The chocolate "chunk" cookie—which came into vogue more recently, but which has multiplied through society even more fervently, with its melty pools of chocolate shards or fèves—even more so. And yet I couldn't help myself. Maybe because when I get a new cookbook, the CCC is the first thing I flip to. I've baked through all the classics many times over: the Toll House recipe, the three-day Jacques Torres one[1] that taught many of us about aging dough, the Claire Saffitz brown butter ones,[2] the Stella Parks Levain Bakery[3] copycats, Dan Pelosi's chocolate chip cookie bars[4], the Natasha Pickowicz buckwheat ones,[5] and a dozen or so other recipes.

After many, many rounds of trying to deconstruct and remake a food that was originally revered for its simplicity, I landed somewhere layered with tips and tricks picked up from other bakers. I'll start with what I do not demand you do: I'm not going to make you toast the sugar, or the flour. Both techniques offered subtle nuance, but with all else going on in my dough, the extra effort isn't necessary. I do, however, ask you to add a bit of buckwheat flour, which offers a grit and warmth and nuttiness without needing to toast it first. I also ask you to brown your butter with extra milk powder (!!!). Milk powder is excellent when added directly to cookie batter, but when it's added to butter as the milk solids in butter are toasted—a trick I learned from Hetal Vasavada, aka @milkandcardamom[6]—milk powder completely jacks up the caramel-toffee notes to a five-alarm browned butter disco-rave. I also ask you to cream the butter and sugar for way longer than seems necessary. I learned about this trick from Carla Lalli Music, who wrote up a detailed description of Kelly Mencin's Radio Bakery cookie.[7] As Carla notes, this amount of creaming dissolves some or all of the sugar—like in a meringue—which contributes extra chewiness. It also cuts down on the amount of puffing followed by deflation in the oven, since you've already aerated the butter within an inch of its life, so these cookies aren't going to spread like tar. I'll instruct you to take some of the all-purpose flour and make it into a tangzhong, a technique best known for making milk bread pillow-soft; I cribbed this from King Arthur, whose test kitchen found that it contributes velvety softness to the cookie centers. (You can almost fold these in two without cracking!) I'm also going to suggest you slam your cookies on the countertop to further deflate them at the end of the bake, a sort of You-Can't-Prove-I-Made-These-Pantsless version of the well-known Sarah Kieffer trick for wrinkly, dense cookies.

I also have you employ a tip I learned years ago from Stella Parks, which is nominally to make the cookies perfectly round, but which I discovered actually makes them chunkier and more consistently chewy around the edges. As I tested through dozens of tweaks, I realized that we all seem to define "chewy cookies" differently; to me, chewiness requires a certain degree of density, so when you bite through the cookie, you leave a clean set of tooth marks in the (ideally underbaked) dense-but-tender crumb. To that end, I discarded bread flour, which added extra protein (and therefore chew), but which also contributed a breadiness that took away from the density.

And last, I'll ask you to age the dough as much as you can bear it for more flavor, then bake these from frozen to reduce spread and keep them chunky. I pull them from the oven while the middles are still molten; you can always bake them a little more, but you can't turn a medium-well cookie into one I'd pen a strange little ballad for, off the cuff, while I had a hundred other more important things to do.

As far as chocolate, I suggest a combination of milk and dark, and also Crunch bars (or anything similar; most fancy chocolate bar brands have one with quinoa or puffed rice you could use) to complement the grit of the buckwheat.

I also developed a recipe for the times when you need a deeply flavored, gooey CCC ASAP (not hours or days after the craving strikes); for that, on page 294, I turn to malted milk powder and the bar shape for chewiness, deeper flavor, and extra browning, and to contain spread.

THE BEST METHODS

FOR OVER-ACHIEVING BROWN BUTTER BAKERY-WORTHY CCCS: Cream the butter and sugar forever, add multiple types and textures of chocolate AND buckwheat, brown the butter with milk powder, and add a tangzhong for plush chew, as on page 290.

FOR INSTANT PERFECT GOOEY MALTED COOKIE DOUGH CHOCOLATE CHUNK BARS: Heed the recipe on page 294.

FOR COSMIC EXTRA-CHOCOLATEY CCCS: See page 296.

MOTHER RECIPE

OVERACHIEVER EXTRA-BROWNED BUTTER BAKERY-WORTHY CCCs

LEVEL

A bit of skill required

TIME

1 hour, plus 6 hours rest (or up to 3 days)

MAKES

Roughly 25 medium-large cookies (or more smaller ones)

If you're looking for a quick fix, go to page 294 and bake a tray of my Gooey Malted Cookie Dough Chocolate Chunk Bars. But if you're here because you've already mastered Toll House chocolate chips, and those Jacques Torres ones with the bread flour and the cake flour, and my all-time favorites, the Natasha Pickowicz cookies with the toasted (!) flour in their dough, then, welcome. After many, many rounds of trying to deconstruct and remake a food that was originally revered for its simplicity, here is where I've landed. I'm not going to make you toast the sugar or flour. But I am going to ask you to add some buckwheat flour. I'll also have you brown your butter and boost it with a good dose of milk powder. You'll need to cream the butter and sugar for much longer than you think is reasonable, and turn a portion of your all-purpose flour into a tangzhong. I'll also recommend a trick I picked up from Stella Parks—it's meant to help shape perfectly round cookies, but I've found it also makes them thicker and chewier. For the chocolate, go with a mix of milk and dark, plus some Crunch bars (or any puffed rice or quinoa chocolate bar) to echo the texture of the buckwheat. And finally, pull the cookies from the oven while the centers are still molten.

BRINGING BROWNED BUTTER BACK TO ROOM TEMPERATURE

There are three ways to do this.

- As I note in the recipe that follows, you can brown the butter, stick it in the freezer, and mix it every 10 minutes or so, until it starts to go solid—then transfer it to the fridge to finish firming up, and finally let it sit on the counter for a few minutes.
- If you have a surplus of ice (I'm sad to say I never do, since I don't have an ice maker), you could also make an ice bath in a large bowl and dunk the saucepan right in that and whisk for a minute or two until the butter comes back to solid-soft form. This is by far the quickest method.
- Or, if you have foresight (ugh, what's it like???), you can brown the butter well in advance and leave it covered in the refrigerator. Pull it out 45 minutes before you're ready to bake.

1 cup (2 sticks/225 g) unsalted butter, cut into tablespoons

3 tablespoons milk powder

Heaping 1⅓ cups (200 g) plus ¼ cup (36 g) all-purpose flour

⅓ cup (50 g) buckwheat flour

¾ teaspoon baking powder

¾ teaspoon baking soda

1½ teaspoons Diamond Crystal kosher salt

¾ cup plus 1 tablespoon (163 g) granulated sugar

¾ cup (149 g) packed light brown sugar

2 large eggs, at room temperature

3 tablespoons (about 42 g) whole milk

1 tablespoon vanilla bean paste or vanilla extract

10 ounces mix of milk chocolate, dark chocolate, and Crunch bars, chopped into chunks of various sizes

Flaky salt or pretzel salt

1. About an hour before you're ready to bake, melt the butter in a small saucepan over medium heat. When it comes to a sizzle, add the milk powder. Whisk. When the foam recedes and the butter solids turn a deep caramel, scrape the browned butter into a container, including all the solids, and put in the freezer to bring it to room temperature, stirring every 10 minutes as it cools for an even texture. (No need to rinse the saucepan; you'll use it again.) When the butter starts to turn solid, let it finish firming up in the fridge, then set it on the counter until it is softened and a finger poke leaves an indent. (If you're a temp guy: about 65° to 68°F.)

2. Meanwhile, in a medium bowl, whisk together the heaping 1⅓ cups (200 g) all-purpose flour, the buckwheat flour, baking powder, baking soda, and salt.

3. When the browned butter is back to soft-solid form, add it to the bowl of a stand mixer fitted with the paddle attachment. Add the granulated and brown sugars and beat on medium speed, stopping to scrape down the sides, for about 10 minutes, until super fluffy, pale tan, and more like the batter of a sponge cake than butter. Pinch some of the mixture between your fingers—it's ready once most of the sugar is dissolved, leaving a texture more like pepper straight from the mill than the crushed glass of fresh sugar. Turn the mixer to low. Add the eggs one at a time, scraping down between each, and mix until incorporated.

4. In the dirtied saucepan, whisk together the milk with the remaining ¼ cup (36 g) all-purpose flour. Place over low heat and whisk just for a minute or so, until the flour absorbs the milk and the mixture becomes a thick, gluey paste. Remove from the heat and immediately add to the creamed butter and sugar as you run the mixer on medium speed. Scrape down the sides of the bowl, then run the mixer on medium and add the vanilla. Add the dry ingredients in two additions, including the chocolate with the second addition, mixing just to combine.

5. Cover the dough and let it rest in the refrigerator for at least 6 hours, and up to 72 hours. The longer you rest, the better they'll be. (I have, in a pinch, baked these immediately, and they're still incredible, but be sure to freeze the dough balls for at least 30 minutes before baking; otherwise they'll spread into a mess.)

6. When you're ready to bake, line two sheet pans or cookie sheets with parchment paper. Roll or scoop roughly 2 large tablespoons (40 g) of dough into balls and set 6 on each of the prepared pans, giving them several inches of clearance on all sides. Pop them into the freezer on their pans for 25 minutes. Heat the oven to 350°F.

7. Bake for about 13 minutes, until the tops look set with a walnut-colored rim around the edges. Pull from the oven 2 minutes before you think you should and slam each pan of soft, hot cookies flat on the countertop a few times to deflate the centers. While the cookies are still hot, take a quart container or jar and flip it over to use the inside of the top rim as a mold to reshape cookies while hot—place it over each cookie, one at a time, while holding the pan steady with your oven-mitted hand and vigorously move the jar in a circle around the hot cookie to round its edges and pull them inward, making each cookie thicker and chunkier as its shape becomes a perfect circle. Return the pans to the oven for about 1 minute, then remove.

8. Sprinkle the tops of the cookies with flaky salt or pretzel salt. Let them cool for about 10 minutes. Repeat steps 5 and 6 to bake the rest of the dough.

GOOEY MALTED COOKIE DOUGH CHOCOLATE CHUNK BARS

LEVEL

Anyone can execute

TIME

45 minutes

MAKES

8 to 16 cookie bars (depending how small you slice them)

These are designed to have the texture of the center of an underbaked chocolate chunk cookie. Because there are moments that are worthy of the type of dough that requires three days to develop an optimal flavor and texture. But most moments are not those moments. Most moments call for melty cookies ASAP. Consider this recipe my apology for the fastidious one on page 290. No rest? No problem. The malted milk powder adds a ton of chew and bolsters the flavor in this dough, since it doesn't age before you bake it (though you totally can age it up to 72 hours before baking for an even more over-the-top cookie bar; just bring to room temp before baking for an even rise). And baking these in a square pan like brownies, then cutting them into squares, means spreading is less of a concern than it would be with balls of cookie dough. I buy Carnation brand malted milk powder online.

1½ cups plus 1 tablespoon (220 g) all-purpose flour

¾ cup (120 g) malted milk powder

1 teaspoon baking powder

1 teaspoon Diamond Crystal kosher salt

¾ cup (1½ sticks/170 g) unsalted butter, at room temperature

⅔ cup (132 g) light brown sugar

½ cup plus 1 tablespoon (113 g) granulated sugar

2 large eggs (110 g), at room temperature

1 tablespoon vanilla bean paste or extract

10 ounces roughly chopped chocolate, dark and milk

Flaky salt

1. Line a 9 × 9-inch pan with parchment paper. Heat the oven to 350°F.

2. In a medium bowl, whisk together the flour, malted milk powder, baking powder, and kosher salt.

3. In the bowl of a stand mixer fitted with the paddle attachment, cream the butter and both sugars on medium speed for about 10 minutes, until extremely pale and fluffy and doubled in volume, occasionally scraping down the sides. (When it's ready, it will look like that cake batter that gets smoothed into a pan in *The Great British Bake Off* opening credits, swoopy and aerated.)

4. While the mixer runs on low, add the eggs one at a time, mixing until incorporated, then add the vanilla. Scrape down the sides. Add the dry ingredients in two additions, including the chocolate with the second addition. Mix on low just until combined. Transfer the batter to the pan and use an offset spatula to roughly smooth the top. Sprinkle with flaky salt.

5. Bake for 26 to 28 minutes, until the dough is golden on top in the center and maple-colored around the edges, with a quaking core that still leaves wet residue when a toothpick is inserted into the center. (These are supposed to be very gooey in the center.)

6. Let cool in the refrigerator or freezer until cold to the touch. This is necessary to slice these cleanly, since they're molten when you take them out of the oven. Slice into bars and serve at room temperature for a super soft, doughy texture, or cold for more of a blondie texture. (If you prefer, you can serve these as a scooped dessert along the textural lines of sticky toffee pudding right out of the oven.)

CHOCOLATE CHUNK THUMBPRINT COOKIES

LEVEL

A bit of skill required

TIME

1 hour, plus 6 hours rest (or up to 3 days rest)

MAKES

Roughly 25 medium-large cookies (or more smaller ones)

I experimented with a number of methods to guarantee gooey puddles in the center of each cookie, including one trial in which I stuffed a cookie dough ball with chocolate chips for a lava cake–like effect. That . . . didn't pan out. But ultimately, the best method I came up with—pressing a "thumbprint" indentation into the center of the just-baked cookies while warm and filling it with ganache—also had a second benefit: It guaranteed a dense, chewy center, from both the compression and the puddle of filling. Sometimes I add a little jam, too, though even just the chocolate puddle is a revelation. The cookies are a little cosmic-looking, which is fitting.

1 batch cookie dough from the Overachiever Extra-Browned Butter Bakery-Worthy CCCs (page 290), rested per the directions

Neutral oil

4 ounces dark chocolate, finely chopped

2 tablespoons unsalted butter

¼ teaspoon Diamond Crystal kosher salt

3 tablespoons raspberry jam (I use seeded but you may prefer to use seedless; optional)

Flaky salt

1. When you're ready to bake the cookies, line two sheet pans or cookie sheets with parchment paper. Roll or scoop roughly 2 large tablespoons (40 g) of dough into balls and set 6 on each of the prepared pans, giving them several inches of clearance on all sides. Pop them into the freezer on their pans for 25 minutes. Heat the oven to 350°F.

2. Spray or rub a circular 1 teaspoon measuring spoon with oil on its underside. (If you don't have one, use your thumb! Wash and oil that.)

3. Make a quick cheaters' ganache: In the microwave or over a double boiler, melt the chocolate with the butter and kosher salt. Mix until completely combined. Keep covered until you use, to keep it molten; you can reheat it the same way you made it, as needed.

4. Bake the cookies for about 12 minutes, until they look puffed and are just beginning to set. Remove from the oven and press the oiled 1 teaspoon measuring spoon firmly into the center (or near-center if there's a chocolate shard in your way) of each cookie, to make a circular indent. Return the cookies to the oven for 1 to 2 minutes more, until the tops look set with a walnut-colored rim around the edges. Remove from the oven and press the 1 teaspoon measuring spoon back into the indents one more time to tamp down any puffiness.

5. Pour the ganache into each indent just to fill it and top with about ¼ teaspoon jam (if using) and a sprinkle of flaky salt. (You can also do jam on one side of the indent and ganache on the other, with salt in the middle.)

6. Let cool for 10 to 15 minutes. Repeat with the rest of the dough.

21

Quivering, Luxurious YELLOW CAKE

MISSION

Yellow cake with a plush crumb and a rich, deep flavor.

WHAT I TESTED

Types of sponge • Creaming method
Leavener • Types of fat • Flavor enhancements

MY MOTHER KNOWS WHAT SHE LIKES.

Like the long line of Wolverton women before her—who all lived in a tiny town in the Appalachian mountains that flooded so badly each year they were forced to pick up and leave for several weeks and then rebuild their lives in the spring—she moves through this world with conviction. When she loves something, she will describe it breathlessly and evangelize its merits broadly. Her friend Joan made her a dish of roasted chicken thighs with olives and lemon wedges in roughly 1992, and to this day my mother makes a batch of what she calls "Joan Chicken" at least once weekly, even though Joan purports to have no memory of this meal. When she dislikes something, you will never hear from her again.

So when I sent her my final yellow cake recipe by email and asked for her thoughts, and didn't hear from her for five days, I assumed I would have to start the recipe from scratch without ever actually having a conversation about it. (You may be familiar, already, with the concept of epigenetics: "When caterpillars attack radish plants, they produce chemicals and grow spines to protect themselves. The offspring of these plants also produce these defenses, even if they live in an environment without caterpillars."[1])

I knew that my mother didn't dislike yellow cake in principle, so the problem had to be my version, with its quaking crumb and fussy brown butter French buttercream. Over the past three decades, I had known her to cycle between two different no-nonsense yellow cake recipes—the white wine cake in *The New Basics* and another one made with mashed bananas—with as much dedication as someone might summon for early-morning church. Neither required her to purchase an uncoated aluminum pan for rise. In fact, my mother is so devoted to these no-nonsense recipes that she once confessed to me that there's a yellow cake out there called "The

Lady Baltimore" that she's always fantasized about but never allowed herself to make, since it would require a diversion from her faithfuls. But she thinks about it every day (she spent twenty-two minutes describing it). She then spent another nine minutes describing one potential use case: a Lady Baltimore molded into the shape of a lamb and piped with white meringue to resemble a fluffy coat of wool.

"Why did you hate my cake recipe?" I asked, phoning her out of the blue—a sneak attack. She paused. "I loved it," she said. "It's by far the best yellow cake I ever baked. It was airy as clouds." It wasn't until she sent me a photo that I realized why she'd been cagey.

"What's that bumpy frosting?" I asked. It was a stark white and piped to look like lamb's wool. "It's yours!" she lied. "Prove it," I said. I'm still waiting for a reply.

Anyone who loves to eat eventually falls in love with yellow cake in some format, because when done well, it's an idyllic canvas for creamy frosting, for fruit, for whipped cream, for custards, for jam. It is a fantastical springboard, a flavor and topping chameleon. It can be a visual delight, with beds of plush crumb swaddled by silky buttercream and glossy jam, a three-dimensional centerfold. It has none of the weird has-been energy of cupcakes. For many, it is sentimental, a reminder of birthdays and Safeway sheet cakes decorated with rosettes.

Here I focused on styles of yellow cake commonly found in American bakeries, though it's worth noting that the global tome of yellow cakes is thick.

There is a time and a place for every style of yellow cake, just as there is an occasion for every type of sleeve, hem, and length on an LBD. The most versatile combination across my trials was a medley of flavor additions and batter that got some lift from a whipped egg white meringue. Too light a sponge and the cake lacked the rich flavor I craved and buckled under substantial amounts of frosting (the correct amount of frosting). No sponge and the cake turned dense and satisfied my cravings for only a few bites.

While I ultimately didn't incorporate the reverse creaming method into my final Mother Recipe on page 304, which rises fairly evenly on its own, the technique of coating the flour in butter early on to inhibit gluten formation is a neat one I'd recommend trying; if you're curious, seek out the Rose Levy Beranbaum recipe in her cookbook *The Cake Bible*.[2] Aerating the cake with whipped cream was another fascinating foray into a unique crumb, one that was plush and dense with flavor.[3] I skipped the whipped cream in my Mother Recipe in favor of a slightly lighter, more tender crumb from egg whites, but I loved the trick so much that I incorporated it into my Strawberries-Three-Ways Cake recipe on page 280.

More Detail (I could talk about cake for sixteen hours without a break):

- Sugar makes baked foods tender—it holds on to water. (To see this for yourself, make a cake recipe with half the sugar; it'll be drier and taller, and less delicious, of course.)
- Fat is so important for flavor, and also for the crumb. It aids sugar in tenderizing the cake by coating the flour, which inhibits gluten formation, i.e. makes it so your cake doesn't

turn into a tough dough or bread. Oil does lend cake a moist quality, since it isn't solid at room temperature, but I can't quit butter in a yellow cake for the flavor.

- I balanced my butter with buttermilk for an extremely tender and tangy result. I chose buttermilk over something like sour cream or crème fraîche because higher water content means it produces a bit more steam in the oven, which contributes to the rise. Melting the butter results in a slightly denser cake, which I was okay with since it gets lift from the egg white, and you aren't beating multiple elements over and over until you give up.
- Tipped off by Natasha Pickowicz in *More Than Cake*, I observed that under-whipping the egg white meringue for sponge batter is far more fruitful than over-whipping it. If you let your meringue get too stiff, it becomes difficult to fold it into the rest of the batter, and you'll end up deflating it as you smash against the lumps, trying to smooth them.
- Let's talk about *wine*!!!! It sounds wild! I know! But actually, there's a whole canon of American cake recipes called "wine cakes," which mostly combine white wine with boxed mix. It makes a ton of sense; there are, after all, lots of liquor-laden cakes out there in the world, from juicy-perfect rum cakes to the Spanish torta envinada. In this one, most of the alcohol flavor bakes away, and you're left with a complex fruitiness that helps to cut through the sweetness and add extra nuance to what can be, in its most boring form, flavorless.

THE BEST METHOD

FOR FLUFFY TENDER CAKE: Fold in whipped egg whites; use melted butter, buttermilk, and white wine (!!!) for tenderness and flavor.

ANGEL FOOD

BISCUIT

AMERICAN
(CAKE FLOUR, MILK)

AMERICAN
(CAKE FLOUR, BUTTERMIL

AMERICAN
(AP FLOUR, WINE)

REVERSE-CREAM

GENOISE

CHIFFON

AMERICAN
(AP FLOUR, MILK)

AMERICAN
(CAKE FLOUR, WINE)

WHIPPED CREAM-
AERATED

POUND

MOTHER RECIPE

SOFT AND TENDER YELLOW CAKE

LEVEL

A bit of skill required

TIME

1 hour

MAKES

Two 8-inch layers

Thirty-seven slices of yellow layer cake into my trials, it became clear that an ideal recipe would combine the rich flavors of a classic butter batter with the pillowy-velvet crumb of a chiffon cake. It would also need to be as wet as possible, so it didn't dry out after a few minutes of air exposure. So I combined elements of several battle-tested recipes, with a whipped egg white meringue helping the baking powder to inflate each cake to roughly twice its batter-volume in the oven (leaving the uncoated aluminum pan ungreased is key for this), melted butter for a pancake-like crumb, and buttermilk for tang. Then I borrowed an old trick from The New Basics, *and added dry white wine for even more flavor and moisture. It sounds wild! I know! The result is a cake so soft that it quivers when you lift a slice out; I'd wear a coat made of it in the winter. It's perfect with the Dark Chocolate Pretzel Buttercream on page 324, or the chocolate variation of the French-ish buttercream on page 320. My little sister, Clem, likes to put a layer of raspberry jam in between the layers before adding frosting, and that's just one reason I think she's a genius. You'll need regular aluminum cake pans that do not have a nonstick coating for this cake. If you're not sure, buy inexpensive unlined aluminum pans; otherwise you'll end up with a dense and underwhelming crumb.*

5 large eggs, separated, at room temperature

1 tablespoon vanilla bean paste or extract

1 cup (230 g) dry white wine

½ cup (130 g) buttermilk, at room temperature

2 cups (400 g) granulated sugar

2½ cups (300 g) cake flour

2½ teaspoons baking powder

1¾ teaspoons Diamond Crystal kosher salt

1 cup (2 sticks/225 g) unsalted butter, melted and cooled so it's not hot to the touch

Frosting of your choice

1. Set an oven rack in the middle position and heat the oven to 375°F. Grab two deep 8-inch aluminum cake pans (make sure they are not coated). Cut out rounds of parchment the size of the pans: Put a sheet of parchment on a cutting board, place the pan on top, and with a sharp knife slice around it like a stencil to make a perfect circle. Set the parchment circles in the pans but don't butter or spray the pans or the parchment paper; this type of batter likes to use the sides of the pan to climb.

2. In a medium bowl, whisk together the egg yolks, vanilla, wine, buttermilk, and 1½ cups (300 g) of the granulated sugar until homogeneous and slightly thick, like pulpy orange juice. Set aside.

3. In the bowl of a stand mixer fitted with the balloon whisk attachment, whip the egg whites on medium-high speed to soft peaks, meaning opaque and fluffy; if you lift out the whisk attachment, it'll bring with it a soft swoopy mountain on its tip. Keep beating as you add the remaining ½ cup (100 g) sugar 1 tablespoon at a time. Beat on medium-high just until shiny with medium-stiff peaks, meaning if you remove the beater and flip it upside down, the evil meringue peak at the end softly slumps over. Don't beat any more! It's critical for this batter that you don't use super firm meringue, which will create lumps of egg whites when you fold it in, and in trying to smooth them all, you will deflate them and end up with a rubbery cake. Sad! So: Stop the mixer at medium-stiff slumpy peaks.

4. In a large bowl, whisk the flour, baking powder, and salt. Make a well in the center. Add the wine mixture and whisk until mostly incorporated. Add the melted butter and whisk just until smooth.

5. Use a silicone spatula to gently and completely fold about one-quarter of the meringue mixture into the batter. Fold in the rest of the meringue until there are just a few errant streaks of white. (Better to very slightly under-mix than over-mix.). Transfer half of the batter to each prepared pan.

6. Lower the heat to 350°F. Set the cake pans on the middle rack and bake for 30 to 33 minutes, until the cakes are golden around the edges and the centers feel softly firm when poked (though a bit spongy).

7. Carefully set a piece of parchment paper and a cooling rack on top of the pans and then flip them onto it, so they can cool upside down on the parchment-lined rack (to retain their fluff). Cool for about 45 minutes, then run an offset spatula or sharp knife around the edges. Invert and cool the rest of the way before frosting and serving.

SOFT AND TENDER
YELLOW CAKE, PAGE 304

DOUBLE-CRUMB COFFEE CAKE, PAGE 308

DOUBLE-CRUMB COFFEE CAKE

LEVEL

Anyone can execute

TIME

1 hour

MAKES

Cake for 8

The only thing better than a soft, flavorful yellow cake is a soft, flavorful yellow cake with a crumb topping. And the only thing better than that is a soft, flavorful yellow cake with twice as much crumb topping as your standard coffee cake. So . . . this is the same as the cake recipe on page 304, with a double layer of chunky crumb. Save me a slice? (If you don't love crumb topping as much as I do, only use about half of it; save the rest and sprinkle it on your cereal.)

FOR THE CRUMB

⅓ cup (40 g) almond flour

⅔ cup (95 g) all-purpose flour

½ cup (99 g) packed dark or light brown sugar

2 teaspoons cinnamon

¾ teaspoon Diamond Crystal kosher salt

⅓ cup (76 g) unsalted butter, cold and cut into ½-tablespoon cubes

FOR THE CAKE

3 large eggs, separated, at room temperature

2 teaspoons vanilla bean paste or extract

½ cup (115 g) dry white wine, like pinot grigio

¼ cup (62 g) buttermilk

1 cup (200 g) granulated sugar

1¼ cups (150 g) cake flour

1¼ teaspoons baking powder

1 teaspoon Diamond Crystal kosher salt

½ cup (1 stick/113 g) unsalted butter, melted and cooled so it's not hot to the touch

1. Make the crumb topping: In a medium bowl, whisk together the almond flour, all-purpose flour, brown sugar, cinnamon, and salt. Add the butter cubes and use your hands—or a fork or potato masher—to integrate them into the dry ingredients until you have consistent-ish pebbles of crumble in varying sizes. (If you pinch one, it should have a smooth interior like sugar cookie dough, versus a lump of butter coated in powder; if you see the latter, keep going.) Chill in the refrigerator until you're ready to use.

2. Set a rack in the middle position and heat the oven to 375° F. Grab a 9-inch uncoated aluminum springform pan (nonstick pans will cause the cake not to rise). Line only the bottom of the springform pan with parchment paper. (Don't butter or spray the pans or the parchment paper; this type of batter uses the sides of the pan to climb.)

3. In a medium bowl, whisk together the egg yolks, vanilla, wine, buttermilk, and ¾ cup (150 g) of the granulated sugar until homogeneous and slightly thick, like pulpy orange juice. Set aside.

4. In the bowl of a stand mixer fitted with the balloon whisk attachment, whip the egg whites on medium-high to soft peaks, meaning opaque and fluffy; if you lift out the whisk attachment, it'll bring with it a soft swoopy mountain on its tip. Keep beating as you add the remaining ¼ cup (50 g) sugar 1 tablespoon at a time. Beat on medium-high just until shiny, with medium-stiff peaks, meaning if you remove the beater and flip it upside down, the evil meringue peak at the end softly slumps over. Don't beat any more! It's critical for this batter that you don't use super firm meringue, which will create lumps of egg whites when you fold it in, and in trying to smooth them all, you will deflate them and end up with a rubbery cake. Sad! So: Stop the mixer at medium-stiff slumpy peaks.

5. In a large bowl, whisk the flour, baking powder, and salt. Make a well in the center. Add the wine mixture and whisk until mostly incorporated. Add the melted butter and whisk just until smooth.

6. Use a silicone spatula to gently and completely fold in about one-quarter of the meringue mixture to the batter. Fold in the rest of the meringue, smoothing out lumps with your spatula. When you see just a few streaks of white, transfer the batter to the prepared pan.

7. Lower the heat to 350°F. Set the pan on the middle rack and bake for about 20 minutes, until the cake has puffed up and begun to set across the top. Carefully sprinkle the crumb mixture across the middle of the cake, leaving about a 1-inch perimeter around the sides. Bake for another 12 to 15 minutes, until the edges of the cake are golden and pulling away from the pan. (The center, where you added the crumb, will compress a lot, but that's okay—it makes for a deliciously dense center with a delightfully puffy rim.)

8. Let cool for about 25 minutes, then run an offset spatula or knife around the edges. Release from the springform pan and serve. (You can make it up to a day in advance and let it sit loosely covered at room temperature.)

SOFT AND TENDER CUPCAKES

LEVEL

Anyone can execute

TIME

1 hour

MAKES

24 cupcakes

It's no longer the year 2010, but the need for a perfect go-to cupcake in one's baking arsenal endures. This one offers endless flexibility—add 2 teaspoons of coconut extract and frost it with the Brown Butter French-ish Buttercream on page 321 and roll the tops in toasted coconut flakes; pipe in vanilla bean whipped cream and call these Twinkie cupcakes. But the recipe is also fabulous in any interation, pillowy with just enough structure to support a mound of any of the buttercreams that follow.

5 large eggs, separated, at room temperature

1 tablespoon vanilla bean paste or extract

1 cup (230 g) dry white wine, like pinot grigio

½ cup (130 g) buttermilk

2 cups (400 g) granulated sugar

2½ cups (300 g) cake flour

2½ teaspoons baking powder

1¾ teaspoons Diamond Crystal kosher salt

1 cup (2 sticks/225 g) unsalted butter, melted and cooled so it's not hot to the touch

Frosting and/or accompaniments of your choice

NOTE: *If the muffin tins have a nonstick coating, you'll need to prepare them to allow the batter to climb the edges: Use a brush or a butter wrapper to grease each with melted butter, swiping in an upward motion. Next, add a spoonful of granulated sugar to each and tap until the entire inside of each well is coated. Tap out any excess.*

1. Set an oven rack in the middle position and heat the oven to 375°F. Grab two uncoated aluminum 12-muffin tins and lay roughly circular rounds of parchment paper in the bottoms. (Leave the sides unlined and ungreased.)

2. In a medium bowl, whisk together the egg yolks, vanilla, wine, buttermilk, and 1½ cups (300 g) of the granulated sugar until homogeneous and slightly thick, like pulpy orange juice. Set aside.

3. In the bowl of a stand mixer fitted with the balloon whisk attachment (or in a bowl with a hand mixer), whip the egg whites on medium-high speed to soft peaks, meaning opaque and fluffy. Keep beating as you add the remaining ½ cup (100 g) sugar 1 tablespoon at a time. Beat on medium-high just until shiny, with medium-stiff peaks, meaning if you remove the beater and flip it upside down, the evil meringue peak at the end softly slumps over. Don't beat any more! It's critical for this batter that you don't use super firm meringue, which will create lumps when you fold it in, and in trying to smooth them all, you will deflate them and end up with rubbery cake. Sad! So: Stop the mixer at medium-stiff slumpy peaks.

4. In a large bowl, whisk the flour, baking powder, and salt. Make a well in the center. Add the wine mixture and whisk until mostly incorporated. Add the melted butter and whisk just until smooth.

5. Use a silicone spatula to gently and completely fold in about one-quarter of the meringue mixture to the batter. Fold in the rest of the meringue. When you see just a few thin streaks of white, split the batter among the wells in the prepared muffin tins.

6. Lower the heat to 350°F. Bake on the middle rack for 15 to 17 minutes, until the cupcakes are golden around the edges and the centers feel spongey.

7. Let the cupcakes cool for about 30 minutes, then run an offset spatula or knife around the edges of each (if your cupcakes have risen well above their molds, use an offset spatula to gently scoot by the cupcake tops to get to the sides). Carefully invert onto a rack, then flip the cupcakes to cool the rest of the way right side up. Frost as desired.

22

Fantasy-Inducing BUTTERCREAM

MISSION

Buttercream that externalizes all that is fantasy-inducing about the category: glossy lightness, balanced buttery sweetness, an ability to be piped or sculpted into towering mounds

WHAT I TESTED

Composition • Preparation
Tweaks for stabilization and flavor

I HAVE THIS THEORY THAT EVERYONE IS EITHER A CAKE PERSON OR A FROSTING PERSON.

Cake people prefer fluffy cookies to dense, underbaked ones. If presented with a bowl of pasta, a cake person would prefer the noodles to the sauce. Frosting people live for gooey centers and extra ragu. We ask for a side of marinara, so we can dip our pizza. We want all the toppings on our sundaes, and we ask for our salad dressing to be applied with a heavy hand. And while almost any cake garnish holds our interest, buttercream is in a class of its own. I imagine I feel about glossy, flavorful buttercream the way a dog feels about cubes of cheese. At a dinner party or a bakery, I am inappropriately focused on the way light glints off a buttercream's curves.

All buttercream is good buttercream. But a few buttercreams were elite, both in mouthfeel and in ability to cradle deep flavor. Almost immediately I noticed that I preferred a meringue- or pudding-style buttercream (like Italian, Swiss, French, Korean, German, or Ermine) to an American-style; those allowed for less sweetness, since body and stability came mainly from butter, egg whites (in most cases), and a simple syrup versus raw sugar whipped with butter to provide structure (which required more sugar). It also meant that the sweetener had been dissolved before whipping, for a more supple mouthfeel.

I zeroed in on French buttercream, which to me was the best conduit for flavor, with its rich yolk or yolk-and-whites base. Even without any additions, it tasted like whipped custard, and when seasoned with salt, it sang. With the addition of Dutch-process cocoa powder, French buttercream turned into something I couldn't stop piping directly into my mouth, and when made with browned butter, it tasted like it could prop up an entire chain of bakeries. I added egg white to my version, for extra volume and stability on a cake. (Some traditional French buttercreams use only the yolks, though using whole eggs or a combination of yolks and whites certainly isn't unheard of.) I also employ a method of streaming sugar syrup into the eggs rather than heating them before whipping, to avoid pulpy overcooked yolk bits.

AMERICAN
CREAM CHEESE
GERMAN
ITALIAN
MELTED CREAM CHEESE
FRENCH
FRENCH (+GELATIN)

SWISS

AMERICAN (SIFTED)

PUDDING

AMERICAN (MILK)

KOREAN

RUSSIAN

SATIN

Other Findings

- I like to use French buttercream as my base for a colorful frosting (pink from blended dehydrated strawberries, or violet from blended dehydrated blueberries, for example), though I don't make hyper-realistic cakes that need to be a perfectly accurate shade. If you do, you probably have another book for that! But if not, my two cents is to use a starkly white buttercream as your base, like Swiss or Italian, to avoid the yellow tint from the yolks.
- When prepared properly, piped French buttercream will keep its shape very well, but as with any meringue-based frosting, you'll need to keep it chilled and let it come to room temperature before serving for optimal mouthfeel. (If you expose it to heat, fine piping will soften, slump, then melt.)
- I know this is heresy, but I . . . don't prefer American-style buttercream. I would still happily eat a bowl of it, but when tasted alongside meringue-based buttercreams, or cream cheese frosting, or even whipped cream fortified with extra ingredients, I found it cloying and a little grainy. I tested about twenty ways to troubleshoot those qualities, including dissolving sugar in cream or butter first, and using corn syrup, and condensed milk (as with Russian buttercream)—but the resulting frostings were always fussy. They curdled too easily, or melted too easily, or required you to take out a double boiler. And American buttercream should be easy! That's its biggest asset: You can whip together butter and confectioners' sugar in 5 minutes, frost a cake, and be done with it. I don't want to leave you in the lurch if you're in need of something super quick, or if the denser texture of American buttercream is your favorite, so I offer my go-to super-simple formula on page 323. No tricks or hacks, just sweet, salty, thick frosting in moments. I use a little more than half as much sugar as many other recipes call for, and if you like your frosting sweeter than this, you can certainly increase the amount up to 6 cups of confectioners' sugar. Of the other classic American variations I tried, my favorite version of American buttercream included cream cheese (whipped first to avoid clumps) or another tangy element to offset the sweetness of the classic formula.
- And, finally, a sleeper hit: The "Satin" method on page 324 comes from a recipe in *Joy of Cooking,* and it could not have a higher payoff for so little effort. All it requires is a bit of melting and then whirring in the food processor to produce a dense, ganache-like chocolate buttercream.

THE BEST METHODS

FOR BUTTERCREAM YOU WON'T BE ABLE TO STOP THINKING ABOUT: Employ a French-ish style, as on page 319.

FOR PRACTICALLY INSTANT, EASY FROSTING: Make American buttercream, on page 323.

FOR A SLEEPER HIT: Try satin buttercream, on page 324.

ACTUALLY MANAGEABLE FRENCH-ISH BUTTERCREAM, PAGE 319

FRUITY FRENCH-ISH BUTTERCREAM, PAGE 320

CHOCOLATE BROWN BUTTER FRENCH-ISH BUTTERCREAM, PAGE 322

SALTY-MILK AMERICAN BUTTERCREAM, PAGE 323

MOTHER RECIPE

ACTUALLY MANAGEABLE FRENCH-ISH BUTTERCREAM

LEVEL

A bit of skill required

TIME

30 minutes

MAKES

Frosting for two 9-inch cakes

I am so sorry, but you should get an instant-read thermometer for this recipe. It's truly worth the $14 and the day of waiting, should you order it online to avoid putting on pants. There are indeed other ways to test if the sugar syrup is at the right stage, but they involve dropping it into a cup of water and seeing whether you can pinch it like softened candy, and I feel as though by the time I got into the full explanation of that you'd be on to a breezier cookbook. Just get the thermometer! I have the Javelin from Lavatools, which I now use at least once a day. Here's my sales pitch on French buttercream: It tastes somehow as rich and glossy as it looks. Once you get the hang of this recipe, you'll never want to use another method; it makes even the drowsiest cake seem dazzling. I use a sort of hybrid method, which includes egg whites along with the yolks. I employ a method of streaming sugar syrup into the eggs rather than heating them before whipping, to avoid pulpy overcooked yolk bits. Am I scaring you? Just make it!

3 large eggs and 1 large egg yolk, at room temperature (important)

1 teaspoon Diamond Crystal kosher salt

1⅓ cups (267 g) granulated sugar

2 cups (4 sticks/454 g) unsalted butter, at room temperature, cut into roughly 1 tablespoon pieces

1 tablespoon vanilla bean paste or extract

1. In the bowl of a stand mixer fitted with the balloon whisk attachment, beat the eggs and yolk and salt on medium speed until doubled in volume, foamy, and the color of pale lemon curd, 5 to 6 minutes. If you remove the whisk attachment and let the eggy material drip, it should sit distinctly for just a few seconds on top of itself then begin to lose form, seeping together. If that happens before the syrup is ready, turn off the mixer.

2. Meanwhile! In a small saucepan, combine the sugar and 1 cup of room-temperature water. Place the pan over medium heat and use a silicone spatula to gently stir until the syrup becomes clear, with no discernable grains—then immediately remove your spatula. Turn up the heat to high. Let the syrup simmer for about 6 minutes, then add your thermometer. You're looking to simmer just until the temperature reads between 235° and 240°F, another several minutes, depending on your burner temperature. Cut the heat.

3. If you stopped the mixer by now, turn it back on to medium speed. As it whips the eggs, slowly pour the hot sugar syrup in, avoiding the whisk or the sides of the bowl. The eggs will deflate a bit. Turn the speed to medium-high and keep beating until the exterior-bottom of the bowl no longer feels warm to

continued

the touch, which could take as long as 8 to 10 minutes; you'll see more deflation toward the end, which is normal and not cause for panic.

4. When the mixture has cooled to room temperature (be patient, okay?), keep the mixer on medium-high and add the butter 1 tablespoon at a time, counting to 10 after each addition. Add the vanilla. If the buttercream seems curdled, you just need to keep beating—it means your butter is too cold relative to the rest, but time will heal. Patience is critical. If the buttercream gets soupy and greasy, the eggs were too hot; just keep beating another 3 to 4 minutes. If it doesn't fluff up, then pop it into the refrigerator to chill for 8 minutes and beat again. You'll know the buttercream is ready to use when it's fluffy and silky-smooth. Use immediately or chill, covered, in the fridge, and when you're ready to use it, let it come to room temperature. If it's gotten a little sad, you can let it come to room temp, then beat on medium speed until fluffy.

CHOCOLATE FRENCH-ISH BUTTERCREAM

Sift in ½ to ¾ cup Dutch-process cocoa powder after you add the butter in step 4, as soon as the frosting comes together, and mix just to fully combine. (Sometimes I add an extra pinch or two of flaky or pretzel salt for a textured layer.)

BROWN SUGAR FRENCH-ISH BUTTERCREAM

Swap in dark brown sugar (133 g) for half of the granulated sugar in step 2. The result is a nuanced, subtly molasses-y flavor that pairs well with spice cake, carrot cake, or oatmeal cookies.

FRUITY FRENCH-ISH BUTTERCREAM

Blend about ½ cup freeze-dried fruit—like raspberries, strawberries, or blueberries—in a high-speed blender until you have a fine powder. After you add the butter in step 4, as the frosting is coming together, add a few tablespoons of the fruit powder with a sifter as the mixer runs until you reach the color and flavor you prefer.

MALTED MILK FRENCH-ISH BUTTERCREAM

Add ¼ cup (or more!) malted milk powder to the buttercream as soon as the frosting comes together and fluffs in step 4 and mix just to fully combine.

NOTE: *People with compromised immune systems should avoid eating raw eggs.*

BROWN BUTTER FRENCH-ISH BUTTERCREAM

LEVEL

A bit of skill required

TIME

30 minutes (plus time to let the browned butter resolidify)

MAKES

Frosting for two 9-inch cake layers

This recipe turns my Actually Manageable French-ish Buttercream (page 319) into something you'll want to eat by the spoonful while you bat away passersby. For more tips on how to get brown butter to resolidify quickly, should you find yourself in a rush to eat a vat of the best frosting known to girl, see the Overachiever Extra-Browned Butter Bakery-Worthy CCCs recipe on page 290. Milk powder provides a boost of toffee flavor; I recommend ordering a bag to keep in your pantry. Either way, this is great as is when used to frost a yellow cake (like the one on page 304), and it's even better covered in toasted coconut flakes. My secret is that after I've toasted the flakes over dry heat, I toss them off the heat with about 3 drops of that artificial coconut extract and a pinch of salt, and then press the cooled flakes into the frosting on the cake. People lose their minds.

2 cups (4 sticks/454 g) unsalted butter, at room temperature, cut into 1-tablespoon pieces

6 tablespoons milk powder

3 large eggs and 1 large egg yolk, at room temperature (important)

1 teaspoon Diamond Crystal kosher salt

1⅓ cups (267 g) granulated sugar

1 tablespoon vanilla bean paste or extract

1. To brown the butter, add it to a small saucepan over medium heat, and let it melt, then foam. As it foams, before it turns toasty-brown, add the milk powder and whisk. Let it continue to cook until the milk solids at the bottom are the color of toast that's one minute away from being too crispy. For the fastest results, transfer to a small metal bowl and dunk its bottom only in an ice bath and whisk until the butter resolidifies to room temp. If you're in no rush, transfer to a sealable container, including *allllll* of the browned bits at the bottom (use a silicone spatula to get them), cover, and let cool in the refrigerator. Stir intermittently to encourage even solidification. You can also do this on the counter if you've got some time. You want it to become solid again, then bring it back to room temperature, so when you poke it, it holds the dent perfectly and doesn't feel chilly to the touch.

2. When the butter is solid, soft, and room temperature, it's time to make the frosting. In the bowl of a stand mixer fitted with the balloon whisk attachment, beat the eggs and yolk and salt on medium speed until doubled in volume, foamy, and the color of pale lemon curd, 5 to 6 minutes. If you remove the whisk attachment and let the eggy material drip, it should sit distinctly for just a few seconds on top of itself, then begin to lose form, seeping together. If that happens before the syrup is ready, turn off the mixer.

3. Meanwhile! Meanwhile, in a small saucepan, combine the sugar and 1 cup room-temperature water. Place over medium heat and use a silicone spatula to

continued

gently stir until the syrup becomes completely clear, with no discernable sugar grains—then immediately remove your spatula. Turn up the heat to high. Let it simmer for about 6 minutes, then add your thermometer. You're looking to simmer just until the temperature reads between 235° and 240°F, another several minutes depending on your burner temperature. Cut the heat.

4. If you stopped the mixer by now, turn it back on to medium speed. As it whips the eggs, slowly pour the hot sugar syrup in, avoiding the whisk or the sides of the bowl. The eggs will deflate a little bit. Turn the speed to medium-high and keep beating until if you touch the exterior-bottom of the bowl, it no longer feels warm, which could take as long as 8 to 10 minutes; you'll see more deflation toward the end, which is normal and not cause for panic.

5. When the mixture has cooled down to room temperature (be patient), turn the mixer on medium-high again, and add the butter 1 tablespoon at a time. Add the vanilla. Note that if the buttercream seems curdled, you need to keep beating—it means your butter is too cold relative to the rest, but time will heal. If the buttercream gets soupy and greasy, the eggs were too hot; just keep beating another 3 to 4 minutes. If it doesn't fluff up, then pop it into the refrigerator to chill for 8 minutes and beat again. You'll know the buttercream is ready to use when it's fluffy and silky-smooth. (If it's truly runny and you can't imagine saving it, add more room-temperature butter 1 tablespoon at a time to fluff it up.) Use immediately or chill, covered, in the fridge, and when you're ready to use, let it come to room temperature, then beat on medium until it's fluffy.

CHOCOLATE BROWN BUTTER FRENCH-ISH BUTTERCREAM

Sift in ½ to ¾ cup Dutch-process cocoa powder after you add the butter in step 5, as soon as the frosting comes together, and mix just to fully combine. (Sometimes I add an extra pinch or two of flaky or pretzel salt for a textured layer.)

MALTED MILK BROWN BUTTER FRENCH-ISH BUTTERCREAM

Add ¼ cup (or more!) malted milk powder to the buttercream as soon as the frosting comes together and fluffs in step 4 and mix just to fully combine.

NOTE: *People with compromised immune systems should avoid eating raw eggs.*

AMERICAN BUTTERCREAM

LEVEL

Anyone can execute

TIME

10 minutes

MAKES

Frosting for two 9-inch cake layers

American buttercream should be easy! That's its biggest asset: You can whip together butter and confectioners' sugar in 5 minutes. My preferred frosting is the Actually Manageable French-ish Buttercream on page 319. But I won't leave you stranded if you're in a rush—this is my no-frills formula for frosting that's thick, salty-sweet, and ready in minutes. It uses a little more than half the sugar most recipes call for. If you've got more of a sweet tooth, you can add up to 6 cups of confectioners' sugar.

1½ cups (3 sticks/339 g) unsalted butter, at room temperature

4 cups (480 g) confectioners' sugar, sifted or whisked to remove lumps

1½ teaspoons Diamond Crystal kosher salt

1 tablespoon vanilla bean paste or extract

¼ cup heavy cream, at room temperature

1. In the bowl of a stand mixer fitted with the balloon whisk attachment (or in a bowl with a hand mixer), whip the butter on medium-high speed for about 2 minutes until it's fluffy, soft, and lightened in tone. Scrape down the sides with a silicone spatula. Add a third of the confectioners' sugar, plus the salt and vanilla bean paste. Whip again on medium until it begins to integrate, then on high until sticky and paste-like. Scrape down the sides. Add a splash of cream and another third of the confectioners' sugar. Beat again until it comes back together. Add the rest of the confectioners' sugar and beat on medium, then high until you have a thick, sticky frosting. Scrape down the sides. While the mixer runs on medium, slowly stream in the rest of the cream, then when it stops splattering, whip for another 20 seconds or so, just until fluffy and set.

CHOCOLATE AMERICAN BUTTERCREAM

Add ½ to ¾ cup sifted or whisked Dutch-process cocoa powder along with the confectioners' sugar. If the texture is too thick, add another splash of cream.

SALTY-MILK AMERICAN BUTTERCREAM

Add 3 tablespoons milk powder along with the confectioners' sugar. If the texture is too thick, add another splash of cream.

CREAM CHEESE AMERICAN BUTTERCREAM

Before you add the room-temperature butter, whip one 8-ounce block of room-temperature cream cheese for about 2 minutes, until fluffy and lightened. Scrape down the sides with a silicone spatula. Proceed with the recipe as written above.

DARK CHOCOLATE PRETZEL BUTTERCREAM

LEVEL

Anyone can execute

TIME

15 minutes

MAKES

Frosting for one 9-inch cake (make a double batch for a layer cake)

This dead-simple method comes from a recipe for Satin Buttercream in Joy of Cooking, *and it could not have a higher payoff. Here I've tweaked the ingredients and ratios and added pretzels for a salty-silky buttercream that anyone can make with just a food processor. I've also thrown in some egg yolks (in a nod to the richness of French buttercream), which you heat through alongside the cream. Use this immediately, ideally on the Soft and Tender Yellow Cake on page 304, or store it covered in the refrigerator for up to 6 days and bring it back to room temperature, then buzz it in the food processor to re-fluff before frosting.*

4 ounces (113 g) salted sourdough pretzels, the darker the crust the better

1 cup (230 g) heavy cream

6 ounces (199 g) unsweetened dark chocolate, chopped or roughly broken

1 teaspoon espresso powder

1 egg yolk

1½ teaspoons Diamond Crystal kosher salt

2½ cups (300 g) confectioners' sugar

7 tablespoons (113 g) unsalted butter, on the slightly chillier side of room temperature (not slumped and melting)

1. Pulse the pretzels in a food processor until crushed to the texture of pebbly sand. Set aside and wipe out the processor bowl, but leave it out.

2. In a medium saucepan, bring the cream to a simmer over low heat, whisking occasionally to avoid scalding. Remove from the heat and add the chocolate and espresso powder. Cover and set aside. After 2 to 3 minutes, when the cream is warm but not hot to the touch, add the egg yolk. Let everything sit another minute or so, to give the chocolate time to melt, then whisk until smooth and melted.

3. Scrape the mixture into the food processor and add the salt, confectioners' sugar, and butter. Process just until smooth, stopping once to scrape down the sides—do not overblend, or it will lose structure and appear slick, soupy, and drippy. The mixture should be thick and spreadable, not a melted stew. (If this happens, chill in the refrigerator for 20 minutes, or until firm, then pulse a few times until spreadable and thick again.)

4. Just before you're ready to use the frosting, add three-quarters of the pretzel crumbs and pulse just once or twice to combine in loose pockets. Use immediately. (To hold off on frosting the cake, refrigerate the frosting before you mix in the crumbs. When you're ready to use the frosting, let it come to room temperature, then add three-quarters of the crumbs and pulse in the food processor until fluffy and spreadable.)

5. Use the reserved pretzel crumbs as a cake topping.

NOTE: *People with compromised immune systems should avoid eating raw eggs.*

BROWN BUTTER FRENCH-ISH
BUTTERCREAM, PAGE 321
DARK CHOCOLATE PRETZEL
BUTTERCREAM, PAGE 324

23

Decadent Flourless

CHOCOLATE CAKE

MISSION

Decadent flourless chocolate cake that toes the line between brownie batter and a sliceable form. Lots of salt. Only a moderate amount of fuss.

WHAT I TESTED

Structural element • Composition
Aeration

TWO-INGREDIENT "MOUSSE" BATTER
ALMOND FLOUR
"TRUFFLE" BATTER
STEAMY OVEN
"CLOUD" BATTER
OAT FLOUR

FLOURLESS CHOCOLATE CAKE IS THE RARE DISH THAT DESCRIBES WHAT IT IS NOT, RATHER THAN WHAT IT IS.

It's a broad category. There is my mother's favorite flourless chocolate cake, the one she makes on Passover and on Thanksgiving. The recipe comes from the late Laurie Colwin's column[1] for *Gourmet*. It's a rich disc of dark chocolate and almond meal, closer in texture to cornbread than to a meringue. There's the much-iterated-upon category called "cloud cakes" after the beloved Richard Sax[2] recipe, in which egg whites inflate butter, yolks, and of course melted chocolate, for a marshmallow-y shell that puffs in the oven, then collapses onto its tender, ethereally soft crumb. There is the chocolate torte category, which itself can range from cakier to delicate and melty, with a high proportion of chocolate as the main structural element. There are TikTok "hacks" for two-ingredient no-bake "flourless chocolate cakes" that get their sweetness and body from apples or sweet potato.

And so for an obsessive person, it's easy to get carried away when deconstructing flourless chocolate cake. One could methodically go down the list, one type of cake at a time, and scale up and down the yolks and whites, whip them or just whisk, melt the butter, swap in and out various types and qualities of chocolate, testing hundreds of variations, until her husband leaves her and takes the dog. Me, personally, I went a bit broader, because I love my dog. Once you have selected one of the wide range of available styles and perfected it to your palate, flourless chocolate cake becomes a sort of back-pocket companion—if you have a recipe you love and trust, it will effortlessly shepherd you from bake sale to birthday to dinner party and then back to bake sale. (Can you tell I've never been invited to participate in a bake sale?)

With the exception of the TikTok apple "cake," most recipes used eggs—either aerated or simply beaten—for structure. In the presence of heat, eggs firm up to provide structure. Cakes with an alternative flour like oat or almond used those finely ground ingredients for structure, too, which turned them dense and cakey, rather than dense and truffle-like.

Across the cakes, flavor came mainly from the chocolate—so the benefits of higher-quality chocolate were perceptible. Flavor could come, too, from cocoa powder, some supporting agents like espresso powder (which deepens the chocolate), and vanilla. Salt was crucial; an undersalted cake was underwhelming and cloying even when its texture was impressive, but cake with an appropriate amount had that transfixing quality of fudgy brownie batter.

I loved the creamy, barely solid texture of the truffle batter (an adaptation of Ruth Rogers's Chocolate Nemesis Cake[3]) best for its buttery softness. But I didn't love how long it took to make; the reference recipe I used baked for 2 hours at a super-low temperature, to produce an elegant texture. I also appreciated elements from some of the other tests I wanted to bring into the truffle version, like the sweetness balance of the cloud batter and the moisture ensured by the steamy oven. So my version is a sort of hybrid. It's not quite as elegant as one baked forever at just a gust of heat, but when it's all said and done (and crusted with salty cookie crumbs), I don't think you'll mind.

THE BEST METHOD

A truffle-like crumb with a salty cookie crust and a mound of whipped cream on top, on page 330.

Densest					**Lightest**
Truffle batter	Simple batter with no egg aeration	Almond flour	Oat flour	Two-ingredient mousse batter	Cloud batter

MOTHER RECIPE

FLOURLESS TRUFFLE CAKE WITH SALTY COOKIE CRUST

LEVEL

Slightly challenging but impressive

TIME

1 hour 15 minutes, plus at least 1 hour to chill the cake

MAKES

Cake for 10

Loyalists to Ruth Rogers's Chocolate Nemesis Cake from the River Café might find my spin on a similar batter, which produces a smaller cake in about half of the time, to be blasphemy. And I get that. The salty Oreo-dust crust and the whipped cream topping take something elegant and simple and make it more of a Whole Situation. But here's what I will say in its defense: Even Lauren—as in, Chicken Lauren, from page 158—has no notes on this cake, especially when it's upgraded to host the Raspberry Ripple Sour Whipped Cream (page 331). Please don't panic when I tell you to take it out of the oven and let it chill until firm; I know, it looks quite . . . underdone. But the beauty of this type of flourless chocolate cake is that it's not even really cake. It's more like very buttery whipped chocolate. If it helps, think of it like a custard or cheesecake—you're going for just-set, not baked through until dry and puffy.

FOR THE CAKE

Scant 13 tablespoons (180 g) unsalted butter, cut into tablespoons, softened to room temperature, plus more to butter the cake pan

4 large eggs (220 g), at room temperature

1⅓ cups (267 g) granulated sugar

10 ounces (269 g) high quality semisweet dark chocolate chips or finely chopped bars

1 teaspoon espresso powder

2 tablespoons Dutch-process cocoa powder

1 tablespoon vanilla bean paste or pure vanilla extract

1¼ teaspoons Diamond Crystal kosher salt

1. Heat the oven to 350°F. Butter a 9-inch springform pan, line the bottom with a circle of parchment paper, and butter the parchment. Butter the sides very well. Wrap the outside of the springform pan tightly in tinfoil, so when it's time to bake the cake in a water bath, no water can get into the bottom seam. Set it in a deeper (i.e. 3-inch) roasting pan. See the Note on page 331 re: the cake pan.

2. Make the crust: Separate the 30 Oreo cookies from their frosting, so you get 60 cookie pieces. Reserve the frosting for another purpose (what you do in your private time is not my business). In a sealed bag, with a wine bottle, rolling pin, or a mallet of some sort, crush the cookies very finely. Reserve about 3 tablespoons of the fine cookie crumbs for later. To the rest, still in the bag, add the melted butter, sugar, and salt, reseal, and use your hands to fully integrate. Press the crumb mixture firmly into a compact layer on the bottom of the cake tin, to form a crust.

3. Set over high heat a kettle and a medium pot each filled with water. Bring to a boil and cut the heat.

4. Make the cake: In the bowl of a stand mixer fitted with the balloon whisk attachment, beat the eggs on medium-high speed with about ⅓ cup (67 g) of the sugar until the mixture inflates to four times its original size, about 5 minutes.

5. While the egg mixture is aerating, in a medium saucepan, whisk together the remaining scant 1 cup sugar with a scant ½ cup room-temperature water. Set over medium heat, whisking occasionally until the sugar dissolves.

FOR THE CRUST

30 Oreo cookies

7 tablespoons (99 g) unsalted butter, melted

2 tablespoons granulated sugar

1 teaspoon Diamond Crystal kosher salt

FOR THE TOPPING

1 cup heavy cream

2 tablespoons granulated sugar (you can use confectioners' sugar if you prefer)

1 tablespoon vanilla bean paste or extract

Pinch of Diamond Crystal kosher salt

⅓ cup sour cream, at room temperature (you can use Greek yogurt if you prefer)

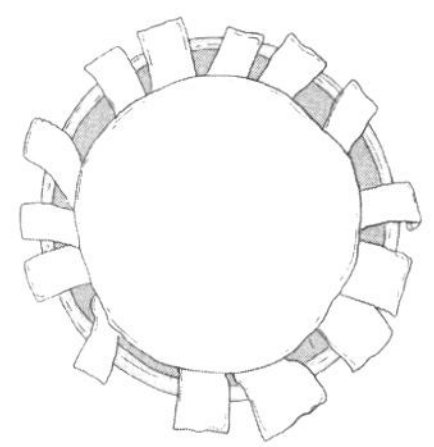

NOTE: *If, like me, you have drawn the line at buying another type of pan, so you stubbornly don't own a springform, you can butter and line the bottom of a 9-inch cake pan with parchment, and then, beneath it, add roughly 6 to 8 thick overlapping long strips of parchment that hang over the sides. You can use these later to airlift the cake out of its pan.*

6. In a large heat-safe bowl, combine the chocolate, softened butter, espresso powder, cocoa powder, vanilla, and salt. Pour the hot sugar–liquid over it. Cover with a towel and let it sit for about 2 minutes, then whisk to combine, until you have a shiny, dark chocolate fudge syrup–textured mixture. (If the syrup doesn't get everything melty enough, just heat in 10-second intervals in the microwave until you can fully mix and combine.)

7. When the eggs have fluffed up, with the mixer running, slowly stream in the chocolate syrup. Scrape down the sides. Beat again until combined.

8. Pour the batter into the cake pan over the cookie crust, slowly so as to not disrupt the crust. Place the roasting pan inside the heated oven and, carefully, add the hot water to the roasting pan to nearly fill it (it's a water bath). If your roasting pan is taller than your cake pan, don't fill it all the way—you don't want to get any water into the cake batter.

9. Bake for 52 to 58 minutes, just until the cake no longer feels sticky to a gentle poke, less like raw brownie batter and more like chewed gum. A toothpick will still come out wet, but the top will look shiny and set and lighter than whatever's on the toothpick. Right when the cake comes out of the oven, run a hot knife around the sides, for easier release later.

10. While the cake bakes, make the whipped cream: In the bowl of a stand mixer fitted with the balloon whisk attachment, beat the cream on medium speed for 2 minutes, or until it stops threatening to splatter. Add the sugar, vanilla, salt, and sour cream. Continue to whip for another minute or so on medium, until it holds stiff peaks. Cover and chill in the refrigerator.

11. Let the cake cool completely in the refrigerator, at least 1 hour. When it feels chilled all the way through, run a hot knife around the edges again, then release the springform sides and use two fish spatulas or offset spatulas to gently lift it from the bottom of the springform pan onto a serving plate.

12. Store chilled and covered for up to 4 days before serving. When you're ready to serve, spread the sour cream whipped cream over the top of the cake and smooth it with an offset spatula or a knife. Dust with the 3 tablespoons reserved cookie crumbs, slice, and serve.

RASPBERRY RIPPLE SOUR WHIPPED CREAM

Try this in place of the sour cream whipped cream. In a stand mixer fitted with the balloon whisk attachment, whip 1 cup heavy cream on medium speed until it stops splattering. Add 2 tablespoons granulated or confectioners' sugar, ⅓ cup room-temperature sour cream or Greek yogurt, 1 tablespoon vanilla bean paste, a pinch of salt, and 3 tablespoons raspberry jam. Whip on medium-high speed for another minute, until soft peaks form. Add half of 1 pint raspberries and turn the mixer to low to let the balloon whisk crush them into the cream, about 15 seconds. Add the rest of the berries and mix on low for just 5 seconds.

FLOURLESS TRUFFLE CAKE WITH SALTY COOKIE CRUST, PAGE 330

24

Butter-Forward
SHORTBREAD

MISSION

Shortbread that is enticing
enough to be your cookie of choice.

WHAT I TESTED

Aeration of butter • Sugar • Fat
Mixing method • Baking temperature
Rest before baking • Flour type

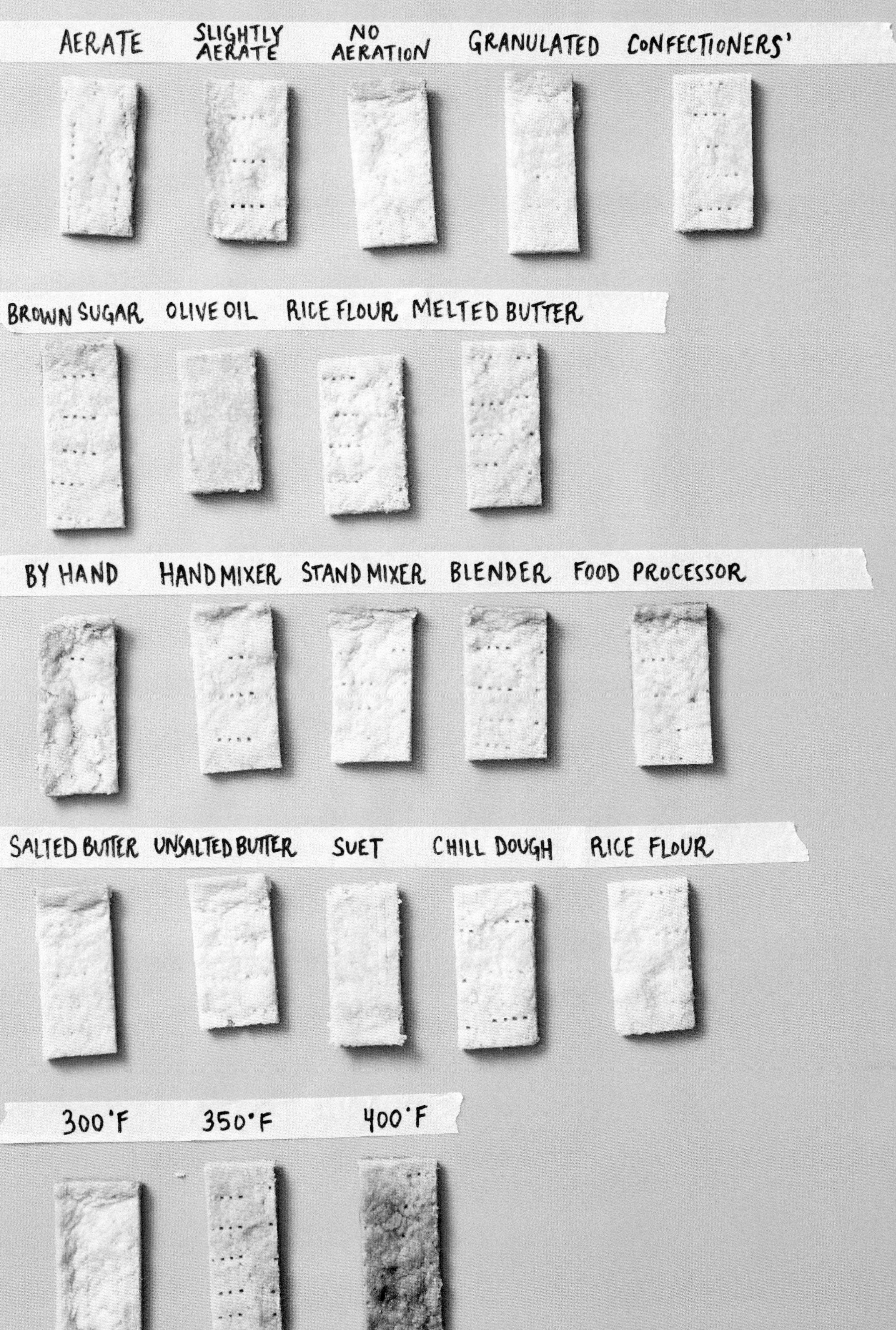
AERATE
SLIGHTLY AERATE
NO AERATION
GRANULATED
CONFECTIONERS'
BROWN SUGAR
OLIVE OIL
RICE FLOUR
MELTED BUTTER
BY HAND
HAND MIXER
STAND MIXER
BLENDER
FOOD PROCESSOR
SALTED BUTTER
UNSALTED BUTTER
SUET
CHILL DOUGH
RICE FLOUR
300°F
350°F
400°F

THINK OF ADDING FAT TO FLOUR AS A BUTTER BLOCKADE.

It effectively shortens chains of gluten by coating glutenin and gliadin proteins. The effect, when baked, is a crumbly, flaky texture, and it's how shortbread got its name. There is such a thing as too crumbly, though, at least in my kitchen. To me, a perfect bar or wedge of shortbread is so tender that it begins to render as soon as it hits your mouth. If plain, it should have a deep buttery flavor, and enough salt to make you want more than one. (As Sohla El-Waylly writes in *Start Here*, "Shortbread is just a way to eat butter."[1])

While most methods of making shortbread work well, the best technique I found for consistently tender shortbread was a combination of a hand mix with a spatula or spoon (to avoid overworking the dough and ending up with something dry and crisp) with a dough rest, and a low baking temperature to keep the insides of each cookie softer than their crusts. You can use your hands to work in the butter, too, like Will Ryan, who makes expert-level shortbread for his pop-up Percy's: "[If] at any point you find yourself frustrated just remember this recipe is pastoral—and you're supposed to be enjoying it," he told me.

I preferred salted butter that had not been aerated (which can cause a rise in the oven and interrupts the classic density). Granulated sugar contributed a sandier, snappier texture, while confectioners' sugar made for a softer, almost powdery cookie. Brown sugar, with its extra moisture, slightly changed the texture and identity of the cookie to something chewier.

THE BEST METHOD

Use a wooden spoon, fork, and/or your hands for the most tender cookie, as on page 340.

TOASTED RICE FLOUR AND
JAM SHORTBREAD, PAGE 342

PERFECT BUTTERY
SHORTBREAD, PAGE 340

SALTY CHOCOLATE BUCKWHEAT SHORTBREAD, PAGE 341

GRAPE-NUTS SHORTBREAD, PAGE 342

MOTHER RECIPE

PERFECT BUTTERY SHORTBREAD

LEVEL

Anyone can execute

TIME

20 minutes, plus 1 hour rest

MAKES

8 to 16 shortbread bars, depending how you cut them

Plain shortbread has a reputation for being a bore. I don't think that's fair. When made properly, with salted butter plus more salt, with your sugar of choice—see page 336 for more detail—a simple recipe will yield a compelling cookie. If you still don't agree after trying these, I've included seven variations to amp up flavor and texture. You should really consider this "Shortbread Unlimited Ways." Citrus-sugar could come from a winter citrus, or be paired with an herb (Carla Lalli Music has a fabulous shortbread recipe with lemon zest and rosemary); Grape-Nuts could be swapped out for Raisin Bran, or Rice Krispies, or Trix. You could swirl any nut butter into the surface before baking, or line the bottom of the pan with a crumb crust. The most important guideline to keep in mind is that you don't want to overwork the dough. When you mix the sugar and butter, do it to combine, not aerate; when you work in the flour, create cohesive crumbles, then stop. Feel free to use your mixer or food processor, but err on the side of undermixing. For neater slices, cut the shortbread into bars before you chill, then cut again out of the oven.

1 cup (2 sticks/225 g) salted butter, cut into tablespoons, at room temperature

¾ cup (150 g) granulated sugar (reserve a spoonful for sprinkling)

1 teaspoon Diamond Crystal kosher salt

1¾ cups (255 g) all-purpose flour (if you aren't using a scale, sift the flour, then scoop it into the measuring cups; go for 2 scant cups)

OPTIONAL

6 ounces semisweet chocolate chips or bars, roughly chopped

2 tablespoons unsalted butter at room temperature, cut into ½-inch cubes

Flaky salt

1. Line an 8 × 8-inch pan with two wide strips of parchment paper, crossing over one another, for easy lift-out later. (You can use a 9 × 9-inch pan, or a 9-inch cake pan, and so on; just start checking the cookies earlier for doneness using the visual cues in step 4.)

2. In a large bowl, use a wooden spoon to combine the butter, sugar, and salt until mostly uniform but still dense; it will look like the store-bought almond paste you'd use to make rainbow cookies. Add the flour. Integrate into the butter mixture with the wooden spoon, or your hands, or a fork, or some combination—the resulting mixture will look like crumbles of streusel, and if you pinch one, the insides should be uniform (not just a clump of butter coated in flour). Press the crumbles evenly into the pan.

3. Cover tightly and chill in the refrigerator for 1 hour, or up to 24 hours.

4. Heat the oven to 300°F. Sprinkle the reserved sugar evenly over the dough. Use a fork to "dock" the surface, i.e. make holes all over that go about halfway down. Bake for 40 to 45 minutes, until barely golden around the edges and just set and dry to the touch in the center.

5. Let cool for about 10 minutes, then lift out of the pan using the parchment overhangs. Carefully cut into 8 square bars, or 16 long rectangular bars.

6. If topping with chocolate, melt two-thirds (about 4 ounces) of the chocolate in 10-second bursts in the microwave, stirring between each one. When melted, add the rest of the chocolate and the butter and stir until melted. Return to the microwave for 10 seconds. Stir. (Repeat if not silky smooth. Chocolate is fickle.)

7. Dip each shortbread cookie into the chocolate to cover it partially. Sprinkle with flaky salt. Set on a rimmed rack in the fridge to let the chocolate harden. Store loosely covered at room temperature or tightly covered in the refrigerator. These also freeze very well, tightly covered, for weeks.

MILK POWDER SHORTBREAD

Swap in ⅓ cup (48 g) whole milk powder for 48 g (roughly a heaping ⅓ cup) of the all-purpose flour; the best way to do this is to measure out the 48 g whole milk powder in a bowl on the scale, and then add all-purpose flour until you reach the full 255 g. These will finish baking about 5 minutes earlier than the standard recipe; start checking at 35 minutes.

VANILLA BEAN–CITRUS SUGAR SHORTBREAD

Just before you make the shortbread, rub 2 tablespoons citrus zest into the sugar. Scrape the insides of 2 vanilla beans or add 1 tablespoon vanilla bean paste into the butter mixture before you mix in the flour.

SALTY CHOCOLATE BUCKWHEAT SHORTBREAD

Swap in 40 g (scant ⅓ cup) buckwheat flour for 40 g (heaping ¼ cup) of the all-purpose flour. Add 40 g (scant ½ cup) cocoa powder. Before making the dough, toast both flours and cocoa powder on a parchment-lined sheet pan at 300°F for 12 to 15 minutes. Let cool, get rid of any lumps with a whisk or fork, and add to the recipe in place of the plain flour.

TAHINI DATE SHORTBREAD

Swap in 3 tablespoons tahini for 3 tablespoons of the butter. Before baking, drizzle the shortbread with tahini, pinches of the reserved sugar, and several pitted, finely diced dates.

TOASTED RICE FLOUR AND JAM SHORTBREAD

Swap in 70 g (scant ½ cup) rice flour for 70 g (scant ½ cup) of the total flour. Toast both flours on a parchment-lined sheet pan at 300°F for 12 to 15 minutes. Let cool, then use in the recipe in place of the all-purpose flour. Before baking the dough, dollop a few teaspoons of raspberry jam on the surface and use a martini pick, toothpick, or knife to swirl it, without integrating it too much (leave the swirls distinct). You could also swirl some peanut butter into the surface. Bake as directed.

BROWNED BUTTER SHORTBREAD

Brown half of the butter in a small saucepan; when it foams, add 2 tablespoons milk powder and whisk. Let the mixture come back to a soft room temperature, then add the rest of the room-temperature butter and proceed with the recipe.

GRAPE-NUTS SHORTBREAD

Sprinkle ¼ cup Grape-Nuts plus 1 tablespoon additional sugar evenly over the parchment in the pan. Press the dough into it as if the sugary Grape-Nuts are a roughly hewn bottom crust. Before chilling the dough, sprinkle an additional ¼ cup Grape-Nuts and 1 more tablespoon sugar over the dough. Press hard so some of the cereal wedges into the top of the dough. Bake as directed.

CHEWY MALTED CHOCOLATE SHORTBREAD

LEVEL

Anyone can execute

TIME

40 minutes (including 30 minutes of rest)

MAKES

16 cookie bars

Try as I did to incite mass worship of the Giant Party Latkes on page 145, every person in my life decided that these shortbread bars were the one recipe that they could not live without. Sounds dramatic, until you try them. (P.S. You'll notice that instead of asking you to make the dough by hand to prevent overworking, I'm calling in the food processor here—the malted milk powder contributes so much chew that these are almost an entirely different cookie from a classic, snappable shortbread. So why not make life easier? You can swap in the same weight of confectioners' sugar for the granulated sugar for a bit more softness.)

Heaping ⅔ cup (140 g) granulated sugar

1½ teaspoons Diamond Crystal kosher salt

1⅓ cups (189 g) all-purpose flour

½ cup (78 g) malted milk powder

¼ cup (24 g) Dutch-process cocoa powder

1 cup (2 sticks/225 g) unsalted butter, cut into tablespoons

OPTIONAL

6 ounces semisweet chocolate chips or bars, roughly chopped

2 tablespoons unsalted butter, at room temperature, cut into ½-inch cubes

Flaky salt

1. Line an 8 × 8-inch metal baking dish with parchment; add a second strip of parchment overhang beneath a longer strip of parchment for help with lift-out.

2. Combine the sugar, salt, flour, malted milk powder, and cocoa powder in the bowl of a food processor. Cover the open spout (or risk dusting your kitchen). Pulse to combine. Add the butter cubes to the dry ingredients and pulse to work the butter in, covering it in the dry ingredients and continuing until the mixture is mostly combined and you can press the dough together into a cohesive ball the texture of modeling clay.

3. Transfer the dough to the lined baking dish and gently press it into the edges in an even layer. You can smooth the top with an offset spatula if you're fussy, but I never do; I love the rippled pattern that forms when you leave the top of the dough rough and irregular. Or maybe that's a defense mechanism since, as we know, I hate extra steps.

4. In any case, chill (tightly covered) in the refrigerator for at least 30 minutes or up to 1 hour. (You could chill longer, up to several days, but if you do, be sure to let the dough sit at room temperature for about 30 minutes before you bake it.)

5. Set an oven rack in the middle position and heat the oven to 325°F.

continued

6. Remove the dough from the refrigerator and dock—poke all over with a fork, about halfway to the bottom. Bake on the middle rack for 24 to 28 minutes, until the edges begin to puff up and the center no longer looks several shades darker than the outsides. Don't overbake or you'll end up with a batch of cocoa crackers.

7. Remove from the oven and let cool for about 10 minutes, then slice into 16 squares with a sharp knife. Let cool for another 5 minutes before attempting to lift the cookies out.

8. If dipping in chocolate, melt two-thirds (about 4 ounces) of the chocolate in 10-second bursts in the microwave, stirring between each one. When the chocolate has melted, add the rest of the chocolate and the butter and stir until all melted. Add back to the microwave for another 10 seconds. Stir. (Repeat if not silky smooth. Chocolate is fickle.) Dip each shortbread cookie into the chocolate to cover partially. Sprinkle the melted chocolate with a pinch of flaky salt. Set on a rimmed rack in the fridge to let the chocolate harden.

PEANUT BUTTER OATMEAL SHORTBREAD

LEVEL

A bit of skill required

TIME

45 minutes, plus
1 hour to chill

MAKES

20 to 22 cookies

I wrote on page 272 about the corn muffins I used to eat to combat my apathy while working in finance; on the mornings I had slightly more time, I would venture over to a cafeteria in another building called "2B." 2B mornings were halcyon: I got oatmeal with an enormous scoop of peanut butter and topped it with honey, banana, and salt. By the time I was back at my desk, the peanut butter had begun to melt into the oats. This is my ode to that breakfast. If you don't have oat flour, which, fair, you can make your own by food processing oats, then weighing out the correct amount of oat flour.

1¼ cups (160 g) oat flour

1 cup plus 2 tablespoons (161 g) all-purpose flour

1¼ teaspoons Diamond Crystal kosher salt

2 teaspoons ground cinnamon

1 cup (2 sticks/225 g) chilled unsalted butter, cut into tablespoons, plus more for greasing

1 cup plus 2 tablespoons (140 g) confectioners' sugar

Roughly ⅓ cup smooth peanut butter

2 ripe bananas

Roughly ¼ cup honey

Flaky salt

1. Line two sheet pans with parchment paper. Let them chill in the refrigerator as you prepare the dough.

2. In the bowl of a food processor fitted with the S-blade, combine the oat flour, all-purpose flour, kosher salt, and cinnamon. Pulse to combine. Add the butter and confectioners' sugar and process for 30 to 45 seconds, stopping to scrape the sides down a few times, until a dough ball forms and begins to zoom around the bowl. Don't overmix; doing so will cause the butter to melt and the dough to become greasy and overly soft; if this happens, put it in the fridge to firm up before moving on to the next step.

3. Roll twenty to twenty-two 1½-inch dough balls (if you want to be fussy—I don't—each ball should weigh about 25 g). Set them 2 inches apart on the lined sheet pans. Use the back of a ½-teaspoon measuring spoon greased with butter to make an indent in each ball going nearly down to the pan, but not quite. You can also use your thumb. Fill each indent with a scant teaspoon of peanut butter.

4. Chill the dough in the fridge for 1 hour, on the pans or otherwise. (You could chill them longer or even freeze them; they'd need to sit on the countertop for 15 minutes before baking; thaw first in the refrigerator if frozen.) Toward the end of the chilling period, heat the oven to 375°F.

5. Bake the cookies for 12 to 15 minutes, until fragrant and a dark khaki color.

6. Remove the pans from the oven and let the cookies cool for 10 minutes. Right before you're ready to serve, slice the bananas into ⅓-inch discs and place a slice atop each peanut butter center. (If you're making the cookies in advance, wait to slice and complete the banana part until just before you're serving.) Finish the cookies by topping each one with a stripe of honey and a pinch of flaky salt.

THE BEST MEATBALLS DO NOT EXIST

The "best" meatballs do not exist, at least according to Elvira, who is not technically a nonna. Though she did fit a particular American idea of the "nonna" with her stern rebukes about the tiny departures I took from her meatball recipe—accidental stutters of my fingertips. She had hurried over to her daughter's friend's home on a Thursday night with short notice when she learned that a journalist would be in Rome trying to find the absolute best way to make Roman-style meatballs. Elvira used to run a restaurant, and according to Debora Lanini, who teaches cooking classes from her home—which is incidentally filled with more than 370 pieces of frog-themed decor—Elvira was known around the city for her meatball prowess.

I had arrived in Rome during the hottest week of the summer to gorge on salty meat. I forgot to check the weather before planning my visit, which spanned a number of appointments to learn the art of the Italian meatball and then an extended visit to the Festival del Prosciutto di Parma in the Langhirano Valley of Emilia Romagna. Anyway, the Langhirano Valley sounded windy, and didn't Rome have all of those fountains? I spent the ten minutes I had to spare between landing and arriving at Debora's home in Trastevere eating a plate of thinly sliced cured jowl and, amid a city built on 2,776 years of culture, scrolling through the online marketing materials for the upcoming prosciutto fest. By the time I made it to the top of two large hills and one steep staircase that Google Maps had innocently obscured and I came face-to-face with the large metal frog-shaped mailbox affixed to the grand double doors of Debora's home (me: red and glistening and grinning, it: chilly and unbothered), I was nearly indistinguishable from the cheerful sow used as the unofficial mascot for the Festival del Prosciutto di Parma.

Soon I learned I was the last guest to arrive. A second frog, dressed in miniature gingham pants, glanced accusingly at me from a glass case. Already there was a married couple who had plans to head to Italy's other meatball capital (Naples) the next day, as well as a friend of Debora's who renounced *all* meatballs shortly after I showed up, citing a wedding diet. There was the bride's fiancé—a local magistrate who was introduced to me and subsequently referred to only as "The Judge"—and the bride's mother, Elvira.

Debora had kindly welcomed me for dinner with her friends on one of her few nights off, after I'd sent a desperate inquiry about wanting to learn the best way to make meatballs. She was the first person of many to tell me that there was no such thing as a "best" meatball, because a meatball was a humble thing, born of leftovers. It would be like flying to an asphalt factory and asking about the most iconic way to make highway pavement. The meatball's historic roots as a use for leftovers is especially evident in one Roman version, called the polpette di bollito: a juicy blimp of days-old stewed beef as tender as short rib, held together by a fried casing like a croquette. (Two great versions can be found at the Mordi e Vai booth at the Testaccio market and the restaurant Trattoria Da Cesare al Casaletto near the Villa Doria Pamphili.)

So Debora and Elvira showed me how to make two types of meatballs, a classic Roman style from ground pork and beef, and another made from boiled potato and tuna fish. Their choreography was precise: They demonstrated how to "ammolare" (presoak) the stale bread with milk just until it stopped sucking up the liquid, then to pour no more. Debora added a parsimonious pinch of salt and grated just a bit of lemon zest into the mix but abandoned the citrus well before she hit the bitter white pith. Elvira added more salt while Debora was turned away, then got to mixing with a black latex glove. We each ate a spoonful of it raw and Debora pronounced it slightly too salty. They demonstrated various sizes and explained potential use cases; one, sized like a newborn's eyeball, could be put in a lasagna. But each time I tried to prod about the best way to chop the parsley, or the best ratio of grated pecorino to meat, Elvira gently corrected me: Meatballs were a matter of personal taste and routine.

Meatballs were so personal, she told me, that you can work out which grandchild (or son-in-law; here, The Judge winked) a nonna prefers by the corresponding tweaks she makes to her meatballs. Still, that doesn't make them the best; they're still just meatballs.

The idea that the best did not necessarily reign supreme the same way it did in America was a sentiment I heard a lot in my travels. I interviewed three generations of a family in Kichijoji, outside of Tokyo, who had won national awards for their senbei—baked rice crackers—made the traditional way in a wood-burning oven in the back of their shop. I had to inquire five or six times before they would show me the framed certificates of honor, hung out of sight behind large bags of senbei. The first four or five times I asked, they deflected and showed me photos of a large retreat of many different families of senbei-makers, whose senbei they described to me in admiring detail. A few days after I left Debora and Elvira in Rome for Emilia Romagna, I watched with a shvitzing Aperol spritz—the Langhirano Valley was not windy that week—as a handful of butchers wearing special mesh gloves competed with one another to hand-carve Parma hams. Their long spindly knives cruised through thick layers of fat and cured pork like violinists' bows for hours, but even when the competition ended, it was unclear who had won. There were pronouncements made about whose slices had been arranged the most artfully on dozens of paper plates, and about who had managed to retain the most yield from each leg of prosciutto, and about whose slices were the thinnest, but it wasn't obvious to an onlooker with a poor grasp of the language who exactly would be going home with the big win. In Tokyo, a few months later, I'd visited the Tokyo Ramen Festa (held fittingly in Komazawa Olympic Park), where for eleven days, dozens of vendors hawked all sorts of types of noodles and broth to 140,000 ramen obsessives from all over Japan. There was grilled potato-miso ramen, a creamy minced chicken version that won something called the "Ramen Grand Prix," and Honke Daiichi Asahi's regional tonkotsu Kyoto bowl, which has lines from 6 a.m. onward in its home city. And yet, when I asked legendary ramen critic and event chairman Hiroshi Osaki—a person who purported to be "the man who

has eaten the most ramen in Japan," at a count of 29,000 bowls—what he thought of a rivaling ramen festival that had popped up about twenty-five minutes from his own, he vacillated, saying something like "all ramen is good, and you should eat the one that you like best."

I might have chalked up this reluctance to claim superiority to a resistance to the American obsession with individual performance—a social distaste toward the ways in which American capitalism has created constant, granular hierarchies, even—if not for what happened that first night in Rome, after I went to Debora's bathroom to wash my hands and dry them on a frog-printed towel. When I emerged, Elvira was standing at the hot plate, quietly crying. No one but me and a stuffed frog peeking out from a potted plant had seemed to notice. The Judge was gesticulating from a love seat as he explained something about local politics, the friend was eating a peach she had brought from home, and Debora was refilling the salt dish. But Elvira, prodding at the contents of one of the two pans, was wordlessly wiping tears as they collected in the corners of her eyes.

Minutes before, she had demonstrated how to get a nice brown crust on each type of meatball. As I approached her at the hot plate, I didn't have to ask what was wrong. One of the skillets looked like it held the contents of an exploded hamster cage, with shavings of tuna and potato withering in the oil, completely untethered from the ball shape they'd held minutes earlier. There was no best way to make a meatball, but apparently she thought there was a worst way. Debora caught notice and ushered me to the side, so Elvira could have a moment with her disappointment while I pretended not to study her. Within five minutes, Elvira was back to chiding me again, this time for flipping the pork and beef meatballs a single second too soon.

Still, the whole incident got me thinking about relativity. Even in a culture (or subculture) skeptical of any one "best," the members of that culture still invent ways—sometimes subtle ones—to call things good or bad. In Japan, when I asked attendees about the best stalls at the rivaling ramen festivals, I was told more than once about Tabelog, the equivalent of Yelp, where restaurants received weighted rankings out of five stars. In Emilia Romagna, at the hand-carving competition, contestant Fausto's 215-gram plate of leaf-thin prosciutto slices generated a gasp from the crowd, while contestant Flaminio's, which was arranged like a school of fish swimming, got only gruff headshakes. And after much inquiry, at the end of a long night that included for some reason a drive-by visit from a local Italian chapter of the Hells Angels, I finally learned who won the carving competition: a butcher named Chantal, who would receive a "winner" sticker to display quietly in the window of her shop for the coming year.

Even where there was resistance to the idea of "the best," where it needn't always be invoked in quite the same way to stoke competition to then stoke the economy, there was still ranking. There was still relativism, at least as a point of organization. Was this just another example of how the algorithmic overlords were creating a monoculture from Silicon Valley?

It didn't totally seem so, in large part because of the lo-fi marketing efforts around most of these events. They felt distinctly local, tangible, and community-oriented, rather than commoditized. Born of a communal urge to celebrate and recognize. Innovation, or hard work, or any combination of the two begets a proverbial window sticker. That existed in America, too, but more often alongside commercially oriented exclusivity: TikTok lists that preyed on the idea that we are drawn to knowing what we aren't meant to know, because we aren't good enough to know it. A posted brag that you, yes you, were the first to discover an under-trafficked taco place in Queens, weeks before the prestigious food critic we all read wrote it up.

And these competitions seemed primarily a way to express identity. No one person, place, or thing needed necessarily to be publicly proclaimed as the best as a matter of mass consensus, but it was important that each individual had an idea of what "the best" meant to them. The titration of garlic in a meatball. The arrangement of prosciutto slices on a plate. These things mattered in that they said something about the person they mattered to. This, too, felt different from the American fixation with "bests," which aspired to be broad, maybe national, likely shared online, in pursuit of consensus and alignment with influential authorities.

These "bests" had little to do with the status anxiety of America, where any sticker one could win in a meat carving contest would no doubt be large and loud, adorned with flashing neon lights and its own social media handle. And so they dissolved seamlessly into the narrative when I did indeed find my personal "best" meatball on the Aventine Hill, the southernmost mound of Rome, a mythical site of an ancient competition to be "the best," in a mostly local way. The legend goes something like: Romulus and Remus decided to hold a contest of augury (basically, birdwatching to guess at the will of the gods), to decide whose name was slapped across the city. Remus set up camp on the Aventine Hill and Romulus, the Palatine. It's fairly obvious what happened next, and it's also fairly obvious why anyone who now owns real estate near the Aventine Hill might dismiss talk of said competition as culturally irrelevant. Still, on one morning of my trip, in an apartment on that Aventine hilltop, I broke into a meatball so tender that it seemed held together by sheer will. A meatball that was juicy and plush, and which percolated fat when sliced in two. I'd watched its creator, a chef and food writer named Daniela Del Balzo, make the mix and fry it, and I asked a million questions. Then I came home and tried to re-create it again and again. Eventually I wrote a recipe. Maybe they will be your ideal, too—or maybe you'll dislike them. I've come to realize that either way, the best meatballs do not exist.

YOU GOT TO THE END!!!

Now Take a Break from Trying to Be Perfect

I won't give you too many instructions here, since this part is about relaxing! You just need to know that the key to an extra-tall chip tower is structural integrity, especially if you're making one of the variations without any dip. The gist is: Start with a wide (wider than you think) layer of chips shingled over one another to form a base. Then use slices of meat or other ingredients (see below for ideas) and/or a "glue" between layers of chips to encourage everything to stick together. Mix and match with as many elements as you like. Once your chip tower is intact, decorate by balancing "ornaments" like olives and capers and torn figs on the edges of chips; you can also use a "glue" beneath each one to help it stick.

MIX AND MATCH CHIP TOWER IDEAS

CHIPS	GLUE	SLICES	"ORNAMENTS"
Sour cream and onion	Fig jam	Prosciutto	Olives
Ridged	Hot honey	Mortadella	Cornichons
Salt and vinegar	Onion dip	Salami	Capers
Cheddar and sour cream	Dijon	Sliced cheese	Cheese curds
Truffle-flavored	Greek yogurt	Thinly sliced apple	Spun sugar
Tortilla chips	Hot raclette	Radicchio	Tiny bits of Brie
Thin, long crackers	Stracciatella cheese	Tuna carpaccio	Torn figs
Shrimp chips	Beer cheese	Smoked salmon	Roe or caviar
Honey butter–flavored	Sour cream	Fruit leather (!)	Smoked almonds
Barbecue-flavored	Homemade ranch	Arugula	Microplaned Parm

CHIPS, FIGS, AND PROSCIUTTO

Layer potato chips with thin slices of prosciutto (or thinly sliced Serrano ham). Balance ripped-apart ripe figs on some of the outer chips, like Christmas tree ornaments.

RIDGED RUFFLES, LIPTON'S ONION DIP, CHIVES, AND ROE

Make onion dip by mixing a packet of Lipton's Onion Soup Mix into about 16 ounces of sour cream. Every layer of ridged Ruffles, pipe a bit of onion dip as glue to hold the chips in place as you construct the tower. Finish with a smattering of finely chopped chives and on the very tips of some of the chips, a little dollop of caviar (or any sort of roe). Serve and eat immediately to avoid soggy chips.

TRUFFLE-FLAVORED CHIPS, MORTADELLA, STRACCIATELLA CHEESE, AND OLIVES

Layer truffle-flavored chips with slices of mortadella (you can tear them if they're too wide). Every few layers, add a draped dollop of stracciatella cheese. Balance olives on some of the outer chips, like Christmas tree ornaments.

SOUR-CREAM-AND-ONION-FLAVORED CHIPS, SALAMI, CAPERS, AND HOT HONEY

Layer sour-cream-and-onion-flavored chips with slices of salami. Every few layers, add a drizzle of hot honey. Balance capers on some of the outer chips, like Christmas tree ornaments.

ACKNOWLEDGMENTS

Making a cookbook is a sprawling process and I'm certain I'll miss three or four critical people, and they'll hate me forever in a quiet, simmering way. But I'll try anyway. Thank you . . .

To my brilliant, patient editor, Cassie Jones. To my unflappable team: Alyssa Reuben, Andrew Schoessel Mondragón, David Stone, Marissa Fine, and the talented legal and contract teams across WME and TFC.

To my creative team: Nikole Herriott, Michael Graydon, Sue Li, Kalen Kaminski, Allison Gelles, Tommy McKiernan, Veronica Martinez, and Chris Johnson. We'll always have DebWear.™ To the designers who loaned us gorgeous props: Sophie Lou Jacobson, Mellow Ceramica, Fredericks and Mae, Totem, Upstate. To Monica Alvarez, for dealing with me at 6 a.m. To Christopher Cristiano, for seeing things differently. To Olivia de Recat, for illustrations I adore. To my mother, Michelle Slatalla, who was my first reader for most of this book.

To the sfogline and pasta pros who showed me their ways: Tania Raimondi at L'Angolo Della Pasta, Robin Frings at L'Erba del Re, Daniela and Monica Venturi at Le Sfogline, Virginia, the instructors at Academia Barilla. To the organizers of the Festival del Prosciutto di Parma, the producers who let me visit and taught me about curing pork—Luca Galloni (Fratelli Galloni), Tanara Giancarlo Spa—and the concessionaires at the Texas State Fair who spoke to me about the American dream. To Katie Parla, and Daniela Del Balzo, and Debora Lanini (and crew!).

To Yukiko and family at 花見せんべい in Kichijoji, the team at UDONZIN in Osaka, "Akai" Kohei for translating and for taking me to your secret family spot for sushi. To Chef Jo Takasaki of Takasaki no Okan, and Scott Peacock, and Brooks Reynolds and everyone who makes the Blue Ribbon Bacon Fest and Porktoberfest happen. To the whole Tokyo Ramen Festa team.

To my researchers, Corey Popowski and Daniel Ajootian. To Adrienne Murr. To Natalie Rousseau.

To the intrepid cooks and bakers who helped me test method after method and recipe after recipe: Mia Glickman (!!!), Ben Weiner, Laura Manzano, Casey Elsass. To my cross-testers: Julie Bishop, Rebecca Firkser, Jessie Levin, Jerrol Golden, Kristina Woo. As cool as it was to travel around Italy with sfogline showing me ancient techniques for dough, or to go to the ramen festival in Tokyo with Nikole and Michael, or to watch at the Prosciutto Festival in Parma as Michael rolled on the ground on his back to get a slicing shot, without a doubt the best part was forcing my friends and family to cross-test recipes. Yes, I had professional cross-testers, and yes, they were critical. But I also wanted home cooks and food lovers of all skill levels to be able to execute even the trickiest techniques. I didn't anticipate how much their differing styles of feedback would make me laugh. Lauren Beck prepared two six-page dossiers with embedded process images for a single recipe. Coulter Kunzel went NSFW with his feedback. My dad, an incredibly sweet man and a famously harsh editor, became the first cross-tester to send me a full run of notes *before* even making the recipe, about perceived wording issues. My mom delivered her feedback like a CIA agent gives a field report and then disappeared into the wind. Allegra Roberts FaceTimed me with her cakes, to ask if I was sure they wouldn't be even better with the lemon frosting she'd been craving. Jaquén Castellanos sent feedback on how those same cakes tasted days later, with lemon frosting. Clementine Quittner took berry decor to new heights and suffered through more than one hundred texts about crumb in the middle of the night. Zoe Quittner and Ray Chang took it upon themselves to increase the cheese every time.

To Linda and Howard Dickey-White, for so many years of kindness and encouragement.

To all the authors whose books I scoured (see page 361), and to everyone who answered my frantic cooking and baking and science questions.

To my many supportive editors, mentors, showrunners, and deeply creative friends for advice and patience: Erika Green Swafford, Allison Davis, Crystal Liu, Tanya Sichinsky, Becky Hughes, Eric Kim, Kim Bernstein. To friends who have tasted endless batches of latkes and crispy smashed potatoes (Colin Stokes, Maddie Wise!). To my husband, who has never sugarcoated his feedback on any dish.

To the wonderful people at HarperCollins, WME, Paradigm, and TFC, who make and who have made everything happen: Nicole Braun, Jill Zimmerman, Liv Guion, James Hansen, Liza Mullett, Kasey Feather, Anwesha Basu, Ben Steinberg, Anna Brower, Shelby Peak, Renata De Oliveira, Julianna Lee, Leda Scheintaub.

VISA
Sfogline
sta fresca

NOTES

INTRODUCTION

1. Edna Lewis and Scott Peacock, *The Gift of Southern Cooking: Recipes and Revelations from Two Great American Cooks: A Cookbook* (Knopf, 2012).

CHAPTER 1: TENDER LAYERED BISCUITS

1. Toni Tipton-Martin, *Jubilee* (Clarkson Potter, 2019).
2. Briana Holt, "Buttermilk Sugar Biscuits," adapted by Eric Kim, *New York Times Cooking*, October 12, 2023, https://cooking.nytimes.com/recipes/1024061-buttermilk-sugar-biscuits.
3. @hailtheface, "Has Anyone Ever Put Vodka in Their Pie Crust?," reply to @jess_we_can, 2009, https://www.reddit.com/r/food/comments/a7vcd/has_anyone_ever_put_vodka_in_their_pie_crust/.
4. Edna Lewis, *The Taste of Country Cooking: The 30th Anniversary Edition of a Great Southern Classic Cookbook* (Random House, 2012).
5. Edna Lewis, *The Gift of Southern Cooking* (Knopf, 2003).

CHAPTER 3: FOOLPROOF POACHED EGGS

1. America's Test Kitchen defines a "poaching" temperature as between 160° and 180°F, though I conducted my "simmer" tests closer to 185° to 190°F. Source: https://www.americastestkitchen.com/cooksillustrated/how_tos/5548-wet-cooking-methods.
2. Jake Davies, "What Do the Eggs You Eat Say About You?," *Farmers Weekly*, October 8, 2012, https://www.fwi.co.uk/livestock/poultry/what-do-the-eggs-you-eat-say-about-you.
3. Irma Rombauer, *Joy of Cooking: Fully Revised and Updated* (Scribner, 2019), 978.
4. Bob Granleese, "Is There a Failsafe Way to Poach Eggs?," *Guardian*, April 12, 2019, https://www.theguardian.com/food/2019/apr/12/is-there-a-failsafe-way-to-poach-eggs.
5. Harold McGee, *On Food and Cooking* (Scribner, 2004), 90.
6. Rombauer, *Joy of Cooking*, 978.
7. Michael A. Gardiner, "11 Different Methods for Poaching Eggs," Tasting Table, February 6, 2023, https://www.tastingtable.com/1190037/different-methods-for-poaching-eggs/.
8. Thomas Keller, "The Perfect Poach," *Bon Appétit*, March 12, 2012, https://www.bonappetit.com/recipe/the-perfect-poach.
9. J. Kenji López-Alt, "Easy Poached Eggs," Serious Eats, August 15, 2023, https://www.seriouseats.com/foolproof-poached-eggs-food-lab-recipe.
10. McGee, *On Food and Cooking*, 90.
11. France Cevallos, "Sous Vide 'Poached' Eggs," Allrecipes, January 11, 2024, https://www.allrecipes.com/recipe/279620/sous-vide-poached-eggs/.
12. Stephanie, "The Easiest Poached Egg Recipe," *i am a food blog*, March 20, 2012, https://iamafoodblog.com/the-easiest-poached-egg-recipe/#:~:text=Chang's%20slow%20poached%20eggs%20are,and%20the%20yolks%20gloriously%20oozy.

CHAPTER 5: CUSTARDY SOFT-SCRAMBLED EGGS

1. J. Kenji López-Alt, "What's the Best Way to Salt Scrambled Eggs?," Ask Kenji, *The New York Times*, April 24, 2024, https://www.nytimes.com/2024/04/24/dining/best-way-to-salt-scrambled-eggs.html.
2. Jean-Georges Vongerichten, "The Softest Scramble," *Bon Appétit*, March 12, 2012, https://www.bonappetit.com/recipe/the-softest-scramble.

CHAPTER 7: CRISPY SMASHED POTATOES

1. J. Kenji López-Alt, "The Best Crispy Roast Potatoes Ever," Serious Eats, November 4, 2024, https://www.seriouseats.com/the-best-roast-potatoes-ever-recipe.
2. *Good Housekeeping* 143, no. 6 (December 1956), via Food52.

CHAPTER 8: DRAMATIC CARROTS

1. Edward P. Montague, *Narrative of the Late Expedition to the Dead Sea* (Legare Street Press, 2023).
2. Harold McGee, *On Food and Cooking* (Scribner, 2004), 283.
3. Dioscorides, *De Materia Medica*.
4. Ganda Suthivarakom, "Noma's René Redzepi Wants to Feed You Really Old Carrots," *Saveur*, October 7, 2010, https://www.saveur.com/article/Kitchen/Rene-Redzepi-Noma-book/.

5. Christopher Kimball, *The Milk Street Cookbook.*
6. Rick Martínez, *Mi Cocina: Recipes and Rapture from My Kitchen in Mexico* (Clarkson Potter, 2022), 63.
7. "Carrot Salad with Harissa, Feta and Mint," Smitten Kitchen, May 17, 2010, https://smittenkitchen.com/2010/05/carrot-salad-with-harissa-feta-and-mint/.
8. Samin Nosrat, *Salt, Fat, Acid, Heat: Mastering the Elements of Good Cooking* (Simon & Schuster, 2017), 222.

CHAPTER 9: BUTTERY BROCCOLI STEMS

1. Kristen Miglore, "Roy Finamore's Broccoli Cooked Forever," Food52, January 13, 2012, https://food52.com/blog/2860-roy-finamore-s-broccoli-cooked-forever.

CHAPTER 11: EXTRA-FLAVORFUL LATKES

1. Molly O'Neill, *New York Cookbook* (Workman Publishing Company, 1992).
2. Rebecca Firkser, "Shockingly Crisp Baked Latkes," Food52, October 18, 2021, https://food52.com/recipes/86641-best-baked-latkes-recipe.

ESSAY: THE BEST VALUE

1. "Buffet of Buffets Las Vegas: History & Why Still Closed," Las Vegas Always, November 1, 2023, https://www.lasvegasalways.com/buffet-pass-las-vegas/.
2. https://www.ebay.com/itm/126271169006?chn=ps&mkevt=1&mkcid=28
3. Anthony Curtis, "Inside the New Las Vegas: Glutton's Paradise: In Today's Las Vegas, with Its Emphasis on Variety and Value, Buffets Offer Choices for Everyone, Even Dieters," *Los Angeles Times*, February 10, 1994, https://www.latimes.com/archives/la-xpm-1994-02-20-tr-25015-story.html.
4. Curtis, "Inside the New Las Vegas."
5. *Los Angeles Times*, April 23, 2013.
6. "Indian Buffet: A Centuries-Old Tradition," NPR, May 1, 2007, https://www.npr.org/2007/05/01/9354102/indian-buffet-a-centuries-old-tradition.
7. Hana Carter, "Don't Get Stuffed: China Bans All-You-Can-Eat Buffets with Secret Police to Search BINS for Wasted Meals After Covid Hits Food Supplies," *The U.S. Sun*, May 7, 2021, https://www.the-sun.com/news/2843546/china-bans-all-you-can-eat-buffets/.
8. The Gourmet Project, https://www.gourmetproject.net/convivium-roman-banquets/.
9. Katharine Raff, "The Roman Banquet," *The Met*, October 2011, https://www.metmuseum.org/toah/hd/banq/hd_banq.htm.
10. Raff, "The Roman Banquet."
11. Edmund A. Bowles, "Instruments at the Court of Burgundy (1363–1467)," *Galpin Society Journal*, July 1953, https://www.jstor.org/stable/841716?read-now=1#page_scan_tab_contents.
12. Lauren Collins, "The Hottest Restaurant in France Is an All-You-Can-Eat Buffet," *New Yorker*, April 1, 2024, https://www.newyorker.com/magazine/2024/04/08/les-grands-buffets-and-the-art-of-all-you-can-eat.
13. Bernard Gordillo, "Feast of the Pheasant, 1454," *Harmonia*, Indiana Public Media, June 9, 2008, https://indianapublicmedia.org/harmonia/feast-pheasant-1454.php.

CHAPTER 12: JUICY ROASTED CHICKEN

1. Carla Lalli Music, "Herbed Faux-tisserie Chicken and Potatoes," *Bon Appétit*, February 18, 2024, https://www.bonappetit.com/recipe/herbed-faux-tisserie-chicken-and-potatoes?srsltid=AfmBOop6UkPFa3cE79c3TnxvqG5rSNrVARUUyZ3HC6VavD8F-amm4MRh.
2. "Zuni Cafe's Roasted Chicken + Bread Salad," Smitten Kitchen, https://smittenkitchen.com/2008/12/zuni-cafe-roast-chicken-bread-salad/.
3. Food52, "Barbara Kafka's Simplest Roast Chicken."
4. J. Kenji López-Alt, "The Food Lab's Complete Guide to Sous Vide Chicken Breast," Serious Eats, October 13, 2024, https://www.seriouseats.com/the-food-lab-complete-guide-to-sous-vide-chicken-breast#toc-the-effect-of-temperature-on-juiciness.
5. Samin Nosrat, "Buttermilk-Marinated Roast Chicken," Salt, Fat, Acid, Heat, https://www.saltfatacidheat.com/buttermilkmarinated-roast-chicken.
6. Souvla, "Feta-Brined Roast Chicken," adapted by Melissa Clark, *New York Times Cooking*, https://cooking.nytimes.com/recipes/1017152-feta-brined-roast-chicken.

CHAPTER 13: PLUSH MEATBALLS

1. Sohla El-Waylly, *Start Here* (Knopf, 2023), 252.

CHAPTER 14: OPULENT SHRIMP

1. Toni Tipton-Martin, *Jubilee: Recipes from Two Centuries of African American Cooking* (Clarkson Potter, 2019), 259.
2. Lidia Bastianich, *Lidia's Italian-American Kitchen* (Knopf, 2001), 571.

CHAPTER 15: SILKY VODKA SAUCE

1. Eric Kim, "What Makes Penne Alla Vodka So Delicious? It's All in the Sauce," *The New York Times*, August 11, 2023, https://www.nytimes.com/2023/08/11/dining/penne-all-vodka-recipe.html.

CHAPTER 16: TWEAKED TOMATO-BUTTER SAUCE

1. Kim Severson, "Marcella Hazan's Tomato Sauce," adapted by *The New York Times*, *New York Times Cooking*, August 5, 2024, https://cooking.nytimes.com/recipes/1015178-marcella-hazans-tomato-sauce.
2. Marcella Hazan, *Essentials of Classic Italian Cooking: 30th Anniversary Edition* (Knopf, 2022).

CHAPTER 18: CREAMY, CRISPY-TOPPED MACARONI AND CHEESE

1. Jessica B. Harris, *High on the Hog* (Bloomsbury USA, 2011), 247.
2. Lesley Enston, "Trinidadian Macaroni Pie," *New York Times Cooking*, October 29, 2021, https://cooking.nytimes.com/recipes/1022707-trinidadian-macaroni-pie.

CHAPTER 19: CLOUDLIKE WHIPPED CREAM

1. Emma Laperruque, "A One-Ingredient Trick to Make Any Cake 1,000 Times Better," Food52, January 25, 2019, https://food52.com/blog/23706-whipped-cream-in-cakes-one-ingredient-hack-change-the-way-you-bake?srsltid=AfmBOoqALanYOOBsdNnftovxtl_PoSWOW9Rerur16yPXEjlISPns5NcS.
2. Rose Levy Beranbaum, "Whipped Cream Cake from Rose's Heavenly Cakes," Real Baking with Rose, June 2, 2021, https://www.realbakingwithrose.com/month/2020/12/29/whipped-cream-cake-from-roses-heavenly-cakes.

CHAPTER 20: SUPERLATIVE CHOCOLATE CHUNK COOKIES

1. Jacques Torres, "Chocolate Chip Cookies," adapted by David Leite, *New York Times Cooking*, January 22, 2025, https://cooking.nytimes.com/recipes/1015819-chocolate-chip-cookies.
2. Claire Saffitz, *Dessert Person* (Clarkson Potter, 2020), 135.
3. Stella Parks, "Levain Bakery-Style Super-Thick Chocolate Chip Cookies Recipe," Serious Eats, February 20, 2025, https://www.seriouseats.com/super-thick-chocolate-chip-cookie-recipe.
4. Dan Pelosi, "Grossy's Chocolate Chip Sheet Pan Cookies," Dan Pelosi, https://danpelosi.com/recipe/grossys-chocolate-chip-sheet-pan-cookies/.
5. Natasha Pickowicz, *More Than Cake* (Artisan, 2023), 32.
6. https://www.instagram.com/milkandcardamom/reel/C3WcIpgxrQV/.
7. Carla Lalli Music, "This Cookie Cured My Self Doubt," Food Processing, January 2, 2024, https://carlalallimusic.substack.com/p/this-cookie-cured-my-self-doubt.

CHAPTER 21: QUIVERING, LUXURIOUS YELLOW CAKE

1. "Epigenetics & Inheritance," Learn.Genetics, https://learn.genetics.utah.edu/content/epigenetics/inheritance#:~:text=The%20offspring%20of%20caterpillar%2Ddamaged,offspring%20through%20the%20reproductive%20cells.
2. Rose Levy Beranbaum and Woody Wolston, *The Cake Bible*, 35th ed. (William Morrow, 2024), 50.
3. Emma Laperruque, "A One-Ingredient Trick to Make Any Cake 1,000 Times Better," Food52, January 25, 2019, https://food52.com/blog/23706-whipped-cream-in-cakes-one-ingredient-hack-change-the-way-you-bake?srsltid=AfmBOoqALanYOOBsdNnftovxtl_PoSWOW9Rerur16yPXEjlISPns5NcS.

CHAPTER 23: DECADENT FLOURLESS CHOCOLATE CAKE

1. Laurie Colwin, Three Chocolate Cakes, *Gourmet*, 1995.
2. Genius Recipes, "Richard Sax's Chocolate Cloud Cake," Food52, July 6, 2021, https://food52.com/recipes/78350-richard-sax-s-chocolate-cloud-cake.
3. Rose Gray and Ruth Rogers, *The River Café Cookbook* (Ebury Press, 1996).

CHAPTER 24: BUTTER-FORWARD SHORTBREAD

1. Sohla El-Waylly, *Start Here* (Knopf, 2023).

OTHER SOURCES

Bailey, Pearl, *Pearl's Kitchen: An Extraordinary Cookbook* (Harcourt, 1973).

Bon Appetit, various food writing and recipes.

Camara, Gabriela, and Malena Watrous, *My Mexico City Kitchen: Recipes and Convictions* (Lorena Jones Books, 2019).

Child, Julia, *Mastering the Art of French Cooking, Volume I: 50th Anniversary Edition: A Cookbook* (Knopf, 2001).

Colwin, Laurie, *Family Happiness* (Knopf Doubleday, 2021).

Crocker, Betty, *Betty Crocker's Cookbook* (Golden Press, 1974).

Dalí, Salvador, *Dalí: Les Diners De Gala*, trans. J. Peter Moore (TASCHEN, 2016).

Dunlop, Fuschia, *The Food of Sichuan* (W. W. Norton & Company, 2019).

Ephron, Nora, *Heartburn* (Vintage, 1996).

Hazan, Marcella, *Essentials of Classic Italian Cooking* (Knopf, 1992).

Hazan, Marcella, *Essentials of Classic Italian Cooking: 30th Anniversary Edition* (Knopf, 2022).

Hazan, Marcella, *Marcella's Italian Kitchen: A Cookbook* (Knopf, 2024).

Interviews with organizers and attendees of Tokyo Ramen Festa, the Blue Ribbon Bacon Festival, and Porktoberfest/the Shingen-Ko Festival; as well as interviews with sfogline and other pasta pros, prosciutto pros, meatball pros, Jo Takasaki, Hirofumi Osaki, and more.

Lewis, Edna, *The Taste of Country Cooking: The 30th Anniversary Edition of a Great Southern Classic Cookbook* (Knopf, 2006).

Lewis, Edna, and Scott Peacock, *The Gift of Southern Cooking: Recipes and Revelations from Two Great American Cooks* (Knopf, 2003).

López-Alt, J. Kenji, for *The New York Times* and Serious Eats, various articles.

Lukins, Sheila, and Julee Rosso, *The New Basics Cookbook* (Workman Publishing Company, 1989).

Lukins, Sheila, and Julee Rosso, *The Silver Palate Cookbook* (Workman Publishing Company, 2007).

McClenny, Rie, and Sanaë Lemoine, *Make It Japanese: Simple Recipes for Everyone: A Cookbook* (Clarkson Potter, 2023).

New York Times Cooking, various food writing and recipes.

Olvera, Enrique, *Tu Casa Mi Casa: Mexican Recipes for the Home Cook* (Phaidon Press, 2019).

Pickowicz, Natasha, *More than Cake: 100 Baking Recipes Built for Pleasure and Community* (Artisan, 2023).

Rombauer, Irma S., *Joy of Cooking: Fully Revised and Updated* (Scriber, 2019).

The author's great-grandmother's and grandmother's recipe boxes.

The patient and kind server at Commerce Inn who asked the kitchen how they make their roast chicken for the author.

ROOM-TEMPERATURE DOUGH
CHILLED DOUGH
FROZEN DOUGH
325°F
350°F
400°F
NO REST
3-HOUR REST
24-HOUR REST
SLAMMED
AP FLOUR TANGZHONG
AP FLOUR + BUCKWHEAT
TOASTED FLOUR
TOASTED SUGAR
SALTED BOTTOM
EXTRA-CREAMED BUTTER
EXTRA YOLK
ESPRESSO POWDER
MALTED MILK POWDER
MILK POWDER
OVERMIXED
HALF OIL

Universal CONVERSION CHART

OVEN TEMPERATURE EQUIVALENTS

250°F = 120°C
275°F = 135°C
300°F = 150°C
325°F = 160°C
350°F = 180°C
375°F = 190°C
400°F = 200°C
425°F = 220°C
450°F = 230°C
475°F = 240°C
500°F = 260°C

MEASUREMENT EQUIVALENTS

Measurements should always be level unless directed otherwise.

⅛ teaspoon = 0.5 mL

¼ teaspoon = 1 mL

½ teaspoon = 2 mL

1 teaspoon = 5 mL

1 tablespoon = 3 teaspoons = ½ fluid ounce = 15 mL

2 tablespoons = ⅛ cup = 1 fluid ounce = 30 mL

4 tablespoons = ¼ cup = 2 fluid ounces = 60 mL

5⅓ tablespoons = ⅓ cup = 3 fluid ounces = 80 mL

8 tablespoons = ½ cup = 4 fluid ounces = 120 mL

10⅔ tablespoons = ⅔ cup = 5 fluid ounces = 160 mL

12 tablespoons = ¾ cup = 6 fluid ounces = 180 mL

16 tablespoons = 1 cup = 8 fluid ounces = 240 mL

EGG
EGG
EGG
EGG
EGG
TIANBO FIRST

INDEX

Note: Page references in *italics* indicate photographs.

 For information, address HarperCollins Publishers, 195 Broadway, New York, NY 10007. In Europe, HarperCollins Publishers, Macken House, 39/40 Mayor Street Upper, Dublin 1, D01 C9W8, Ireland.

HarperCollins books may be purchased for educational, business, or sales promotional use. For information, please email the Special Markets Department at SPsales@harpercollins.com.

hc.com

FIRST EDITION

Case design by Chris Cristiano
Endpaper design by Julianna Lee
Designed by Renata De Oliveira
With consultation by Chris Cristiano
Photographs by Michael Graydon and Nikole Herriott
Illustrations by Olivia de Recat

Library of Congress Cataloging-in-Publication Data has been applied for.

ISBN 978-0-06-335768-6

Printed in Canada

26 27 28 29 30 TC 10 9 8 7 6 5 4 3